The Complete Idiot's Reference Card

Top 100 Investment Club Stocks

Each year, *Better Investing* magazine, a publication of the National Association of Investors Corp. (NAIC), publishes a list of the top 100 stocks held by NAIC-member investment clubs. The 100 most popular stocks for 1999 are listed as follows:

1. Intel (INTC)
2. PepsiCo (PEP)
3. Merck (MRK)
4. Lucent (LU)
5. Home Depot (HD)
6. Cisco Systems (CSCO)
7. AFLAC (AFL)
8. Diebold (DBD)
9. Motorola (MOT)
10. Clayton Homes (CMH)
11. Tricon (YUM)
12. Coca-Cola (COKE)
13. Microsoft (MSFT)
14. McDonald's (MCD)
15. RPM (RPM)
16. General Electric (GE)
17. Johnson & Johnson (JNJ)
18. Wendy's (WEN)
19. Abbott Labs (ABT)
20. Walt Disney (DIS)
21. Oracle (ORCL)
22. Pfizer (PFE)
23. Compaq (CPQ)
24. Hewlett-Packard (HWP)
25. AT&T (T)
26. Wal-Mart (WMT)
27. Boeing (BA)
28. MCI WorldCom (WCOM)
29. Walgreen (WAG)
30. Amgen (AMGN)
31. Centurytel, Inc. (CTL)
32. Invacare (IVC)
33. Synovus (SNV)
34. Newell (NWL)
35. Gillette (G)
36. Medtronic (MDT)
37. Sara Lee (SLE)
38. Starbucks (SBUX)
39. Schlumberger (SLB)
40. Callaway Golf (ELY)
41. Procter & Gamble (PG)
42. Citigroup (C)
43. ConAgra (CAG)
44. Staples (SPLS)
45. Biomet (BMET)
46. Harley-Davidson (HDI)
47. Colgate-Palmolive (CL)
48. ADC TeleCom (ADCT)
49. SYSCO (SYY)
50. Safeskin (SFSK)
51. Automatic Data Processing (AUD)
52. Bank One (ONE)
53. Stryker (SYK)
54. Cracker Barrel
55. Dana (DCN)
56. Dollar General (DG)
57. Exxon (recently merged with Mobil) (XOM)
58. Schering-Plough (SGP)
59. Applied Materials (AMAT)
60. Deere & Co. (DE)
61. Global Marine (GLM)
62. Philip Morris (MO)
63. OfficeMax (OMX)
64. US Filter
65. Mylan Labs (MYL)
66. Avery Dennison (AVY)
67. Federal National Manufacturing Assoc. (FNM)
68. Hannaford (HRD)
69. SBC Communications (XTX)
70. MBNA Corp. (KRB)
71. PeopleSoft (PSFT)
72. Applebee's (APPB)
73. Network Assocs Incorporated (NETA)
74. Sun Microsystems (SUNW)
75. Emerson Electric Co. (EMR)
76. Albertson's (ABS)
77. 3Com (COMS)
78. Texaco (TX)
79. Johnson Controls (JCI)
80. Mobil (recently merged with Exxon) (XOM)
81. Bristol-Meyers (BMY)
82. Thermo Electron Corp. (TMO)
83. Gateway 2000 (GTW)
84. Nucor Corp. (NUE)
85. Modine (MODI)
86. IBM (IBM)
87. Federal Signal (FSS)
88. Campbell Soup (CPB)
89. Claire's Stores (CLE)
90. Andrew Corp. (ANDW)
91. Monsanto Co. (MTC)
92. American Power Technology, Inc. (APTH)
93. Kellogg (K)
94. Atmos Energy (ATO)
95. Linear Technology (LLTC)
96. Wolverine World Wide, Inc. (WWW)
97. ServiceMaster (SVM)
98. Thermo Instrument Systems (THI)
99. American Home (AHID)
100. Eli Lilly and Co. (LLY)

alpha books

Investment Club Meeting Checklist

Continuously review these basic steps to keep your investment club meetings organized and running smoothly.

- ❏ Find a comfortable place to meet, with room for club members to spread out and work.
- ❏ Recite your club goals at the beginning of every meeting.
- ❏ Make sure that all members are acquainted, and don't forget to introduce any new members. Consider nametags if your club is large.
- ❏ Encourage members to get to know one another on a social level as well as a business level.
- ❏ Choose and maintain a full slate of club officers.
- ❏ Limit the length of your club's meetings.
- ❏ Take attendance at every meeting.
- ❏ Limit the number of meetings that each member can miss during a year.
- ❏ Insist that members show up and your meetings start on time.
- ❏ Get everyone involved with both the work and social aspects of the club.
- ❏ Have your club's books open to all members at all times.
- ❏ Set and follow an agenda at every meeting.
- ❏ Designate part of every meeting as educational, and try to have club members learn something new each month.
- ❏ Understand that disagreements are sometimes unavoidable.
- ❏ Insist that all members are respectful of one another, even when they don't agree.
- ❏ Don't let one or two people dominate decisions concerning the club's investments.
- ❏ Make sure that every member does his or her share of club work.
- ❏ Have good outside help available, and call on it when you need to.
- ❏ Remember that mistakes happen and that the club shares responsibility for investments that don't do as well as you'd like.
- ❏ Keep your club meetings fun.

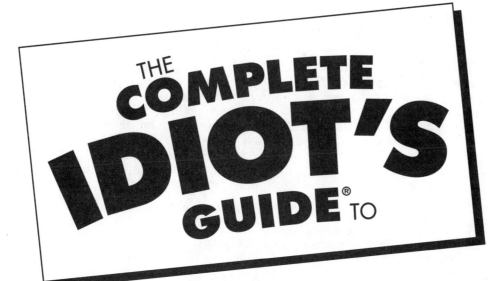

THE COMPLETE IDIOT'S GUIDE® TO

Starting an Investment Club

by Sarah Young Fisher and Susan Shelly

alpha
books

Macmillan USA, Inc.
201 West 103rd Street
Indianapolis, IN 46290

A Pearson Education Company

This book is dedicated to the founders and members of all investment clubs—past, present, and future.

Copyright © 2000 by Sarah Young Fisher and Susan Shelly

International Standard Book Number: 0-02-863587-6
Library of Congress Catalog Card Number: Available upon request.

02   01   00   8   7   6   5   4   3   2   1

Interpretation of the printing code: The rightmost number of the first series of numbers is the year of the book's printing; the rightmost number of the second series of numbers is the number of the book's printing. For example, a printing code of 00-1 shows that the first printing occurred in 2000.

Printed in the United States of America

Publisher
Marie Butler-Knight

Product Manager
Phil Kitchel

Managing Editor
Cari Luna

Acquisitions Editor
Randy Ladenheim-Gil

Development Editor
Nancy D. Warner

Production Editors
Billy Fields
Christy Wagner

Copy Editor
Abby Lyon Herriman

Illustrator
Jody P. Schaeffer

Cover Designers
Mike Freeland
Kevin Spear

Book Designers
Scott Cook and Amy Adams of DesignLab

Indexer
Amy Lawrence

Layout/Proofreading
Svetlana Dominguez
Gloria Schurick

Contents at a Glance

Contents

Appendixes

Foreword

Since 1951, NAIC (National Association of Investors Corporation) has been the leading proponent of investment education for individuals in the United States. Our vision is to "Build a Nation of Individual Investors," and we encourage everyone to learn about investing in common stock. We believe that anyone can learn how to invest successfully and that they can participate in the market, even with very small amounts of money. Stocks present a wonderful opportunity for everyone to participate in the success and growth of our economy and in so doing, all involved in the process will benefit: the shareholders, the corporations, the brokers/dealers, the markets, and the communities where all of these people live, work, and interact. Over the years, NAIC has helped millions of people learn about the benefits of investing. Our members have proven that you do not need to be rich or have formal financial training to get started. A willingness to learn and a commitment to follow a regular focused methodology can enable anyone to take control of their financial future.

One of the best vehicles for a person to use to learn about investing and develop the confidence to participate in the stock market is an investment club. *The Complete Idiot's Guide to Starting an Investment Club* clearly and entertainingly presents important points to consider when starting a club and what to watch for once you are underway. A club should be formed with the right people and dedicated to pursuing a sound investment philosophy. A club where all are willing to learn and share in the effort, risks, and rewards can make its members truly wealthy by providing years of friendships, social opportunities, education, and a brighter financial future for all. NAIC has encouraged the formation of, and participation in, investment clubs to those interested in getting started. It has seen many of its members learn and apply their knowledge to create successful clubs and then use the same abilities to build their own personal portfolios. After several years, most members have two to three times more invested in their own accounts than in the club! The club's success continues, however, because of the forum it provides for learning, sharing, supporting, and socializing.

This *Complete Idiot's Guide* contains a wealth of reference material and straightforward discussion of club startup and operation. There are too many reasons why people continually fail to start an investing program, and we want you to start today. Read this book! Gather some friends from family, work, or school. Agree on an investing approach and agree to follow it. Schedule regular meetings and define and maintain your educational program. Adopt a club agreement and elect officers. Have fun naming your club and make sure to register it. Start learning and investing today, regardless of what others are saying about the market and where it's going.

Whether you decide to invest within a club or on your own, in individual stocks or mutual funds, NAIC can provide you with the educational programs, materials, and support to help you reach your goals. Our proven conservative philosophy is well suited to the beginning investor. It allows you to learn about investing with a minimum of money and risk. Don't fear the stock market. Learn to invest wisely and join millions of others who are benefiting from our nation's growth. We are available to help you at any time, and would urge you to read this book and get started today!

Robert A. O'Hara
VP of Development, NAIC

Introduction

All across the United States and in other parts of the world, as well, people are joining investment clubs.

These clubs are becoming increasingly more popular year after year. Why? Because they give regular folks like you and me the opportunity to invest in the stock market without risking our life's savings.

A modest initial investment and a small monthly contribution is all it takes to begin building considerable assets. Investment clubs have helped thousands and thousands of people to build up their retirement savings, pay for their children's college education, pay off mortgages, buy vacation homes, or simply live with the knowledge that they had money available if it was needed.

The success that so many investment clubs realize is due primarily to their commitment to education. Education is, or should be, the most important goal for investment clubs. When it is, both experienced investors and brand-new members benefit greatly.

Investment clubs are nothing new. There have been clubs in the United States for more than a century. The great surge in membership in recent years, however, is testimony to the fact that these clubs work. Members of investment clubs make money, learn firsthand about investing, and have fun while they're doing it.

If you've picked up this book, it probably means that you're interested in starting—or at least in joining—an investment club. If that's the case, congratulations. You're joining hundreds of thousands of others across the country who have already done so.

By getting involved in an investment club, you're taking the initiative to control your own finances. You're not sitting around, hoping that Social Security will still be available when you're ready to retire, or thinking that your retirement savings will fund the lifestyle you hope to be able to have.

If you're young and getting ready to join an investment club, you're to be admired for your foresightedness. You'll definitely be ahead of the game later in life, and you'll have lots of time to enjoy the rewards of your initiative.

If you're, well, not quite so young, you're still doing yourself a big favor by getting involved with an investment club. It's never too late to improve your financial situation, and careful, smart investing is a great way to do so.

This book will serve as a guide as you start or join an investment club. Hopefully, it also will inspire you and make your investment club journey one that is enjoyable and profitable.

What You'll Find in This Book

The Complete Idiot's Guide to Starting an Investment Club is written in six parts.

Part 1, "The Great World of Investment Clubs," will cover the history of investment clubs, and some of the different kinds of clubs that are around. No two clubs are alike—that's for sure—because all clubs have different members, ideas, and ways of doing things. Online clubs are hot these days, and we'll look at how they work, and their advantages and disadvantages.

Also in Part 1, we ask you to be honest with yourself, and decide whether or not getting involved in an investment club is the right move for you. While we think clubs are great, and many, many people have benefited from them, they're not for everyone.

Part 2, "The Basics of Starting a Club," will point out the things you need to know to get a club off the ground. You know, the basics. You'll learn that choosing members is a little more involved than you might think, and that some people are more likely to work successfully together in a club than others.

We'll cover topics as basic as choosing a name for your club and the nuts and bolts of holding a meeting. We'll also go into important subjects such as choosing the best legal structure, writing an operating agreement, and hiring lawyers, accountants, and other outside help you might need.

Part 3, "Details, Details," will focus on issues beyond the basics of getting your club up and running. You'll need to think about keeping records—they're extremely important to all aspects of your investment club. And you'll need to consider how your club will handle taxes—Uncle Sam isn't going to let you off the hook, you know!

We'll tell you how to find a broker who's right for your club, and discuss how much each member should pay in monthly dues and initial contributions. This part covers a lot of important topics that can affect your club significantly.

Part 4, "It's Time to Do Some Homework," will look at the stock market, and some other types of investments your club might want to consider. It's extremely important to develop an understanding of how the market works before you start investing. You'll need to learn a bit about the different types of mutual funds, stocks, bonds, and the companies that offer them. You'll have to consider such topics as evaluating stocks, the mechanics of buying stock, and the risk factors involved with different stocks.

Part 5, "Keeping Track of Your Investments," will cover the ins and outs of trading stock. You'll learn that, although investment clubs generally buy and hold their stock for the long term, there are times when it just makes more sense to sell. You'll learn to recognize those times, and how to sell stock if you decide that it's necessary.

We'll discuss those things called dividends, and the concept of reinvesting dividends to make your investment grow even faster. We'll also explain how to read stock reports and tell you about other methods of tracking your investments.

Part 6, "The Evolution and Life Span of Your Investment Club," will deal with the ebbs and flows of a club or other type of organization. We all know that nothing stays the same, and your investment club will be no exception. While we hope your club runs fairly smoothly, there almost inevitably will be some rough spots along the way.

Those rough spots are a lot easier to handle if you can anticipate possible problems, and develop strategies with which to deal with them when they occur. We'll talk about changing officers and evaluating your outside help. And you'll learn that if your club eventually stops working and disbands, it's not the end of the world.

The knowledge that you'll gain from being a part of an investment club will help you start another club, or use the skills you've acquired to invest on your own. One thing is for sure: Your investment club experience will be of great benefit in many, many ways.

Extras

Last, but not least: This book contains a lot of miscellaneous definitions, tips, warnings, and interesting facts in the form of sidebars. These tidbits of information are given particular names. Here's how they stack up:

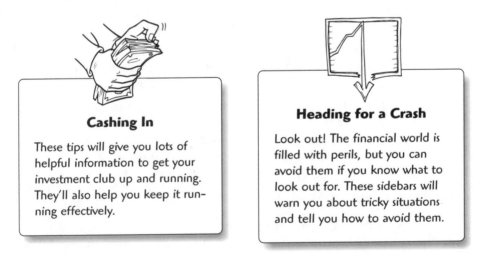

Cashing In

These tips will give you lots of helpful information to get your investment club up and running. They'll also help you keep it running effectively.

Heading for a Crash

Look out! The financial world is filled with perils, but you can avoid them if you know what to look out for. These sidebars will warn you about tricky situations and tell you how to avoid them.

Taking Stock

Dividends, initial public offerings, common stock, preferred stock, the NASDAQ—what's it all mean? These sidebars will set the record straight with simple, to-the-point definitions of these and other tricky terms.

Take This to the Bank

These are fun bits of information that you're not likely to find in stock reports or those serious annual reports that show up in your club's mailbox.

Acknowledgments

The authors would like to thank the many people who provided time, information, and resources for this book. Especially we would like to thank our editors at Macmillan USA, Inc.: Randy Ladenheim-Gil, Nancy D. Warner, Cari Luna, and Christy Wagner.

We also extend a warm thank you to Bert Holtje of James Peter Associates.

Thanks also to Robert O'Hara and the other good people at the National Association of Investors Corporation in Royal Oaks, Michigan. The NAIC was very generous in providing information and help for this book. Our thanks go to Clint Slonaker and Harry Glah, who took their time to answer numerous questions, confirm information, and provide valuable insight and experience.

A very special thank-you to our families and friends, especially to Carol A. Turkington, a great friend and extraordinary listener; to Mike McGovern, who can always be counted on for encouragement and some laughs; and to Sara and Ryan McGovern, who make every day special. And as always, thank-you to three very special and patient people: Chuck, Rob, and Catie Fisher.

Special Thanks to the Technical Reviewer

The Complete Idiot's Guide to Starting an Investment Club was reviewed by an expert who double-checked the accuracy of what you'll learn here, to help us ensure that this book gives you everything you need to know about starting an investment club. Special thanks are extended to Wilma Sirota.

Trademarks

All terms mentioned in this book that are known to be or are suspected of being trademarks or service marks have been appropriately capitalized. Alpha Books and Macmillan USA, Inc. cannot attest to the accuracy of this information. Use of a term in this book should not be regarded as affecting the validity of any trademark or service mark.

Part 1

The Great World of Investment Clubs

Investment clubs are becoming more and more popular, with new clubs springing up every day. They're not, however, a new concept. Investment clubs have been in operation in the United States for many years.

The first part of this book looks at the history of investment clubs and examines the recent surge in interest and club membership. It also gives you some tips from experienced club members and discusses the possibility of starting an online club, rather than a traditional one.

Also, we'll examine the advantages and disadvantages of starting your own club, rather than joining an existing one.

Chapter 1

What's All This Talk About Investment Clubs?

In This Chapter

➤ Defining investment clubs

➤ Exploring the history of clubs

➤ More and more people are joining up

➤ Reasons why people love their clubs

➤ Understanding that investment clubs aren't for everybody

➤ A look at who's joining and forming clubs

Investment clubs are big. In fact, investment clubs are huge.

Ever since the gray-haired ladies from Beardstown, Illinois, captured the attention of investors everywhere by announcing that they were pulling in greater than 23 percent returns on the investments they made as a group, clubs have been sprouting up across America like mushrooms during a long, damp spring.

Of course, the Beardstown Ladies' Club is no longer considered the epitome of investment clubs (remember that little mix-up in 1998 when it was revealed that the ladies had miscalculated, and their actual return was more like 9 percent than 23?), but such clubs continue to flourish.

The National Association of Investors Corporation (NAIC), a nonprofit, Michigan-based organization that helps investors organize and run clubs, calls the surge in the number of clubs being formed "the Investment Club movement."

New clubs are being formed every day, and they're credited with providing investment opportunities and education to thousands of people.

In this chapter, we'll take a look at exactly what these clubs are, and who is getting involved with them. We'll consider the history of investment clubs, and look at some of the attitudes people have about them. When we finish, you'll have the information you need to decide whether you want to consider joining a club—or maybe even forming one of your own. So, let's get started!

Taking Stock

An **investment club** is a group of people with similar interests and outlooks, who research the investment pros and cons of various stocks, then use their pooled resources to buy those stocks that members feel will give them the best returns.

Exactly What Is an Investment Club?

An *investment club* is a group of people who decide to get together, throw some money into a pot, and invest that money in stocks that they all like.

Yep. It's that simple.

Well, maybe not *quite* that simple. While that's the basic premise of an investment club, there's a little more to consider.

Club Expectations

Members of investment clubs are expected to do a bit more than put up some money and smile at one another as they agree to buy McDonald's stock. They're expected to participate in researching the companies whose stock they propose to buy, and to adhere to the guidelines of the club.

Cashing In

The three "R"s of investment clubs aren't reading, 'riting, and 'rithmatic, but *research, rules,* and *regulations.* Research is critical to making smart choices about the stock a club purchases, while having rules and regulations in place gives the club cohesiveness and structure.

Research is a vital element of an investment club. Members are expected to make reasonable, knowledgeable decisions about companies and their stock, based on information revealed through research.

No self-respecting investment club member, for instance, would suggest that his club purchase stock in the Mattel Corporation, simply because he had fond memories of playing with Matchbox cars when he was a kid. A suggestion to buy Mattel (or any other) stock should be based on what the club member learns about the company through research, the performance of the stock, and its outlook for the future.

Rules and regulations are another important mention when talking about investment clubs. Experts say that, while clubs don't need to be extremely formal, they should follow some rules and guidelines. This assures that all members have the same expectations about what will occur within the club and understand what is expected of them. Regulations also will make club meetings proceed more smoothly.

Club Dynamics and Personality

Probably no two investment clubs are exactly the same. Each group has its own dynamics and personality, based upon its members, their philosophies, and how the club is set up and run.

Some factors, however, should be common to all clubs. Consider the following:

➤ Members should agree on the stocks the club will purchase. Some clubs require that an investment vote is unanimous, while others require only a majority. Your operating agreement will guide your club (refer to Chapter 8, "Establishing Operating Rules").

➤ The amount of money that each member is required to contribute to the club should be pre-determined. Some clubs require each member to invest the same amount, while in other clubs, the amount varies (see Chapter 11, "Exactly How Does an Investment Club Operate?").

➤ The club should have guidelines in place to deal with potential situations, such as someone dropping out or new members wanting to join. Such guidelines are included in your club's operating agreement (see Chapter 8).

➤ The club should be organized with a spirit of cooperation, and the goal of having all members benefit from club activities (see Chapters 7, "Getting Your Investment Club off to a Good Start," and 23, "How're You All Doing by Now?").

All of these points will be dealt with more thoroughly in later chapters, so we won't spend any more time discussing them now. Just remember for now, that while there are guidelines to follow when setting up or joining a club, the basic premise of investment clubs is simple. All club members must work together for the benefit of the membership. And hopefully, everyone will learn a lot about investing, and have a lot of fun.

Investment Club History 101

Cruise around the Internet for a while, or take a walk through your neighborhood bookstore. You'll find dozens of Web sites relating to investment clubs (see Appendix B, "Resources," in the back of the book for a listing of some of the better ones), and more than a couple of books on the same subject.

Take This to the Bank

A Texas railroad master named A. L. Brooks started the first investment club in 1898. Legend has it that Brooks started the club in hopes of keeping his workers from squandering their paychecks.

Don't be fooled into thinking that all that information is about something that's new. Investment clubs have gotten a lot of publicity during the past few years, generating a lot of new interest. Such clubs, however, have been around in the United States for more than a century.

Back in the Day

The earliest U.S. investment club was established at the end of the nineteenth century. The early clubs were made up primarily of people (almost all men, you can be sure) who had similar social backgrounds and were interested in investing a little money, though they didn't focus on educating their members or researching companies and stocks, as clubs typically do today.

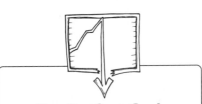

Heading for a Crash

Don't be tempted to join an investment club in which members are looking to "get rich quick" or make a killing in the stock market. These clubs traditionally fall apart quickly. The long-lived clubs are those that focus on education and experience.

Investment clubs, as we know them today, got their start in 1940, when Frederick C. Russell founded the Mutual Investment Club of Detroit.

You'll get a better idea of the mindset of the members of the Detroit club if you consider the circumstances of the time.

While Americans were still recoiling from the Great Depression, much of the rest of the world was already in turmoil from war and aggression. Japan had invaded China in 1937, the same year Italy dropped out of the League of Nations. Hitler had taken over Austria in 1938, and the following year occupied Bohemia and Moravia. World War II got underway with a vengeance in 1939, prompting President Franklin D. Roosevelt to declare U.S. neutrality, while at the same time placing the country under a limited national emergency.

Times were, to say the least, uneasy.

So, when Russell, who was out of work and looking to buy a small business, rounded up some folks (some of them were his fraternity brothers) with whom to start an investment club, he wasn't doing so for the tea and crumpets that may have been served at the meetings. Russell hoped to use his share of the club's profits as start-up capital for a business, and he was dead serious about making the club work.

It's focus was on safe investing, and all members were encouraged to become as educated as they could about investment opportunities. Obviously, the club's philosophy was right on track.

Take This to the Bank

The Mutual Investment Club of Detroit really does set the standard for all clubs. The club has survived and flourished for 60 years. By doing their homework and investing modest amounts of money each month, long-term members make money to send their kids to college, pad their retirement funds, and upgrade their lifestyles.

Thousands of investment clubs have been organized since the 1940s. Until recently, however, they were a quiet presence. People were meeting regularly, researching stocks, and making money (or not) from their investments, but doing so without much fanfare.

National attention really didn't focus on investment clubs until the Beardstown ladies made the news, and people all over the country decided that if a group of women from Illinois could do it, so could they. Let's have a closer look at the number of clubs that are around today, and why people are joining them in record numbers.

The Membership Surge

There's no question about it, the number of people who are joining or forming investment clubs is on the rise. More than half a million people belong to U.S. investment clubs, according to a survey by *USA Today,* with the number rapidly growing. Membership in the National Association of Investors Corporation doubled between 1996 and 1998. By the end of 1999, the NAIC counted more than 37,000 clubs among its membership. Although it's impossible to know how many clubs exist that aren't NAIC affiliated, there surely are many thousands.

Those in the know say it's no surprise that people are becoming increasingly interested in investment clubs. Interest in nearly all areas of personal finance is on the rise, and the investment club boom mirrors the trend for people to get involved and take control of their money.

Online investing has prompted many folks to take charge of their own *portfolios* by managing their stocks with their computers. Some schools have started offering courses in personal finance, or setting up investment clubs for students. In fact, all-student investment groups are a fast-growing segment of the investment club movement. And, more and more businesses are coming up with 401(k) retirement plans, many of which require participants to choose their own investments as part of the package.

Investment clubs and 401(k) plans are known as sort of "crash courses" in investing. That's because both of them force participants to learn about and get involved with their investment choices. If your employer offers a 401(k) plan, be sure to take full advantage of it, especially if the company is willing to match—or partially match—your savings.

It's about time that people get more involved with their money, experts say. No one, not even a really good financial advisor, has the same stake in your money as you do. And, ultimately, you're responsible for how your money is used and invested. Learning about where your money is going, and how it's working for you, is a great way to assure your financial health.

Taking Stock

Your investment **portfolio** is the listing and value of all your investments.

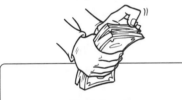

Cashing In

Although experts say that socializing shouldn't be the primary focus of an investment club, a certain amount of chit-chat is encouraged. Club members who feel comfortable with one another are more likely to feel free to express their views and exchange ideas than those who aren't comfortable. So, don't be afraid to loosen up a little bit, as long as the socializing doesn't get out of hand.

Why Do People Love Investment Clubs?

People love investment clubs for lots of reasons—not all of them are the right ones.

Some people love the clubs because they think they'll join up, make a large profit very quickly, and move on. Hopefully, we don't have to tell you that this is not a good reason to love your club. Investment clubs aren't "get rich quick" schemes—at least they shouldn't be considered as such.

Others love investment clubs because they give them the opportunity to get together with acquaintances, do a bit of socializing, and learn a little something about investing.

While the social aspect of investment clubs is important, it shouldn't be a person's primary reason for joining. If socializing is what you want to do, plan to have dinner, or coffee and dessert, before or after the meeting. This allows you to have social time, while reserving your meeting time for business.

Safety in Numbers

A wide appeal of investment clubs is the "safety in numbers" feeling that many members have. In most clubs, while each member is responsible for researching particular stocks or other types of investments, the membership must fully, or mostly, agree before any investment is made. If there's a goof, the blame normally doesn't fall solely on one person, but is shared by the group.

The person who researched the investment will no doubt feel somewhat chagrined if he or she recommended that the group purchase a particular stock, and the purchase turns out to be a bad decision. Still, the blame has to be shared because the majority of the club agreed to buy it.

In addition, the philosophy behind investment clubs traditionally is that it's easy to make some mistakes. After all, club members are all learning together, and no one is expected to be perfect.

A club should provide a comfortable environment, where a mistake, or two or three, isn't looked at as the end of the world.

Painless to the Pocketbook

Another major appeal of investment clubs is that they're relatively painless to the pocketbook. Most clubs require members to shell out between $10 and $50 a month, an amount that most people find manageable.

Take This to the Bank

If your investment club requires you to throw in $25 a month, consider what else you might do with that money. The average fee for bouncing a check is around $25, so you could do that. Or you could take the kids to Burger King. Or you could take your spouse to the movies and maybe have enough left over for popcorn. Consider your $25 monthly contribution to your club money well spent.

While most clubs allow members to contribute more than the minimum amount, keeping the monthly payments fairly low gives members flexibility. Let's face it. We all have those financially challenging months, when scraping together even $25 or $30 can be a chore. Knowing that it's not necessary to come up with large sums of money in order to stay in the club is a big plus for many people.

Knowledge Builds Confidence

The acquisition of knowledge and resulting self-confidence are additional reasons why so many people love their investment clubs. Consider a middle-aged woman (we'll call her Karen), who has always deferred to her husband's opinions on their investments. He's handled the money for their entire married lives, while she managed the house and arranged for the kids to get to soccer practice, Girl Scouts, Boy Scouts, cheerleading practice, choir practice, the dentist, and to visit their grandparents.

One day, a friend invites Karen to join an investment club, and Karen accepts. Following the recommendations of the club, Karen begins researching various companies. She learns about financial statements and annual reports. Not only does she know what they are, but she knows how to read them, as well.

She learns about the stock market. Soon, phrases like "cyclical stock" and "Dow Jones Industrial Average" are creeping into her vocabulary. She's excited because she's learning about things she barely knew existed. She joins in party conversations about finances and investments—something she never would have done before joining her club.

Karen knows she's on to something—and she loves it. Her newly acquired knowledge, all due to joining the investment club, has given her a wonderful sense of confidence. She thinks that joining the club is one of the best moves she ever made.

As you can see, there are different reasons, some of them quite intangible, why so many people love their investment clubs. Some people, however, aren't as thrilled.

Not Everybody Thinks They're Great

While many people report extremely positive investment club experiences, there are some who are less enthusiastic about the clubs.

Jack, a friend in central Florida, started an investment club in the mid-1990s in his neighborhood. All was well for the first year, and he was excited about how the club seemed to be progressing. Members were enthusiastic about the club, and gladly followed through with their research. Everyone was making regular contributions, and doing his or her share of the work to keep the club afloat.

In addition, the neighbors were getting to know each other better because of the club, and people were friendlier to each other than they'd been previously. Club members even got together every couple of months to go out to dinner.

Take This to the Bank

It's estimated that about half of all investment clubs fail within the first 18 months. Oops!

Slowly, however, things fell apart. Jack was left to try to pick up the pieces.

Some of the members started complaining that the research took too much time, and overall research efforts decreased. If an investment turned out to be a bad one, certain members would blame others, and bad feelings resulted. People started skipping meetings without notifying Jack, and meetings no longer seemed fun, but were filled with tension.

Jack says he knew the club was doomed on the night that about half of the people in attendance got into a bad argument about whether or not to buy a particular stock. He doesn't think anyone even cared that much about the stock (in fact, he can't even remember what company's stock it was). Member relations were so strained at that point, Jack says, that no one needed much reason to start a fight.

"We should have broken up [the club] a couple of months before that happened," Jack says. "I guess it really was my fault for letting it go for so long, but I didn't realize just how bad things had gotten."

The club dissolved shortly after that fateful evening, amidst numerous arguments about how the money should be divided and returned to members.

"It took a while for the neighborhood to recover from the investment club experiment," Jack says. "I don't think we'll be starting any more clubs any time soon."

Certainly, there are many clubs that tried and failed, for whatever reasons. There are personality clashes, people who want to enjoy the benefits of a club without doing their share of the work, and members get frustrated when they realize it's going to take a while before the club makes any money.

Cashing In

Anticipating club problems before they occur can help you deal with them more effectively. Consider adding a clause to your club's bylaws that allows the group to terminate the membership of anyone who misses a certain number of meetings, doesn't do his share of the work, or doesn't make monthly payments.

Investment clubs, like anything else, aren't for everyone. They require work, commitment, and dedication. Still, for many thousands of people, they're definitely the way to go. Let's take a look at who's joining clubs—and who's forming them.

Who's Joining Investment Clubs?

Family members, sorority sisters, priests, stockbrokers, golfing buddies, women's groups, men's groups, neighborhood groups, housewives, steelworkers, teachers, senior citizens, chefs, college students, co-workers, Generation X-ers, Baby Boomers, and even kids are joining investment clubs, just to name a few.

It would be difficult to find a professional, socioeconomic, ethnic, or religious group that's not represented by an investment club. That, of course, is a big reason that many people find the clubs so appealing. They're encompassing, accessible, and affordable. And surveys show that they work.

Take This to the Bank

Financial writer Doug Gerlach reports in a 1999 article found online at www.investorama.com that the majority of clubs that belong to the National Association of Investors Corp. are outperforming the Standard & Poor's 500 Index. That's a much higher number than mutual fund managers who outperform the index.

At least as many women as men are joining investment clubs, with the Beardstown Ladies' Club being largely credited for the increased interest among women. And, club membership (both men and women) in other countries is on the rise, as well.

Many people who belong to investment clubs also are seasoned investors on their own. That's good news to the other members of their clubs, who can benefit from their expertise. But, a lot of investment knowledge shouldn't be a requirement for joining a club. Willingness to work hard and learn is more important.

Who's Forming Investment Clubs?

Grandmothers and grandfathers who want to help their families achieve financial security, teachers who want their students to learn about finances, and motivated employees who want to create opportunities for themselves and co-workers are forming investment clubs. Generation X-ers, who don't believe there will be any Social Security for them when they retire, and college students looking to start out their financial futures on the right foot are joining in as well.

Those forming investment clubs are mostly ordinary people who recognize the power of these clubs and believe that they can help them achieve financial security. The founders are informed and intelligent, and not afraid to work hard to achieve results.

There is much help available for those interested in forming investment clubs. In addition to this and other books and Internet sites, the National Association of Investors Corp. offers a large selection of information and resources for anyone who's thinking of starting a club.

Hopefully, the information you read in this chapter will help you decide if the idea of joining or forming an investment club is appealing to you. In the next chapter, we'll look at some successful clubs, and what they've done to make themselves successful. If you're not yet convinced that investment clubs are your cup of tea, keep reading. Maybe seeing what others have done to put their financial futures on the fast track will convince you that investment clubs are the way to go.

Cashing In

For more information, contact the NAIC at its toll-free number, 1-877-275-6242. Or check out its Web site at www.better-investing.org.

The Least You Need to Know

➤ Investment club members must commit to doing the work involved with keeping a club up and running.

➤ Investment clubs have been around for more than a century, but have only recently become the focus of so much attention.

➤ Joining investment clubs is one way, but not the only way, that people are getting more involved with and taking charge of their personal finances.

➤ There are many reasons why people love investment clubs, but joining a club may not be the right decision for everyone.

➤ Nearly every group of people imaginable is represented by an investment club.

Chapter 2

Some Successful Clubs and What They've Done

In This Chapter

➤ Learning from the experience of others

➤ The granddaddy of all investment clubs

➤ Making mistakes is okay

➤ A family club that gives back

➤ Keeping it simple works best

➤ Using the expertise of the NAIC

Experience is a great teacher. Too often, we're tempted to reinvent a wheel that works perfectly just the way it is.

When starting your investment club, you'll probably have all kinds of ideas about what you want to do, how you want the club to run, the structure of the club, and so forth. All of these considerations, when put into action, will determine your club's character.

If every investment club were exactly the same, it would be easy to start one. You'd simply get a step-by-step plan and put it into action. No two clubs are the same, however, for a variety of reasons.

First of all, the people who will join your club are different than those in the investment club your cousin's boyfriend started last year. The membership of any club makes it unique.

Secondly, your club most likely won't be set up exactly like the one your cousin's boyfriend started. You may choose to have a different legal structure, or you'll meet at a different time. Maybe you'll decide you want an online club, which is very different from a traditional one.

Regardless of how you choose to set up and run your investment club, there are many clubs that are already up and operating, and there are many lessons that you can learn from them.

Internet Clubs

Although we've included only a few clubs here, you can access many more on the Internet, many of which offer helpful suggestions and information. Some clubs even tell you how many shares of stock they hold in particular companies, and share information such as how much money they contribute each month, how they keep records, and so forth.

The Aloha Investors

Located in Honolulu, Hawaii, the Aloha Investors have been a group since October 1997. The club's primary objectives are to buy stock in companies that have high potential for substantial growth, and to educate its members. The club has 19 members.

Its Web site includes meeting minutes, a list of officers, and the club's partnership agreement and portfolio. You can find the site at members.aol.com/kkh737/thealohainvestors.html.

The Yong Fah Investment Group

Yong Fah is Chinese for Prosperity Forever, and members of the Yong Fah Investment Group in Tampa, Florida, are hoping their club's name is an omen for what lies ahead of them.

The Yong Fah Web site includes market trends and stock quotes, links to other finance-related sites, and lots of information about the club. Check it out at home1.gte.net/ginajen/index.htm.

The Black Monday Investment Group

The Black Monday Investment Group was started in 1995 by a group of co-workers in Santa Ana Heights, California. The 14-member group started out strictly adhering to NAIC stock analysis methods, but, as members gained experience, started trying other methods.

The Black Monday Investment Group has been placing its orders online since 1996, and has found the service to be "simple, powerful, and economical." Its Web site includes meeting minutes and links to other financial and investment sites. It's on the Internet at www.gordian.com/users/blackmonday/.

The Neighborhood Investment Club

Located in Pullman, Washington, the Neighborhood Investment Club is an NAIC club, and uses NAIC software, investment strategies, and the NAIC philosophy.

Its Web site includes the club's portfolio, reports on recent meetings, links to other sites, and information about the club. You can access it at www.mme.wsu.edu/~kurt/N.A.I.C./index/html.

The Investment Analysis Group at Stern

This high-powered investment club is associated with the Stern Business School at New York University in New York City. The club attracts guests such as John Bogle, founder and senior chairman of the Vanguard Group, and focuses on education as well as investing.

Its sophisticated Web site includes information about the companies the club has researched, its calendar, press releases about past and upcoming events, and information about the group's stocks and mutual funds. You can find it on the Internet at www.stern.nyu.edu/~iag.

Many clubs give e-mail addresses and encourage visitors to visit their Web sites to contact club members with any questions or comments. We encourage you to take advantage of the willingness of many clubs to share their ideas and experiences.

Meanwhile, let's have a look at some successful clubs, and get some tips on what they've done to achieve their success and keep the clubs operating smoothly.

The Mutual Investment Club of Detroit

We'd be sorely remiss if we didn't mention the Mutual Investment Club of Detroit—often called "the granddaddy of all investment clubs."

Formed in 1940 and still going strong, this club truly is an inspiration for members of investment clubs everywhere. We've chosen to use, with permission, the Mutual Investment Club's operating agreement as a sample in this book. It's a great example of what an agreement should include. It's readable, useable, and contains everything your club will need.

Frederick C. Russell organized the Mutual Investment Club of Detroit in February 1940. Russell, like many people at that time, was out of work. He formed the club as a means of raising money to use to buy a small business.

One member was a broker and several were Russell's fraternity brothers. The club continued operating during World War II, although some of its members were off fighting for their country.

When the war ended, the club was up to a dozen members, with between $4,000 and $5,000 invested. Its members, by that time, were deeply committed to the concept of group investing, and news of their club began to spread.

The club determined at the very start that it would do three things:

➤ Invest every month

➤ Reinvest all its dividends

➤ Buy growth companies

By following these guidelines, and by hanging tough when the market was at its bleakest, the Mutual Investment Club of Detroit has set an example for thousands of other clubs over the years.

The original members who stayed with the club for the long haul realized significant gains. By 1982, the Mutual Investment Club members who'd been investing $10 to $20 a week had gains of more than $200,000 each.

Starting and Running a Profitable Investment Club, the official guide from the National Association of Investment Corp. (more about that organization later in the section "The National Association of Investors Corporation"), gives us statistics on one of the original members of the Mutual Investment Club of Detroit.

Take This to the Bank

The Mutual Investment Club of Detroit was one of four Michigan clubs that founded the National Association of Investors Corporation in 1951.

By starting in 1940 with a $10 monthly contribution, which he later increased to $20 a month, the club member was able to take $70,000 in earnings when he retired to pay off his mortgage. Although his monthly investments over the years totaled less than $10,000, his piece of the investment club's pie is worth more than half a million dollars.

If that's not an inspiration to aspiring or fledgling club members, we're not sure what would be.

All this isn't to say that the club's portfolios haven't taken some hits. After all, the market has had plenty of ups and downs in the past 60 years. During the 1970s, in fact, the Mutual Investment Club of Detroit, along with many other individual investors and investment clubs, watched as the value of its portfolio dropped nearly by half.

It took conviction and confidence for the club to keep investing in that market, but that's exactly what it did. Eventually, as we all know, the market recovered, and the Mutual Investment Club came out a winner.

The club's longevity, tenacity, and professionalism have combined to make it a model for other clubs.

The Beardstown Ladies' Investment Club

Almost everyone has heard of this club, which has been both heralded and ridiculed. The Beardstown (Illinois) Business and Professional Women's Investment Club (its official name) first started in 1980.

It was formed in response to a suggestion from the national office of Business and Professional Women (BPW) that its local chapters across the country form investment clubs so that members could learn more about handling their finances.

The original club, made up of members of the Beardstown chapter of BPW and other community members, was a bit unwieldy with about 36 members.

Women in the club concentrated on learning about all kinds of financial issues, while contributing between $5 and $30 a month for investing.

The club met regularly for three years, and then disbanded, as specified in its charter.

Some members of the original group were unwilling to let the club die. Twelve of the most active members, along with four other women, committed to reforming the group.

They used the same name as the former club. As the club gained recognition, however, it became better known as the Beardstown Ladies' Club.

The Beardstown Ladies, meaning the second group, set three goals as their club's mission. The goals are ...

➤ Education

➤ Enjoyment

➤ Financial enrichment

Cashing In

The reputation of the Beardstown Ladies may have suffered a bit, but their book, *The Beardstown Ladies' Common-Sense Investment Guide,* is a great read. It's entertaining, informative, and you even get some interesting recipes, such as Lillian's Chicken Supreme, Carnell's Favorite Ham Loaf, and Shirley's Stock Market Muffins (guaranteed to rise!).

The order in which the goals are listed is significant, for that's the order of priority as noted by the Beardstown Ladies.

You may have already heard how the Beardstown Ladies, after much public acclaim and recognition, discovered they'd made a serious accounting error. The 23.4 percent return on their investment that had made headlines and was publicized on the covers of the books they wrote, turned out to be incorrect.

Oops! Apparently, the Beardstown Ladies actually did have a 23.4 percent return during a two-year period in 1991 and 1992. Over the 10-year period between 1984 to 1993, however, the Ladies' return was just 9.1 percent, which is well below the 15 percent return of the overall stock market, with dividends reinvested, during the same period.

The giant accounting firm Price Waterhouse audited the Beardstown Ladies' books, and reported that the overall average annual rate of return for the club between 1983 and 1997 was 15.3 percent.

While that's certainly not a bad return, it pales in comparison to 23.4 percent.

As it turns out, the Beardstown Ladies' Club hadn't added their club dues to the returns, which badly skewed their results.

Betty Sinnock, longtime club treasurer, said the mistake was due to a computer input error—probably her own. She wrote an open letter to the treasurers of all clubs affiliated with the National Association of Investors Corp., in which she explained her mistake, and said she was sorry if she had misled anyone.

"We are truly sorry and pray that the people who have bought our books did so because they wanted to learn about investing in the market and not because the 23.4 percent was printed on the cover," Sinnock wrote.

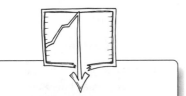

Heading for a Crash

The Beardstown Ladies' mishap sends a needed warning to other investment clubs. If you don't take the time and make sure you have the expertise to keep the proper and necessary records, you'll be heading for serious trouble.

So, why are we calling the Beardstown Ladies a successful club, and spending all this time writing about them?

The Beardstown Ladies, arguably, did as much, or more, than any other investment club to get people interested in the club movement.

Thousands of people have read their books, which are written in a very user-friendly, easy-to-read manner, and were inspired by the club's determination and success. They no doubt spurred hundreds of people to start investment clubs, who may not have done so without the influence of the Beardstown Ladies.

All-women clubs have been and remain extremely popular, and we must assume that many of them started in response to the Beardstown Club. There are many clubs that are made up primarily of older people, and we have to believe that's also at least partially due to Beardstown influence.

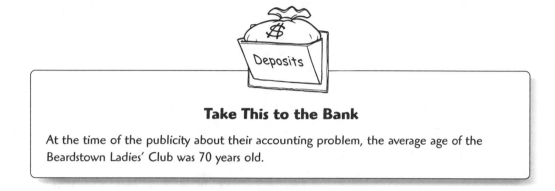

Take This to the Bank

At the time of the publicity about their accounting problem, the average age of the Beardstown Ladies' Club was 70 years old.

Another noteworthy aspect of the Beardstown Ladies' Club is its policy of not investing in what it calls "personal misery" companies. These are companies involved with gambling, tobacco, or liquor industries. We think there's much to be said for socially responsible investing, and the Beardstown Ladies have inspired other clubs to do the same.

The Washtenaw Women's Investment Team from Ann Arbor, Michigan, adopted the Beardstown Ladies' policy of socially responsible investing. In addition, the Washtenaw group decided that it wouldn't purchase any stocks in the defense industry.

So, while the Beardstown Ladies may have ended up publicly embarrassed, they still must be given great credit for their initiative and the inspiration that they provided for many people.

The Moore Money Club

Waymon Moore, of DeKalb County, Georgia, started the Moore Money club because he wanted to teach his younger relatives about investing. He also thought it would be nice to get far-flung cousins, aunts, uncles, nieces, and nephews communicating with each other.

"My first motivation was to get them acquainted," Moore was quoted as saying in an article that appeared in the February 7, 1999 edition of the *Atlanta Journal and Constitution*. "They had never had any reason to get together."

The Moore Money club is made up entirely of Moore's relatives, and has been together for nearly six years. Twenty-four relatives joined when Moore founded the club, and the membership has remained essentially the same.

The Moore Money Club is a great example of a well-run, responsible family club.

Their annual returns have been close to 20 percent, and the value of their portfolio exceeds a quarter of a million dollars.

After a successful career in the insurance industry, Moore was able to offer an extra incentive to those relatives who joined the family club. Moore asked for a $500 initial investment from each member, which he then matched. Needless to say, his generous gesture was met with much enthusiasm.

The Moore family club is particularly noteworthy because of its habit of tithing. The club donates 10 percent of its gains each year to its favorite charities, many of which are church-related.

Cashing In

Betty Taylor, a representative of the National Association of Investors Corp. who lectures frequently about family investment clubs, says that family clubs are becoming increasingly popular, with many people eager to start one. "They see that clubs are very profitable, and they say, 'Why not do it with the family?'" Taylor says.

The Fresh Start Investment Club

There's an investment club in Lancaster, Pennsylvania, in which all the members are middle-aged, divorced women. A number of the 10-women club had been stay-at-home moms who were forced to return to work after they separated from their husbands.

Most of these women, who didn't want their names used, are struggling a bit financially, and are under additional pressure because they're only about 10 years away from retirement age.

In other words, there isn't a lot of money to spare among the members of this club. Each of these women, however, recognized the fact that it was imperative that they started investing some money. Their present savings aren't enough to take them comfortably through retirement, and they're all looking to generate some additional capital for when they're no longer working.

Each member of the Fresh Start Club makes it a point to save $50 a month to invest. It's tough sometimes because there's not much left over after all the expenses have been paid. These women, however, are committed to investing, and nobody has missed a month's contribution since their club was formed in early 1999.

We've included this club in this chapter because of the spirit and drive of these women who chose to take control of their futures by saving a little bit to invest each month.

In addition to the benefits that investing will bring, the women say they're learning more from each other about finances than they ever thought they would know. They're getting involved in 401(k) plans at work, and building up other retirement accounts whenever possible. A few of them had to learn to balance a checkbook after their divorces—they'd never been involved with the family finances.

Belonging to the investment club makes it possible for these women to buy stock that they wouldn't be able to get on their own. It's also provided them with a great support system, and has been the impetus for a lot of education.

We say congratulations to all of the ladies of the Fresh Start Investment Club. Keep up the great work.

The Ten Thousand Club

Members of the Ten Thousand Club are all members of the Atlantic Health System, based in Florham Park, New Jersey. Julie McGovern, director of organization development, training, and recruitment, organized it.

McGovern put her considerable organizational skills to work to form the club because she was interested in learning about investing and knew that some of her co-workers were, too.

"We used to talk about investing quite a bit," McGovern says. "Everybody's interested in making their money work for them. Forming a club seemed like a natural way for us to help each other do that."

The club works, McGovern says, because they keep it simple. The Ten Thousand Club's bylaws are a simple three-page document. The bylaws outline topics such as membership requirements (membership is limited to Atlantic Health System employees, all members must attend at least 75 percent of the club's scheduled yearly meetings, and all members must participate in stock research and reporting), and the duties of officers.

The bylaws establish when meetings will be held and that 75 percent of members must be there to establish a quorum. Without a quorum, no voting can occur. And, the bylaws state that each member will contribute $50 a month, and that each contribution is worth one unit in the member's capital account. They also cover what happens when a member withdraws from the club, and the distribution of his or her capital.

McGovern said that the simplicity of the bylaws is a plus, because members can easily read and understand what's expected of them, and how the club will operate.

"That's been very helpful," McGovern says. "We refer to our bylaws a lot, and it's nice to have something that we don't have to debate. Everyone understands what the bylaws state."

Club members take turns researching and presenting possible investments to the rest of the club. Everyone understands the importance of doing their homework and having a report ready to share with other members.

The National Association of Investors Corporation

Somewhere around 37,000 investment clubs from all parts of the country belong to the National Association of Investors Corporation (NAIC). And, a recent survey of NAIC clubs showed that nearly 43 percent of them equaled or exceeded the return of the Standard & Poor's 500.

The club was founded in 1951 by the previously mentioned Mutual Investment Club of Detroit and three other clubs, and is largely responsible for the current investment club movement.

The president and CEO of the NAIC is Kenneth S. Janke Sr., and the chairman of the board is Thomas E. O'Hara. Robert A. O'Hara, the NAIC's Vice President of Development wrote the forward to this book.

We'll tell you more about the NAIC and how your club can become affiliated with the organization in Chapter 9, "Ensuring That the Club Runs Smoothly."

The NAIC can be an extremely valuable resource for your club, offering materials such as a stock selection guide, a monthly newsletter, accounting software, seminars and other educational programs, and much more. Because the organization has been around for almost 50 years, it has invaluable experience, which it willingly shares with its members.

Even if you're not a member of the NAIC, you can get some valuable information from its Web site at www.better-investing.org.

The Least You Need to Know

➤ There are many successful clubs out there, many of which are willing to share tips and ideas.

➤ The Mutual Investment Club of Detroit, in operation for more than 60 years, is a model for other clubs to follow.

➤ The Beardstown Ladies' Club made mistakes and took its share of ridicule, but it still serves as an inspiration for many other clubs.

➤ Family clubs offer special rewards and challenges.

➤ Keeping the operating rules clear-cut and simple assures that all club members have the same expectations.

➤ The National Association of Investors Corp. is a great source of help to both new and experienced investment clubs.

Chapter 3

Online Investment Clubs—the Wave of the Future?

In This Chapter

➤ Learning the basics of online investment clubs

➤ Looking at the pros and cons of online clubs

➤ Figuring out how to find an online club that works for you

➤ Starting your own online club

➤ Keeping alert for con artists and scams

We buy books and CDs from Internet sites. We buy clothing, collectibles, and gifts. We chat with people on the Internet we probably will never meet, from places we'll never visit. And we research topics that we perhaps didn't even know existed.

As the Internet becomes more and more pervasive in our society, its uses have, and will continue, to grow. So, it should be no surprise that increasing numbers of people are starting online investment clubs.

Online clubs definitely offer some advantages that face-to-face clubs don't. Most notably, they allow people who are not able to get together to conduct club business on their computers. And online clubs allow members to communicate with each other when it's convenient—not just at specified meeting times.

For many people, however, communicating by computer is no substitute for face-to-face conversation and interaction. For that, and other reasons, online clubs don't appeal to everyone. Besides, we need to remember that there is still a significant group of people who don't have or use personal computers.

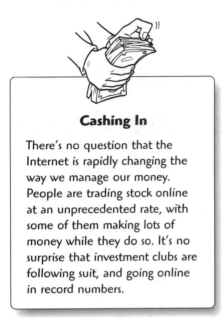

Cashing In

There's no question that the Internet is rapidly changing the way we manage our money. People are trading stock online at an unprecedented rate, with some of them making lots of money while they do so. It's no surprise that investment clubs are following suit, and going online in record numbers.

In this chapter, we'll take a look at online clubs and examine how they compare to face-to-face clubs. We'll look at the similarities and differences between the two kinds of groups, and tell you where you can find out more about online investment clubs. We'll also look at some possible problems with online clubs and examine online investing in general.

What Are Online Clubs?

If you think back to Chapter 1, "What's All This Talk About Investment Clubs?" you'll remember that we defined investment clubs simply as groups of people who decide to get together to share research, contribute money, and invest in stocks that they all agree upon.

Well, online investment clubs are almost exactly the same thing, except their members get together via computer, rather than meet face to face.

A great many investment clubs operate exclusively online, some by choice, others by necessity. Some online clubs started as traditional clubs that chose to go online rather than disband when members moved away and regular meetings became impossible. Other clubs started online, preferring that method of doing business rather than holding actual meetings.

Online club members use message boards, mailing lists, and Web pages to buy and sell stocks in a single portfolio. They research stocks on their computers and communicate information about stocks to other club members by e-mail.

Like traditional clubs, online clubs have (or certainly should have) membership agreements, club rules, and common goals identified for all members. Club participants should be on the same page (or screen, perhaps) when it comes to what's expected of them, and what their membership in the club entails.

The focus of online clubs, just as that of face-to-face clubs, should be on education and learning. Get-rich-quick schemes have no place in any kind of investment club.

How Many Online Clubs Are out There?

While it's difficult to establish an actual number of online investment clubs, it's easy to determine that the number of these clubs is rapidly increasing.

Officials at the National Association of Investors Corporation (NAIC) say that online clubs have played a major role in the great surge of investment clubs during the past five years.

About 37,000 clubs were registered with the NAIC in late 1999. A significant number of them are online clubs, although the exact number isn't known. And there are many more online clubs that aren't NAIC affiliated. You'll read more about the advantages of joining the NAIC in Chapter 9, "Ensuring That the Club Runs Smoothly."

Take This to the Bank

The number of investment clubs (both online and the old-fashioned kind) that are registered with the National Association of Investors Corp. more than tripled between 1994 and 1999.

Experts anticipate that the number of online clubs will continue to increase rapidly, as people become more and more accustomed to using computers and the Internet for daily activities.

Comparing Online Clubs to the Old-Fashioned Kind

Earlier in this chapter, we talked about some similarities between online and face-to-face investment clubs. Both types of clubs operate best when there are membership agreements and club rules in place. Online clubs and their face-to-face counterparts should stress education, and encourage members to learn all they can about stocks, investing, and other financial matters.

While there are many similarities between online and personal clubs, there are some differences as well. The biggest difference, obviously, is that members of online clubs don't physically meet with each other. Some clubs get together every six

Cashing In

Online clubs that are NAIC members often hold periodic meetings at NAIC functions, which are held regularly around the country. For more information about these meetings, contact the NAIC at its toll-free number, 1-877-275-6242. Or check out its Web site at www.better-investing.org.

months or once a year to evaluate where the club stands and where it's going—or just so members can get to know each other on a different level than they do over their computers. Other clubs, however, never meet.

That works for some people, but not for everyone. A friend who belonged to an on-line investment club for more than two years left the group recently. She said it suddenly started to seem absurd for her to be spending large amounts of time at her computer, communicating about financial matters with people she didn't know. She's since joined a club that holds regular meetings, complete with prebusiness chit-chat and refreshments.

Deciding what kind of investment club you want to join is something you'll need to do for yourself. To help you, let's examine some advantages and disadvantages of on-line investment clubs.

Are Online Clubs Better?

People who belong to online investment clubs say there are many advantages. Let's have a look at some of them:

➤ Online clubs are convenient. Online investment club members say they like being able to communicate with other members at their convenience, instead of only at specified times. It's great for people who work different shifts from other club members, or who just keep different schedules. Clearly, the convenience factor is a major attraction to many Internet users—not just online investment clubs. Online shoppers say that sitting at the computer in their pajamas at 10 P.M. with a cup of hot tea next to the mouse pad definitely is more convenient and relaxing than fighting crowds in department stores.

➤ Online clubs allow greater flexibility and faster decisions. When a member recommends that the club buys or sells a particular stock, other club members can cast their votes via e-mail, instead of waiting to vote at a face-to-face meeting. Online clubs say this is a great asset, because it allows them to act quickly when opportunities arise.

➤ Online clubs allow members to get a broad perspective. Investors who belong to clubs whose members are spread out geographically say the distance helps provide a broader sense of various demographic trends, and gives club members a better idea of what's happening financially in other areas than they could get with a locals-only club.

➤ Online club members have access to incredible information on the Internet. Of course, members of traditional investment clubs also can jump on the Net and get the latest stock news, and many do. Online club members, however, are already online, and tend to access information from the Internet more than members of traditional clubs.

Take This to the Bank

The Genie OnLine Discoverers (G.O.L.D.) Investment Club claims to be one of the oldest online clubs in the country. It was formed in 1992 on the Genie telecommunications service, and now operates on the Internet. With more than $10,000 in assets, the club has been featured in *ComputerLife* magazine and on the Motley Fool Web site.

➤ Online clubs encourage more research. For whatever reasons, people who belong to online clubs say they spend more time researching companies and stocks than they did when they belonged to traditional clubs. The reason for that could be that the Internet is full of sites that assist with research. There are on-line brokerages, financial news services, and sites that specialize in investment advice. Two such Web sites to check out are www.winninginvesting.com and 4investmentadvice.com.

➤ Online clubs keep people in touch. Online clubs are popular with families or groups of friends that have spread out to different areas. Some members say that keeping in touch with families and friends through online investment clubs is as important to them as making money.

➤ Online clubs make joining one possible for some people who may not otherwise be able to participate in an investment club. The Internet has been a tremendous benefit to millions of people. Among those who especially benefit from the technology are people with physical challenges. An acquaintance who is deaf says that the Internet has made communicating easier than she ever thought was possible. People who are unable to walk, or even those with anxiety or other kinds of problems that make it difficult for them to leave their homes certainly could benefit from online investment clubs.

These are a few advantages of online investment clubs—no doubt there are many more. Now let's have a look at why some people say they don't like online clubs.

Or Are Online Clubs Not as Good?

Nothing's perfect—not even online investment clubs. Listed below are some factors that make them not so appealing to some investors:

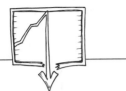

Heading for a Crash

Because stuff happens, don't rely completely on technology when conducting investment club business online. Be sure you back up important notes and information. You might want to keep a written log of what stocks have been purchased, at what cost, and so forth. Computers are great, but it doesn't hurt to take precautions.

➤ An online club is only as good and reliable as the technology it uses. Let's face it. The Internet is far from being problem free. How many times has your program shut down just as you were getting ready to send a lengthy e-mail? Or an e-mail mysteriously disappears from your online mailbox? Of course, there also are problems associated with face-to-face clubs—your car could break down on the way to a meeting, or a snowstorm could force you to cancel. Don't assume, however, that running a club via computers will be problem free.

➤ Online clubs just aren't personal enough. For some people, the only "real" way to communicate is face to face. They like to know what the people with whom they're dealing look and sound like. They feel uncomfortable communicating via computers, and because of that, online clubs aren't appealing.

➤ You've got to be careful of state requirements. Online clubs are likely to include members who live in different states. After all, if you're conducting business via computers, it really doesn't matter where your club's members live. The problem is that different states have different regulations concerning investment clubs. You've got to make sure all your members are on the same page, and your club is adhering to the regulations of the state in which it will be registered.

➤ You don't get refreshments with an online club. Well, maybe it's not the refreshments that are important (although we'd sometimes kill for a good piece of cheesecake), but some people say that the social aspect of their meetings is what makes belonging to an investment club really enjoyable. For those people, online clubs just don't measure up.

Online enthusiasts and face-to-face proponents could argue for hours about which type of club is better. What it comes down to is figuring out in what kind of club you think you'd be more comfortable. While some people conduct most of their business and other communication by e-mail, others are more comfortable on the telephone or in a personal meeting. It's a personal decision that you'll need to make.

Where to Find Online Clubs

If you decide that an online investment club sounds right for you, there are two things you can do:

➤ Find a club to join

➤ Start your own

If you think you'd like to join an existing club, there are several ways to go about finding one. You could put out some feelers, much the same as you would do if you were looking to join a face-to-face club. Start by asking friends, acquaintances, co-workers, and relatives if they know anybody who trades stocks online or is involved with an online club. Ask them to let you know if they hear of anyone who does.

If you meet up with somebody who trades online, don't hesitate to ask her if she's aware of any online clubs. She may know of some, regardless of whether or not she's a member.

Take This to the Bank

Online investment clubs are advised not to advertise for new members, as they could risk violating the Security and Exchange Commission's rules on unregistered financial advisors. Some clubs, however, mention on their Web sites that anyone interested in joining is welcome to send an e-mail. If you're looking for an online club to join, spend some time browsing with the search engines, and you'll probably find one.

Another way to find an online club is to go online. Many investment clubs, both online and those that meet in person, have their own Web sites, and you can get plenty of information about the clubs, their investments, philosophies, operating policies, and so forth.

A couple of Internet sites that will help get you started in your search for an online club are …

➤ **www.computerland.net.** This site has an extensive list of investment clubs from every state in the United States, plus Canadian and online clubs.

➤ **www.investmentclub.miningco.com.** This site is well organized and easy to use, listing both face-to-face and online clubs.

➤ **www.investorama.com.** Gives you about 50 online clubs, plus lots of general information concerning investment clubs.

Other online resources are included in the Appendix B, "Resources."

With investment clubs of all sorts starting up in record numbers, it shouldn't be too difficult to find an online club. Some clubs put potential members on waiting lists if they're currently full. Don't hesitate to get your name on a list while you continue to look around for something immediately available.

Choosing an Online Club That Makes Sense for You

After you locate and learn about some online clubs, you'll have to choose the one in which you think you'll be the most comfortable.

Be sure to learn as much about each club you discover as possible. There are many philosophies when it comes to buying stock, and you should make sure that yours is in tune with that of the other members.

Take This to the Bank

Members of some investment clubs buy only what they consider to be socially responsible stocks. The Beardstown Ladies' Club wouldn't invest in any of what it called "personal misery" companies, meaning companies involved in gambling, tobacco, or liquor industries.

Some clubs, for instance, buy only sexy, high-tech stocks, while others prefer more mainstream, predictable ones. Many online clubs with their own Web sites include descriptions of their philosophies on their sites.

Look also at the number of members of each club you explore. Some people like a bigger club because it's more diverse and the club has more money to invest, while others prefer small, more intimate groups.

And don't forget to check out each club's rules and regulations, such as how much money you'll need to invest each month, how much say you'll have in investment decisions, and so forth. You don't want to hastily join a club, only to find out afterward that you're required to invest $300 a month!

After you do your research and decide what kind of club you're looking for, don't be afraid to trust your gut. If a particular club really feels right for you, it probably is.

Starting an Online Club

If you decide to start your own online club, there's some important information you'll need to know. We cover all the basics of starting a traditional investment club in Part 2, "The Basics of Starting a Club." There are some guidelines and parameters, however, which apply especially to online clubs.

Take This to the Bank

You have to wonder about some of the names of online clubs listed on the Internet. Some that we came across include Rampaging Bulls Online, Broken Bayou Partners, and High Seas Traders. Rampaging Bulls? It's great to have fun with a club name, but experts do advise that the name should reflect the club's purpose.

If you don't want to have only people you know in your online club, you can go online to find other members. Use the sites listed in the "Where to Find Online Clubs" section earlier in this chapter, or you could post a message announcing that you're looking to start a club. The Motley Fools have an investment club message board on which you can post a notice about your club. That site is at www.boards.fool.com.

If you get a lot of replies, be careful that your club doesn't get too big. Experts say that online clubs should have no more than 25 members, or they get too cumbersome to operate effectively.

Also, the law requires that all members of investment clubs registered in the United States must be U.S. citizens, so you'll need to keep that in mind. If there's doubt about a person's citizenship, you'll need to ask for proof. If you're not sure, it's best to politely decline his or her request to join, and find somebody else.

Cashing In

Members of the National Association Investors Corp. (NAIC) can get a Web site that will be maintained by Yahoo! A NAIC-Yahoo! site includes portfolio tools, an events calendar, and virtual meeting rooms. Check out www.clubs.yahoo.com/naic.html. Non-NAIC members can get sites at Yahoo! Clubs or Excite Communities (www.excite.com/communities/directories), but those sites don't have all the features of the NAIC-Yahoo! site.

When you get a group of potential members in place, you'll need to figure out how you're going to communicate with one another. Most online clubs just use group e-mails, and that might be the simplest way. Some clubs, however, set up private Web sites.

Just like any investment club, an online club should have a partnership agreement (see more about the agreements in Chapter 8, "Establishing Operating Rules"). The agreement must be submitted to state officials when your club is registered.

An online club can register in any state in which one or more of its members reside. If your club includes members from different states, be sure you shop around before deciding where to register. The cost and hassle involved with registering will vary greatly from state to state. You'll learn more about that in Chapter 8.

Once you've found members and have registered your club, you're ready to go. There are other rules and regulations of which you'll need to be aware, and they'll be covered in later chapters.

Just be sure that all your members understand exactly how your club will operate, and how you'll do business online. It's really important that all members have the same understanding about how the club will work.

Watching Out for Tricky Situations Online

If the Internet is the next great frontier, as it's sometimes been described, it is no less without peril than the Wild, Wild West was 150 or so years ago.

Heading for a Crash

If it sounds too good to be true, it probably is. That old saying is especially applicable for Internet users, who are bombarded with all kinds of information and messages, and might not be as alert as they should be to possible scams. If you want to know more about what's going on, check out the Securities and Exchange Commission's investor alerts at www.sec.gov.

You've no doubt heard or read those awful stories about kids and teens who were lured into horrible situations by people they "met" on the Internet. Or of long-married spouses who suddenly leave home for a chat-room lover. If it's scandal you're looking for, the Internet will provide.

Financial sites are no more immune to bad situations than the rest of the Internet, though they tend to be a little different from chat-room scandals. Internet financial scams of all kinds have been reported, and anyone using the Web should be aware of what could happen.

Con artists seem to concentrate on online investors, of which there are more and more all the time. There are bogus stock newsletters, in which companies pay to have their stock promoted to online investors. There are online discussion groups, in which con artists post messages promoting worthless stock to gullible investors. There's even been a case in which online investors were convinced to invest in nonexistent eel farms.

While you shouldn't assume that everyone you come across online is looking to bilk you out of your hard-earned cash, maintain a healthy dose of cynicism. You should also use caution when starting, or joining, an online investment club.

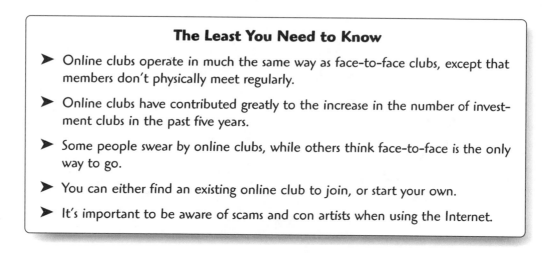

The Least You Need to Know

➤ Online clubs operate in much the same way as face-to-face clubs, except that members don't physically meet regularly.

➤ Online clubs have contributed greatly to the increase in the number of investment clubs in the past five years.

➤ Some people swear by online clubs, while others think face-to-face is the only way to go.

➤ You can either find an existing online club to join, or start your own.

➤ It's important to be aware of scams and con artists when using the Internet.

Chapter 4

Deciding If an Investment Club Is Right for You

In This Chapter

➤ Investment clubs are great, but they're not for everyone

➤ Taking a good, hard look at your personal finances

➤ Good things about joining a club

➤ Not-so-good things about joining a club

➤ Making the decision

You know that thousands of people all over the world belong to investment clubs, and the number of new clubs has climbed dramatically over the past couple of years.

You understand that many people are learning more about stocks and the stock market through their clubs than they ever thought was possible. And you're aware that many of these people are doing themselves a big financial favor by participating in clubs and making smart investment choices.

Despite knowing and understanding the numerous advantages to joining an investment club, maybe you just haven't done it yet. For whatever reasons, you're wavering. You just can't decide whether to join a club or not.

If this is the case with you, don't feel bad. While many people are happy and productive members of investment clubs, we acknowledge that these clubs are not for everybody. There's no law that says you have to join one.

Let's face it. Some people do better on their own than they do in groups. They're more comfortable being solely responsible for their decisions than they are in sharing that responsibility. Also, Internet trading has made it easy for people who like going it alone to get and stay in the action.

In this chapter, we'll get you thinking about the current state of your personal finances. If they're not where you'd like them to be, maybe now is not the time to think about joining an investment club. Even though it's not typically a lot, you need to have some extra money to invest each month.

We'll take a look at the advantages that investment clubs offer, and discuss the disadvantages of being a club member as well. After all, nothing is perfect.

Hopefully, this information will give you the basis on which to decide whether or not to join a club. If you've already joined one, keep reading anyway. You never know what you might learn.

Where You Stand Financially

You need money in order to be able to invest it. And, although most investment clubs don't require you to come up with huge sums of money every month, belonging to a club still means that you're going to need a little extra.

So, before you commit to joining a club, you'd better take a good, hard look at your personal financial situation. You'll need to evaluate where you stand right now, and where you're heading for the future.

Get Control of Your Situation

If you're thinking about joining an investment club, then presumably your personal finances are reasonably sound. We have to assume that you have a means of income, and you manage your money fairly well. Hopefully, you pay all your bills each month.

If you're not doing those things, however, then you'll need to get a handle on your personal finances. If you have trouble paying all your bills, or you're living paycheck to paycheck, or, worse still, you're buying more with credit cards than you can pay for when the bill comes in, you need to form a plan to improve your situation. Investing is a really smart plan, but, if you're paying close to 20 percent on a high credit card balance, it will be to your benefit to get that under control either before or as you begin investing.

Just think about it for a minute.

Suppose that, between three credit cards, you're carrying a balance of $2,000. It makes no sense for you to plunk down $50 (or whatever) at your investment club meeting if you're carrying high-interest debt on those credit cards. While you're hoping that your Motorola stock is going to eventually pad your retirement accounts, you're losing big bucks to the credit card companies in the meantime.

If your credit card interest rate is 17 percent (that's about average), and you owe $2,000, you'll pay $340 in interest a year—or $28 a month.

It makes more sense to pay off your credit card debt than to take your $50 and use it to buy stock. Or, begin investing $25 a month, and put the other $25 toward your credit card debt. Paying off credit card debt is one of the best ways to get your personal finances on track. Remember that the longer you carry a balance on your card (or cards), the deeper into debt you're getting.

Get Control of Your Credit Cards

If you're having trouble controlling credit card spending, think about stashing your cards and going the cash route. Many people (including us) find that they spend less if they have to hand over cash for every purchase. Coming up with two crisp twenties and a ten for that blouse you've had your eye on is a lot more difficult somehow than sliding a credit card across the checkout counter. Of course, there are situations in which you'll need a credit card, so be sure that at least one of your cards is accessible—but not too easily accessible.

Credit cards are great to have, but they do require some discipline when you use them. And, if you owe a lot of money on your cards, you should start taking care of that debt immediately.

Get Control of Your Expenses

You also should take a look at your monthly expenses. Are they under control, or do they seem to be more than you can handle? If you're uncomfortable with how much you're spending each month, it might be time to take a good look at exactly where your money goes.

If you're spending big bucks on clothing, entertainment, the gym, and so forth, you're in a good

Heading for a Crash

More than 60 million households in the United States have balances on their credit cards that they're carrying over from month to month. The average amount of this revolving debt is between $6,000 and $7,000. Credit card debt is a real killer, so be sure to keep it under control.

Cashing In

If you're still paying an annual fee on your credit card, write a letter to the credit card company right now and ask to have the fee waived. If the company won't do it, think seriously about canceling that card and finding another one. Increased competition has forced most companies to lower or drop annual fees. If your credit card company won't, there are plenty of others that will.

position to trim your spending and use the money you save for investment club contributions. There are many ways to spend less. Just a few are …

➤ **Forget designer labels.** You can spend thousands of dollars on clothing, which mostly remains in your closet. You can only wear one outfit at a time, the rest of your wardrobe hangs.

➤ **Work out at home.** Belonging to a gym is nice, but it's not necessary. Plenty of people get the exercise they need by walking, running, or lifting weights at home.

➤ **Buy store brands.** The next time you go to the drugstore for a bottle of cold medicine, compare the national brand to the store brand. Chances are that the store brand contains the very same ingredients, but costs at about one third less than the national brand.

➤ **Trade in your car.** Sure, you gotta have wheels. But, do you really need that fancy little Saab convertible? There are lots of cars to choose from, and some cost a whole lot more than others. If you're paying a lot each month on your car, consider getting something less expensive. In addition, if you are considering buying a new car because things are going wrong with your old one, first look into fixing your old one. It will be a lot less expensive to pay $500 now, than to start paying a $300 monthly car payment.

➤ **Look at little things.** Cable TV with premium channels, restaurant dinners two or three nights a week, cell phones, weekend getaways, more shoes, more jewelry, soda and a candy bar on your break, etc. While these extras sound nice, they can be real budget busters. If you're enjoying little luxuries a bit too often, you might want to think about cutting back. Do you really need to pay for manicures every other week, or could you do your nails yourself? Little expenses add up to big ones—fast.

Cashing In

Don't overlook the coupons that are included with your Sunday newspaper. They make it possible to save big bucks on groceries, household products, and personal items—all you have to do is spend a few minutes clipping and organizing. Saving $10 a week with coupons gives you $40 a month to invest with your club.

No matter how careful you are, there's no question that it costs a lot to live these days. Many younger people are trying to pay off college loans, in addition to coming up with money for rent and normal living expenses. Folks who are a little older might be looking at large mortgage payments, while trying to save for college for their kids, and put something aside for their own retirement.

If you're feeling a bit pinched financially, know that you're not alone. Nearly everybody could use a few extra bucks from time to time.

Take This to the Bank

About half of all college grads in this country have borrowed money to pay for their education. The average college debt is between $12,000 and $15,000.

Where You're Heading Financially

After you take a look at where you stand financially, take a look at where you're heading. Think about your short-term financial goals, your intermediate goals, and your long-term goals.

Consider how much money you'll need in the future, and how you might go about accumulating the money you'll need. Investments (such as those you might make as part of a club) are great. Don't, however, overlook other ways to save and make the most of your money.

While we don't have space here to go into great detail about saving money, there are a few things that should be mentioned.

401(k) Plans

If your employer offers one of these, jump in with both feet. Introduced in 1982 as a way for employers to save the money they'd been putting into pension plans, *401(k)s* allow employees to contribute a portion of their paychecks to a company investment plan until they retire or leave the company.

At that time, the employee's money can be either left where it is, rolled over into another retirement account, or claimed by the individual, who usually will face some penalties and an income tax liability for taking the money early.

The real beauty of 401(k)s is that you might get an employer to match your contributions. If you're really lucky, your employer will match your contribution dollar for dollar up to a certain percentage of your paycheck. The most typical match is that for

Taking Stock

A **401(k)** is a type of retirement savings plan that allows employees to contribute a portion of their paychecks to a company-sponsored investment plan. 401(k)s are different from pension plans, which are employee-sponsored retirement plans from which retirees get fixed, periodic payments.

every dollar an employee contributes the employer throws in 50 cents. By taking advantage of the match, you get an automatic 50 percent return on your money.

Be aware that some companies require a year of employment before you can begin adding money to a company 401(k) plan. If that's the case, check out the possibility of starting a traditional IRA account, then roll the money over when your 401(k) kicks in.

Also, be sure to find out your company's 401(k) policy for employees who leave to go elsewhere. Some companies don't let you take the money that they matched—only the part that you've contributed.

If you're not taking advantage of a 401(k) opportunity, and many employees are not, be sure to look into it as soon as possible. It's too good a deal to pass up.

Taking Stock

Mutual funds are investments that pool the money of many investors and place it in stocks, bonds, and other holdings. The money is managed by a portfolio manager and a team of researchers.

Mutual Funds

Mutual funds are popular because they don't require a lot of money to get started. When you put your money in a mutual fund, it's pooled with the money of lots of other people, and invested in stocks, bonds, and other holdings. Mutual funds are managed by portfolio managers and teams of researchers who are responsible for finding the best places to put your money.

Mutual funds come in two flavors: no load and load. No-load funds let you avoid paying a sales commission on your transactions, while load funds charge a sales commission that's paid to a broker or financial adviser. There are advantages and disadvantages to each kind of mutual fund, so make sure you do a little research before diving in. A good place to get basic information about mutual funds and other areas of personal finance is *The Complete Idiot's Guide to Managing Your Money,* by Robert K. Heady and Christy Heady.

Taking Stock

Money market accounts are accounts held in banks, on which you receive interest. **Money market funds** are held within mutual fund companies, and also pay a yield, or interest.

Money Markets

When people talk about money markets, they're talking about either *money market accounts* or *money market funds.* Money market accounts are accounts held in banks and insured within the Federal Deposit Insurance Corporation (FDIC). Money market funds are held within mutual funds companies, and they're not insured. Their safety depends on the safety of the investments within the funds. An example of such a fund is a U.S. Treasury Money Market Fund, which is very safe because the Treasury Notes are insured even though the fund itself is not.

Money market accounts and money market funds typically pay a bit more interest than savings or checking accounts. Both types of money markets normally allow you to write up to three checks a month to a party other than yourself for free. The check normally has to be for a minimum amount—often $250. Although you get higher interest on a money market account or fund than you do with regular savings account, it's not a good idea to leave large sums of money sit in a money market for a long period of time. You can do much better with other types of investments.

There are various types of money market funds. Some are invested in only U.S. Treasury obligations and aren't subject to state income tax liability. Other types carry different tax advantages.

Both money market accounts and money market funds are "dollar in, dollar out," meaning that if you put $500 in, you'll get $500 out—plus interest. Your return on money market accounts and funds is the yield, or the amount that your financial institution pays on your money. Money markets are good places to "hold" money that you may need within a short time, or until you decide on other investments.

Certificates of Deposit

These are accounts that require that you deposit your money for a specific amount of time. It might be days, months, or years, depending on the type of *certificate of deposit* (*CD*) you choose. The financial institution that holds the CD pays you a certain interest rate and yield for the time that it has your money.

Normally, the longer time you keep your money invested, the higher the rate of interest you'll get on it. If you take your money out of a CD before the specified time agreement, you'll be charged a penalty.

Interest rates on CDs can vary greatly, so check around if you're thinking of putting money in one. Most pay fixed interest rates, but some pay variable rates. If you have a variable rate, the amount of interest you'll get will fluctuate. If you're interested in CDs, watch for specials. Interest rates for CDs tend to mirror the interest rates in the general market.

Taking Stock

A **certificate of deposit** (**CD**) is an investment that pays a certain interest rate on your money if you keep it invested for a specified amount of time. You will pay a penalty for early withdrawal.

Consider Everything

These are just brief explanations of some of the vehicles available for saving money. More detailed information can be obtained by reading or consulting a financial expert.

What we want to stress is that, when you're thinking about joining an investment club, you should consider all areas of your personal finances. Look at where you are, where you want to be, and how you're going to get there. Once that information is clear in your mind, you'll be able to see more clearly whether or not joining an investment club makes sense for you.

Cashing In

For a great book on investing, check out Ken Little's *Sams Teach Yourself Investing in 24 Hours.* It will provide you all the definitions of different investment instruments as well as explain the "numbers."

Cashing In

If you're thinking about joining an investment club, it's important to learn all you can about them. In addition to this book, read *Investment Clubs: A Team Approach to the Stock Market,* by Kathryn Shaw, or *The Investment Club Book,* by John F. Wasik.

Advantages of Joining a Club

We already mentioned in Chapter 1, "What's All This Talk About Investment Clubs?" some of the reasons why people like investment clubs, so we won't spend too much time discussing them here.

If you're trying to make up your mind whether or not getting into a club is right for you, however, it will be helpful for you to consider the pros and cons of investment clubs.

Let's have a look at some of the advantages of joining a club in this section, and we'll discuss the disadvantages a bit later on.

It's Affordable

If your personal finances are on track, and you're not looking at overly daunting monthly bills or high debt from credit cards or other sources, you'll probably find that joining an investment club is quite affordable.

Typically, investment club members contribute between $20 and $50 a month. Take a minute and think about how easily you spend that much money on unnecessary items in a typical month.

➤ If you buy a cup of coffee and a bagel on the way to work in the morning, you're probably out at least $30.

➤ A first-run movie for two with sodas and popcorn goes for between $25 and $30 in most areas.

➤ Drinks and dinner for two in a decent restaurant can easily top $50 or $60.

➤ There's that sweater at the mall that you think is just great. It's not that you really need it, but it's just so cute. Say goodbye to another $40.

Well, you get the point. Most of us could find ways to cut between $20 and $50 from our monthly spending. Just remember that the money you contribute to an investment club is not only money saved, but hopefully, will earn money for you.

It's Educational

While turning a profit from your investments may be the top priority of most clubs, learning more about investing should be a close second.

The most successful investment clubs are those in which members are committed to researching and learning. Members of these clubs use the knowledge they obtain to make thoughtful, intelligent decisions about where and how much to invest.

Knowledge is a powerful tool, and financial knowledge can be particularly useful. Learning about the stock market and how to invest in it can be a great personal benefit from which you'll experience rewarding results.

It's Structured

While some of us might be organized and disciplined enough to research and buy stocks or other investments on our own, many of us wouldn't take the time or make the effort to do so.

Take This to the Bank

The National Association of Investors Corp. (NAIC) defines investment clubs on its Web site as "groups of 12 to 20 people who come together for fun, education, and profit ..." Note the order in which the purposes are listed.

Belonging to an investment club provides the structure that many people need to do the work necessary for making smart investments. It gives you time frames within which certain tasks must be completed. The expectations of other members are a strong incentive to do what's required of you, and do it on time.

If you work better and more effectively on your own, then the idea of structure might not seem important. But for many people, structure is not only desirable, but it is necessary.

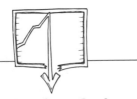

Heading for a Crash

Some investment clubs are very social, and that's okay, as long as all members are comfortable with the atmosphere. It can get to be a real problem when some members expect club meetings to be primarily social occasions, while others want businesslike proceedings. Be sure that everyone understands the focus of your club right from the start, and everyone has the same expectations concerning the club atmosphere.

It's Fun

There are lots of investment club members out there who enjoy their club meetings as social events.

They like the camaraderie of sharing common goals with other people, and of working together toward those goals. They enjoy the companionship that club meetings provide, and consider other members to be their friends.

In fact, there are plenty of investors who started clubs as a means of keeping in touch with friends and family members.

Belonging to an investment club shouldn't be a stressful experience. If you ever find yourself in a club that's so serious that it's uncomfortable, it's time to look for a new club. Each club has to find a balance, and decide how much of its time and energy will be devoted to business, and how much will be for fun. All the guidelines for pulling out of an investment club should be covered in your operating agreement. We'll get into more detail about it in Chapter 24, "The Ebbs and Flows of an Investment Club."

Disadvantages of Joining a Club

While many people swear by investment clubs, you should know that club membership comes with some potential disadvantages.

While the obvious disadvantages are far fewer than the advantages discussed above, they're worth a mention for those trying to decide whether or not to join an investment club.

It Requires a Commitment

When you agree to join an investment club, you're making a commitment to help advance the goals of a group of people. It's not too unlike being a member of a sports team. Just by being on the team, you accept (or should accept) an obligation to do your very best so that your team can win.

And, while we said that investment clubs shouldn't be so serious that there's never any fun, we do believe that people who join investment clubs should be serious about helping move the clubs ahead.

If you're joining the club just to get out of the house one evening a month, with no intention of making the necessary commitment, maybe you could consider joining a card club or aerobics class instead.

It'll Take Some Time

Along with some commitment of effort on your part, belonging to an investment club will take some time. In addition to meetings, you'll have to devote some hours to researching various companies so that you can decide whether or not your club should buy their stock.

While many people find this research exciting and interesting, it can be a bit tedious or even stressful for others. If you're not prepared to take the time necessary to complete the work you're expected to do, then you'd better think twice about joining a club.

Take This to the Bank

John Sortino, the founder of the Vermont Teddy Bear Company and author of *The Complete Idiot's Guide to Being a Successful Entrepreneur*, has some good advice to keep yourself from getting overly involved. Pick one thing to which you're committed (he coaches Little League), and give it your absolute best. When you're asked to do something else, simply say that you can't, because you do Little League (or whatever). Be firm about not taking on anything else, he says, and people will soon know that you're serious and stop asking.

Talk to some people who already belong to investment clubs. Ask how much time they typically spend on club business between meetings, as well as the length of an average get-together. Once you have the information, be honest with yourself about whether you have the time you need to devote to a club.

It's very easy, and unwise, to commit to something for which you don't have the necessary time. If you're already in a position where you can't finish everything you need to in a day, then now is not the time to take on a new activity. Many of us are overly committed, juggling jobs, families, kids' activities, a house, a social life, and so on. If joining an investment club is going to be a problem instead of a positive experience, consider putting it off until your schedule is less hectic.

Yes or No?

Okay. It's time to make a decision. So far in Part 1, "The Great World of Investment Clubs," you've gotten a bit of history about investment clubs and learned exactly what they are and why they've become so popular.

You've read about successful clubs and what they've done and learned about online clubs and their growing popularity. We've gone over the pros and cons of belonging to an investment club and told you about some of the resources available to help investors.

Now, it's up to you. After considering everything you've read, it's time to decide whether or not belonging to a club is right for you.

Hopefully, what you've read has made you excited about investment clubs, and eager to learn more. If that's the case, you won't be disappointed as you move through the rest of the book.

Or, maybe you're discouraged about joining a club because it sounds like too much work, or it will take too much time. If that's the case, then keep reading because you might change your mind.

We definitely think that joining a club is the way to go. But only you can decide for yourself. If you've decided you want to join a club, again, keep on reading. You'll learn everything you need to know to get started and involved in a successful club.

The Least You Need to Know

➤ Many factors will contribute to your decision of whether or not to join an investment club.

➤ It's important to make sure your financial situation is stable before deciding to join an investment club.

➤ Consider your financial goals and how joining a club might affect those goals.

➤ Some of the advantages of financial clubs are that they're affordable to most people, and they offer education, structure, and fun.

➤ Potential disadvantages of investment clubs are that they require firm commitments from members, and that they take time.

Chapter 5

Join the Club or Start Your Own?

In This Chapter

➤ Advantages and disadvantages of joining a club in progress

➤ Finding a club with which to hook up

➤ Using networking skills you might not know you have

➤ Advantages and disadvantages of starting your own club

➤ Making the decision

Nobody knows for sure just how many investment clubs there are out there. It's very safe, however, to say that there are a lot.

The National Association of Investors Corp. (NAIC) counted 37,156 clubs among its membership in the middle of 1999, and 704,000 individual members. And there are many more clubs that aren't NAIC members.

The point is, if you've decided you want to join a club, you shouldn't have too much trouble finding one. If you don't find one that interests you, or you decide that you'd like to have more control over who's in your club and how it's run, you can always start your own.

In this chapter, we'll look at the pros and cons of joining a ready-made club and those of starting your own club. Just as whether or not to join a club should be your own decision, so is the decision of whether to join an existing club or start one of your own. There are various considerations to keep in mind when making your decision.

Maybe you're a person who likes to call the shots. If so, starting your own club is the right choice for you. If you don't enjoy being in a leadership position, or you don't have the time or energy to devote to starting a club, you'd probably be better off joining an existing club.

Joining Up

There are some obvious advantages to joining an existing club instead of starting your own. This pertains pretty much to any situation—not just investment clubs.

Joining a group is generally easier than starting one, regardless of what kind of group it is. If you're looking to get together with a group of people and buy organically grown food, for instance, it surely would be easier to locate and join a food co-op than to start your own.

Think about it. To start your own organic food co-op, you'd have to find and organize your own group of like-minded organic food enthusiasts. You'd have to sell them on the idea of your co-op, and make them willing to join up. You'd need to track down farmers who grow, or suppliers who handle organically grown food, then make sure the food is up to your standards. You'd have to negotiate prices, find a place out of which to operate, and work out the terms of the co-op agreements.

After all that, you'd have to run, or find someone else to run the co-op.

If you join a food co-op, your job is a lot easier. Sure, you'd still have to locate one that's accepting new members, and make sure it meets your needs. You'd need to find out all you could about the co-op, and make sure you understand how it operates and what your role in it would be.

At the end of the day, however, joining a co-op instead of forming one will save you a lot of time and effort.

The same thing is true with an investment club.

Take This to the Bank

As of 1998, more women than men in the United States were joining investment clubs. The National Association of Investors Corp. (NAIC) reported that while female membership totaled only 37.5 percent in 1986, it had jumped to 60.3 percent in 1998.

Please don't think we're trying to discourage you if you've got your heart set on starting your own club. We'll tell you just how to do so in Chapter 6, "Bringing Club Members on Board." All we're saying is that you shouldn't ignore the possibility of joining an existing group or the benefits that doing so can offer.

Some Good Things

In addition to maybe making it easier on yourself, joining a ready-made investment club has some other advantages:

➤ You're joining experience. When you join a club that's been around for a while—or even one that's fairly new—you can benefit from the experience of the other members. They've been there—done that—and presumably have learned along the way. Joining an existing club allows you to learn from the past successes and mistakes of its members, and allows you to benefit from their experiences.

➤ You can get started faster. Starting your own club has its own advantages (we'll get to them in just a few minutes), but it does require some time and work. If you're in a hurry to get started in a club, think about joining one already in progress. You'll eliminate the up-front time and effort and can concentrate on getting started investing your money.

➤ You avoid the responsibility of leadership. Let's face it, it doesn't always pay to stick your neck out. While some people thrive on the challenges of being a leader, sometimes it's nice to pitch in and do your share, without being primarily responsible if things don't go as planned or the group hits some rough spots.

These are just a few advantages of joining an existing investment club instead of starting your own. You'll no doubt come up with some ideas of your own as you continue reading.

Some Not-So-Good Things

While there are advantages to joining a club, there also are some concerns that you should be aware of:

➤ You might be inheriting problems. Along with experience, a ready-made club could have ready-made problems. It's a fact that many investment clubs fail, and many others experience serious problems. That's not to say that problems are exclusive to investment clubs. If you've ever belonged to any kind of group, you're probably aware of the potential for personality conflicts, leadership conflicts, and other sorts of snafus.

53

Take This to the Bank

American women are not the only ones standing in line to join investment clubs. The World Federation of Investors (a group affiliated with the National Association of Investors Corp.) reports that membership among European women also is on the rise.

➤ You'll have little say at first in how the club is organized and run. You'll be able to put in your two cents later on, but when you join a group already in progress, it's generally a good idea to limit your opinions until you're an established member. Sure, do share if you have something valuable to contribute. But, if you jump right in with your ideas on how the club can be improved and what its members are doing wrong, you're likely to generate big-time resentment.

➤ You might not agree with the group's investment choices. If four people in your family have died from lung cancer caused by cigarette smoking, there's a good chance that you're going to balk at investing in Philip Morris stock. If you join an existing club, it's your responsibility to find out ahead of time what its investments are. We'll talk a lot more later on about choosing investments and socially responsible investing, but you should be aware that investment clubs have widely ranging opinions concerning what stocks they should buy.

➤ You may inherit capital gains taxes. If the group you join bought AT&T stock for $20 a share in 1978, and sells it for $80 a share in 2000, it's going to owe some capital gains tax on its profit. As a club member, you might be required to pay your share, even though AT&T stock was already worth $75 a share when you joined the club.

➤ You might have to work your way into the "in crowd." Joining an existing club, in which other members have worked together and come to know each other, could mean that you'll be an outsider—at least at first.

Cashing In

Although nobody likes a know-it-all, don't feel that you must be totally silent when you first join a club. Most people value well-intended suggestions that are offered in the spirit of cooperation and helpfulness. Just don't try to take over a club you've just joined.

We don't want to be overly alarming; we just want to alert you to the possibility of problems. Many people join existing clubs with very positive results, and chances are, if that's the way you decide to go, you will, too.

Finding a Club to Join

If you do decide to join an existing club, how do you go about finding one? More importantly, how do you go about finding one that you like, and that you feel you'll be successful with?

Start Networking

The best way to find a good investment club is through *networking*. What exactly is networking? Basically, networking is using your connections, or your *network*, to obtain information or get help.

We network all the time, often without even realizing what we're doing. Consider these examples of networking, and then think about how you might use your network when looking for an investment club.

➤ The school play is on Thursday, but you're not sure what time it starts, and you seem to remember something about baking for the reception afterward. Unfortunately, the pertinent information that your son brought home from school has gone out with last week's trash. You get on the phone and call your friend, Molly, who's always up to date about school events. Sure enough, Molly tells you the play starts at seven, and you're on the list for two dozen lemon squares.

➤ You just found out that your 10-year-old car—the one with well over 100,000 miles on it—is going to need $2,500 worth of repairs. After thinking about the matter, you decide it's not worth fixing and that you'd be better

Cashing In

Really successful, well-run investment clubs often have membership waiting lists, and require potential members to attend meetings for several months before they can join. If you want to join a top-notch group, be aware that it might require some waiting time.

Taking Stock

Your **network** is the people you know, and the people they know. They're your connections. **Networking** is being able to locate a person within this web who can help you, or tell you who can help you, with a particular situation.

off getting another car. The problem is, you've got appointments to keep, and you can't afford to be without a car for more than a few days. You call your friend, Jack, who knows the guy who writes the weekly automotive column for the local paper. Jack gets on the phone with Nick, who not only writes about cars, but also knows all the local car dealers. Nick makes a couple of calls, and finds out that the local Honda dealer happens to have some really good used cars on his lot, and is looking to make a deal. You drop by the Honda place, tell the salesman that Nick sent you, and make a great deal on a used car.

➤ Your boss just chewed you out for no apparent reason for the third consecutive day, you haven't gotten a raise for a year and a half, and you're completely fed up with that lousy advertising job of yours. Instead of moaning and groaning, you go home that night and call your friend Sharon, who happened to mention at a party over the weekend that her company was looking to hire some new design people. She confirms that there will be some additions to the staff, and tells you whom to direct your resumé to. Six weeks later, you hand in your notice to your old boss and plan a week's vacation before starting your new job.

➤ You've just moved back in with Mom and Dad after ending a long-term relationship in California and coming home to New Jersey. Along with finding a new job, you find out you're no longer able to live with your folks. Getting an apartment is no problem, there are lots available. Furnishing the thing, however, is another story. Your former significant other got custody of all the furniture, and you're more than a bit strapped for cash. Fortunately, your mom is first-rate networker. She puts out feelers to all her friends, who let their friends know that you're looking for furniture. Pretty soon your apartment is filled with the Wilson's old sofa and loveseat, the bedroom suit that the Martins no longer needed because they converted their guest room to an office, and the refrigerator and dining set the Hamiltons discarded when they had their kitchen redone. Good going, Mom!

There are hundreds of situations in which we use our networks. Networking comes very naturally to some people, while others have to work at it. Learning how to network, and using your network effectively, can help you solve all kinds of problems, and can get something done much easier than it would be otherwise.

If you have difficulty thinking about the people you know as a network, that's okay. Just think of them as people you know, some of whom might be able to help you find an investment club. They won't be able to help, however, if they don't know that you're looking for a club.

Put the Word Out

Just as Charley's mom spread the word about Charley needing furniture, spread the word that you're looking to join an investment club.

Tell everybody who might be able to help you, and don't be shy. Remember that investment clubs are popping up all over the place, and nearly everyone knows someone who's in one. Consider these networking possibilities:

➤ Cheryl Ann—you know—Bobby's mom. The one you've sat next to every Saturday morning as you watched your kids run up and down the soccer field. It won't hurt to mention to her that you're interested in joining an investment club. Who knows? Maybe Cheryl Ann's sister just happens to be starting a club for professional women and is looking for members.

➤ Dave, the new guy in your tennis group, is a real estate developer and seems to know just about everybody. The next time you're out for a few beers after your match, ask him if he's familiar with investment clubs. If he is, chances are he'll know some folks who are already in them.

Cashing In

Don't feel that you're imposing upon your network when you start putting out feelers about joining an investment club. Most people like to help others— especially their friends and acquaintances.

➤ The holidays are coming and you're running hot and cold about the approaching cocktail parties and open houses. On one hand, it's nice to go and see who's there, but on the other hand, you often have trouble keeping the conversation up and running. This year, introduce investment clubs into the cocktail chatter, and listen to others. Odds are that you'll meet people who are already in clubs, or who know people in clubs.

➤ Your friend Jim is one of those guys who can talk to anybody about anything—and frequently does. He always has information to share about topics of every sort, making you wonder just where he picks up all those tidbits. Chances are that he knows all about investment clubs, and probably knows some people who are already in them. Don't forget to tell him that you're looking for a club to join.

➤ Don't overlook the obvious. The next time your parents come for dinner, tell them that you're looking to join an investment club. Do the same with your siblings, friends, and neighbors. Get the word out.

Heading for a Crash

Be careful not to rush in and join the first club that shows an interest in you. Be sure that you find out as much about the club as you can before you agree to join. Different clubs have very different philosophies and personalities, and it's important to find one in which you'll be comfortable.

While you're out there networking, don't forget to contact the places where clubs meet. Some clubs meet at the homes of members, but others meet in churches or synagogues, schools, or community buildings. A secretary or events planner may be able to put you in touch with a club representative.

There are plenty of clubs out there, and some of them are looking for serious-minded members who are willing to do their share to make the club successful. Don't be discouraged if you don't find a club the first week you begin looking. Just keep at it, and eventually you'll find one that's a perfect fit.

Starting from Scratch

If you don't join a ready-made club, you can start your own. There are advantages and disadvantages to starting your own anything—and investment clubs are no exception.

Some people have no qualms about starting up and running clubs or organizations. You've probably known some of these folks. They're the ones who started the girls-only or boys-only clubs at age eight, then went on to form babysitting clubs in junior high, homework clubs in high school, and all-night study clubs in college. They don't blink when they're asked to organize and run the school's fundraising drive, chair the parent-teacher group, or plan the company's holiday party.

They're organized organizers, and the thought of starting an investment club is challenging and exciting to them.

If that description sounds like you, then starting a club might be the right choice for you.

But first, let's take a look at some of the good things about starting your own club, and at some of the not-so-good things. Then you can decide.

Some Good Things

There are lots of advantages to starting your own club. Let's have a look at some of them:

➤ You get to establish the club philosophy and decide how the club will be run. Of course, you'll need to consider input from other members, but you can establish the framework under which the club will operate.

➤ You can handpick members. Not to sound rude, but when you join a ready-made club, you're stuck with the people who are already in it. Hopefully, everybody will be great and there will be few conflicts. It could be, however, that you'll have trouble relating to some of the other members, or that you'll be walking into some big-time personality conflicts. When you start your own club, you get to decide who joins.

➤ You start with a clean slate. If you start your own club, you can be sure that you're not inheriting another club's problems.

➤ You establish yourself as a leader. If you're the kind of person who likes to be in charge, being the one to organize the club puts you in a position of leadership. Other members will look to you for decision-making and guidance.

While there are some definite advantages to forming your own club, there also are some potential disadvantages. In the next section, we'll take a look at some of the drawbacks.

Some Not-So-Good Things

When you start your own investment club, there are some potential problems that you should know about and keep in mind:

➤ You need to find enough members to fill the club. If there are a lot of clubs in your area, there may not be many people looking for one to join. If that's the case, you might have to use your networking skills to find enough of the kind of members you want for your club.

➤ You may shoulder more than your share of the club's problems. Every group runs into occasional problems, and, as a leader, you're likely to be called upon when problems crop up. Some people love troubleshooting. If you don't, maybe you should think twice about starting an investment club.

➤ Starting and maintaining a club will take considerable time. If you can barely finish in a day what you need to do now, you should think long and hard about committing yourself to starting an investment club. Once you get the ball rolling, other members will be depending on you to follow through. If you don't have sufficient time to do so, it would be better not to start something you can't finish.

Heading for a Crash

If you decide to start an investment club, be sure that you don't become too possessive about it, or too demanding of other members. You're the one starting the club, but you don't own it. Insisting that everything be done your way will be a big turn-off to other members, as well as potential members.

Cashing In

If you decide to start your own investment club, make it clear from the beginning that all members are expected to do their share of the work. Don't let yourself get stuck doing 90 percent of the work, just because you're the one who got the club going.

➤ Your club might fail. We sure don't want to discourage you from joining or starting a club, but you should realize that, for a great variety of reasons, a significant percentage of investment clubs fail. If you start a club, you need to be prepared for the possibility that it could happen to your club. If you're the kind of person who can't stand to fail at anything, you might be better off joining an existing club.

We could go on and on, listing both advantages and disadvantages associated with joining versus forming an investment club. You, no doubt, will come up with some of your own. Consider your own feelings, and think carefully about what you've read in this chapter. All that's left to do after that is to make your decision.

Making Your Decision

We've spent considerable time discussing the pros and cons of ready-made clubs and clubs you start yourself. Now it's time to decide what to do.

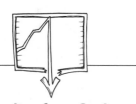

Heading for a Crash

If you work for a company that offers a pension plan, don't let yourself become too dependent on the thought of that money. Many companies are cutting back their pension plans, with millions of workers being forced to take reduced benefits. If your employer has assured you that you will receive a pension, you're likely to get it. If you count on it as your sole source of retirement income, however, you're likely to be sorely disappointed.

Remember though, that the most important thing isn't whether you join an existing club or start your own. The most important thing is that you get yourself into an investment club.

Let's face it. The days of working 30 or 40 years for the same employer and retiring with a pension that would keep you comfortable into your old age are over.

Also, it's clear that we'd better not depend on Social Security to see us through our old age. Many people, including those who work with the Social Security Administration (SSA), warn that the fund will run out of money before many of us are even close to retiring.

Dorcas Hardy, who was the commissioner of the SSA under President Ronald Reagan, has said publicly that, unless the system is overhauled, it will run out of money between 2020 and 2030. Retirees are living longer and longer, and, as a result, consuming more Social Security money than anyone thought they would. Workers are forced to pay more and more to keep the benefits rolling, but it appears right now to be a losing battle.

The state of pension plans and Social Security should serve as wake-up calls to all of us who are concerned about having enough money in our retirements. It's up to us to take action to ensure that we'll have enough, and getting into an investment club is a great way to get started.

So, join an existing club, or start your own. The important thing is that you get into a club, and get your money working for you.

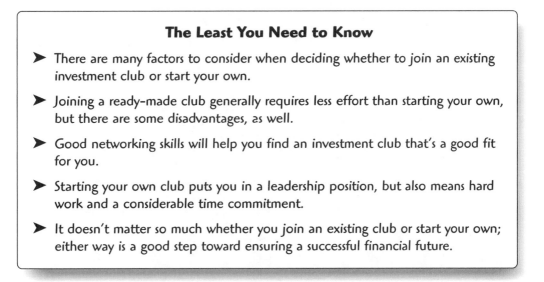

The Least You Need to Know

➤ There are many factors to consider when deciding whether to join an existing investment club or start your own.

➤ Joining a ready-made club generally requires less effort than starting your own, but there are some disadvantages, as well.

➤ Good networking skills will help you find an investment club that's a good fit for you.

➤ Starting your own club puts you in a leadership position, but also means hard work and a considerable time commitment.

➤ It doesn't matter so much whether you join an existing club or start your own; either way is a good step toward ensuring a successful financial future.

Part 2

The Basics of Starting a Club

Getting an investment club started isn't all that difficult, but it's important to get your club off to a good start.

Part 2 will help you understand why it's so important to get the right mix of members, choose an appropriate meeting place, and even choose the right name for your club.

We'll explain what officers your club should have, and the duties each one will be expected to perform.

It's extremely important that your club has a good set of operating rules. You'll learn in this part what should be included in your agreement. We even included a sample agreement that you can use as a guide.

Also, we'll give you some tips for making your meetings run smoothly and keeping club members enthusiastic.

Chapter 6

Bringing Club Members on Board

In This Chapter

➤ Determining how many members your club should have

➤ Finding potential club members

➤ Avoiding personality conflicts

➤ Understanding different kinds of investors

➤ Getting everyone to do his or her share

➤ Making sure everyone's on the same page

We hope that the first five chapters of this book were enough to make you excited about getting into an investment club.

Assuming that they were, and that you're now fully committed to getting a club up and running, it's time to really get down to business.

One thing is for certain: You can't have a club without members. Granted, your club doesn't need to include a great many people, but a handful at least is a definite necessity.

Finding the right members for your club is extremely important. Let's face it. Some people are just easier to get along with than others. We've probably all known people who seem to get along with everyone, and others who don't like anybody. The last thing you need in your newly formed investment club is a lot of bickering among people who can't get along.

While it's important to choose members that are likely to get along socially, it's also important to choose people whose investment philosophies are within close range. There are different kinds of investors, and they don't always see eye to eye.

Also in this chapter, we'll learn why it's important that everyone has the same expectations regarding the club, right from the beginning. Many clubs have been forced to disband because their members couldn't agree on what kind of group they were going to be.

So, let's get started. Pay close attention, and you'll be getting ready to organize your first meeting any day now.

Choosing and Finding Members

You know that it's important to choose the right members for your investment club, but how do you know who's right for your club?

There are many, many different types of investment clubs out there, most of them chugging merrily along. Some are all business, while others barely manage to work in investment matters between the gossip, dessert, and coffee. Some clubs require fairly large monetary contributions, while others might ask that you throw in as little as $20 a month.

The type of club you want to have is up to you. Before you begin asking people to join, however, you should have a clear idea about what your group will be like. Think about what you might include in your operating agreement (refer to Chapter 8, "Establishing Operating Rules," for more information), and what you want the atmosphere of your club to be. It's important that you choose members who will be comfortable in your club, and with whom you'll be comfortable.

Your club membership can come from a variety of sources. There are many different kinds of clubs, including those listed in the following sections.

Family Clubs

There are thousands of family investment clubs including members of all ages. Some families allow even young children to be members, but without voting rights. Once the kids get older, they get to help decide what stocks to buy. Proponents of family clubs say they're great for teaching young people how to save and invest for the future. Plus, they like the idea of sharing a profitable venture with other members of their families.

Sharing investment club membership also serves as a good way of keeping family members in touch. Online clubs are popular among families that are spread out across the country—or world. Family clubs have been known to backfire, however, so consider the pros and cons before setting up one with your relatives. Money does funny things to some people, and many family relationships have been strained or broken over financial matters.

It's important to have rules for any investment club, and family clubs are no exception. In fact, family clubs may have to address special issues in their bylaws, such as what happens if two members get divorced.

Friends

Many investment clubs are organized by groups of friends who use them to stay in touch, as well as to try to make some money. Golf buddies, fraternity brothers, sorority sisters, and school chums have formed clubs, often bringing other friends on board with them. These groups can be all women, all men, or mixed, and the ages of their members often vary.

Cashing In

The National Association of Investors Corp. (NAIC) offers information about family investment clubs. Check out its Web site at www.better–investing.org, or write to P.O. Box 220, Royal Oak, MI, 48068.

Women Investors

Sure, there are plenty of investment clubs in which only men are members, but all-women clubs are extremely popular. More women have joined investment clubs, many of which are exclusively women's clubs, within the past decade. Why? Women are increasingly taking control of their own financial future. Women's earnings average 75 percent of men's earnings, and women live an average of seven years longer than men do. That means that many women have to plan carefully for their retirements and see investment clubs as one way to help them do so.

Heading for a Crash

If you ask friends to join your investment club, be sure that you don't let friendships affect your objectivity concerning the investments the club will make. There have been some really bad investments made because club members didn't want to alienate the friends who suggested them.

Co-Workers

Clubs in which only co-workers are members are fairly common, but not everyone thinks they're a great idea. Some experts feel that club members should be of varied backgrounds in order to bring different viewpoints to the group. Others, however, argue that people who work together are likely to have varied viewpoints on most topics, despite their workplace proximity. An advantage of being in a club with co-workers is that you see each other nearly every day, making it easy to keep up with club business.

Special-Interest Groups

There are investment clubs in which only dentists are members. There are clubs in which membership is limited to musicians, stockbrokers, members of particular ethnic groups, and so forth. Critics might say this limits a group's diversity, but many of these clubs have been together for a long time and do quite well.

While there are many types of investment clubs, most are mixtures of friends, families, co-workers, and each with special interests. Just be fairly certain that everyone you ask to join will be compatible and have reasonably similar investment philosophies.

Cashing In

Some experts recommend that you look for "valuable" club members, such as someone with a financial background, an experienced investor, or someone who has experience doing research. While these qualities are desirable, we don't think they're necessary. Enthusiasm and willingness to learn are every bit as important.

How Many People Should You Ask to Join?

Membership in investment clubs ranges from 3 to more than 50. It is more a matter of personal preference than a magic number.

Most clubs have between 10 and 25 members—that's probably a good range. Consider these points when deciding how many members you want in your club:

➤ There's a certain amount of work required to keep a club up and running. Too few people can mean there won't be enough man (or woman) power to complete all the necessary tasks.

➤ You need enough members to research and recommend (or refute) a wide variety of stocks. It's good to have some diversity among your portfolio, and you learn more from 15 people reporting on 15 stocks than from 3 people reporting on 3 stocks. A larger group of members assures more diversity than a small group.

➤ Too many people can be difficult to keep track of and manage. Fifty people going in 50 different directions can be a nightmare when you're trying to work together as a group. Larger groups can become unmanageable if you're not careful.

➤ Overly large groups often have trouble making decisions that everyone is happy with. Diversity is great. Too many widely ranging opinions, however, can snarl the decision-making process and bring your group to a halt.

➤ You've probably noticed that everybody seems to be extremely busy these days. Our lives are filled with time busters such as work, getting the kids to and from their activities, and helping out at school or church. Many of us help care for older parents and attempt to maintain some kind of social life. Attending meetings is one more commitment for investment club members, so it probably will be difficult to find a time that suits everyone. The more members you have, the more schedules you need to try to work around.

➤ Groups with too few members can get sort of, well … boring. If you have only three or four members in your investment club, chances are that your meetings will get to be pretty predictable—pretty fast. Larger groups tend to be a bit livelier.

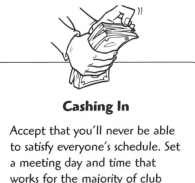

Regardless of how many members you decide to have in your club, pick a number and stick to it. If you decide on 20 members, then find 20 members and don't let in anyone else until someone leaves the group.

It's important to attain and maintain continuity within your club. A constant number of members helps you do so.

Cashing In

Accept that you'll never be able to satisfy everyone's schedule. Set a meeting day and time that works for the majority of club members and stick to it. If there are people who can't attend meetings, they simply won't be able to be members of your club.

Take This to the Bank

The National Association of Investors Corp. advises that 15 members is an ideal number for investment clubs. Many groups, however, have found that more or fewer members works equally well, so don't feel obligated to have 15.

Don't Assume Everyone Has Money to Invest

It's important, when looking for people to join your investment club, to consider the financial situation of each prospective member.

While it's great to have a range of ages and backgrounds, you need to make sure that each prospective member is in a position to make monthly contributions.

Don't assume that everyone can afford to contribute even $25 or $30 a month to an investment club. Young people might be struggling with college debt and not-so-great-paying jobs. Older people might be trying to stretch fixed incomes.

Some clubs require an initial lump payment of $100, $200, or more from each member, while others ask only for a monthly contribution, with no additional money up front.

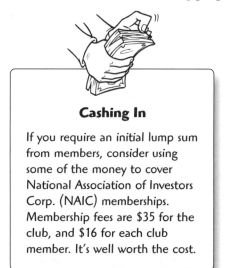

Cashing In

If you require an initial lump sum from members, consider using some of the money to cover National Association of Investors Corp. (NAIC) memberships. Membership fees are $35 for the club, and $16 for each club member. It's well worth the cost.

Whether or not your club requires a lump sum may affect the people you get as members. But, be sensitive to the financial positions of the people you want in your club. Many clubs operate on a share, or unit basis, where the monthly payment of each member is counted as one unit. The number of units each member contributes affects his ownership in the club, and may, or may not, affect how votes are taken. If a person can't contribute any money one month, he simply isn't credited with a unit, and his total ownership in the club declines.

This is a good way of handling the situation should a member be unable to contribute. Other clubs, however, insist that every member contribute every month, and members may have to withdraw if they don't have the money.

Minimizing a Clash of the Titans

Unless you have psychic powers, you can't see into people's heads to know what makes them tick. And, as hard as you try to get people in your club who are compatible, you can't guarantee that there won't, at some point, be some personality clashes. As long as people are people, you'll occasionally have conflict. How many people do you get along with *all* the time?

You can minimize the possibility of conflict in your club, however, by paying attention to the personalities of prospective members. Here are a few personality traits you should be aware of as potential problems for your investment club. If you encounter any of these when sizing up prospective members, you might want to think carefully before agreeing to let them join.

➤ **Very strong or overbearing personalities.** An investment club should be a group effort, not a one-person show. If you get someone in your club who insists on running things, you could encounter big trouble. Sure, it's nice to have someone who will take charge and get things moving, but too much of a good thing is not a good thing.

➤ **Procrastinators.** If someone you're considering for your club has a track record of promising to get something done, but not delivering, think long and hard before agreeing to allow him or her into the group. Investment clubs require effort from everybody. If someone isn't willing to pull his weight, he doesn't belong in the club.

➤ **Extremely shy or self-conscious people.** The purpose of an investment club is to have all members get involved and be active. If somebody is just too shy or self-conscious to participate, she probably should consider investing on her own.

➤ **Extremely argumentative people.** Sure, any investment club will have its share of disagreements among members about which stocks to buy, how much you should pay for them, and how long you should hold them. Such discussion is to be expected, and it's healthy. What you don't need, however, is someone who argues about everything, simply for the sake of disagreeing. An extremely argumentative person can slow down club proceedings and reduce your overall effectiveness.

➤ **Disrespectful, rude individuals.** While a certain amount of arguing is to be expected, it should always be conducted with respect. When people become rude and disrespectful of other club members, it's time to ask them to leave the group. We'll tell you how to do that, and how their share in the club gets dispersed in Chapter 24, "The Ebbs and Flows of an Investment Club."

Heading for a Crash

If there's somebody in your club who's making club life miserable for other members, the worst thing you can do is to ignore the situation. Many clubs have failed because of fighting among members, so any trouble should be promptly dealt with. We'll discuss this in much more detail in Chapters 9, 22, 23, and 25.

You can't ever guarantee that you won't get two, or more, people in your club who simply don't like each other. Some folks just don't seem to be able to get along. If that happens, you and the other club members will have to deal with it. When looking for prospective members, however, you should do what you can to reduce the risk of personality conflicts within your club.

Tuning In to Different Investment Philosophies

You already know that everybody has his or her own, unique personality. Some people are upbeat and cheerful, while others seem to moan and groan constantly about every little thing.

Some people are always serious, while others look for fun in all they do. You might not realize, however, that investors also have different personalities and philosophies.

Some investors are the aggressive, make-me-rich-quick kind that want to make a killing—right away. Others are the middle-of-the-road type. They want their investments to do well, but aren't willing to take huge risks. Then, there are those investors who just want a nice, safe place to put their money, something they won't have to worry about.

In this section, we'll take a closer look at each of these investment philosophies. It's important to understand them and to know the different investment philosophy of each prospective club member before you get your club rolling. It's not a good idea to mix extremely conservative investors with high-risk folks. Doing so nearly guarantees trouble. The graph that follows demonstrates the Security Market Line. It shows that while from time to time, safer asset classes will outperform higher risk assets, it is a temporary phenomenon and will quickly reverse itself.

To increase return, you must also allow increase risk.

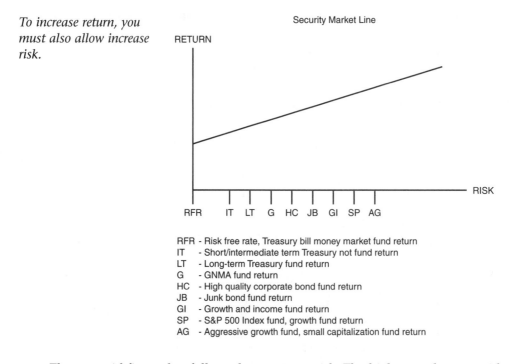

Security Market Line

RETURN

RISK

RFR   IT   LT   G   HC   JB   GI   SP   AG

RFR - Risk free rate, Treasury bill money market fund return
IT   - Short/intermediate term Treasury not fund return
LT   - Long-term Treasury fund return
G   - GNMA fund return
HC   - High quality corporate bond fund return
JB   - Junk bond fund return
GI   - Growth and income fund return
SP   - S&P 500 Index fund, growth fund return
AG   - Aggressive growth fund, small capitalization fund return

The pyramid figure that follows demonstrates risk. The higher up the pyramid you go, the higher the chance for loss of principal, as well as the chance for capital appreciation. The lower on the pyramid, the lower the loss of purchasing power along with the safety of your principal.

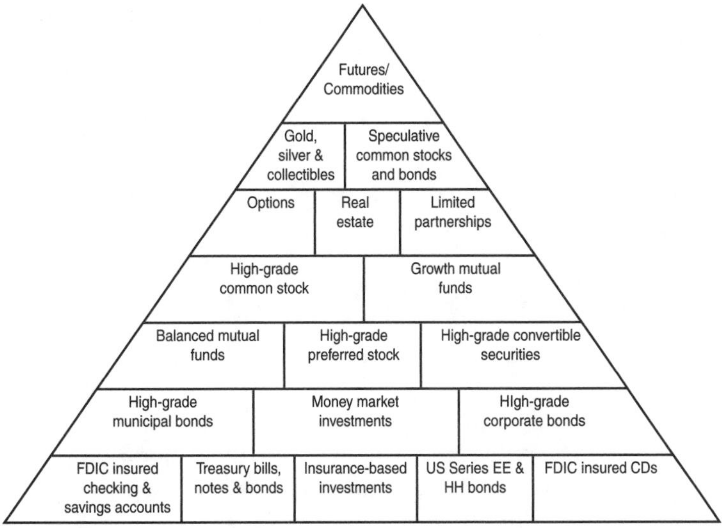
Futures/
Commodities
Gold,
silver &
collectibles
Speculative
common stocks
and bonds
Options
Real
estate
Limited
partnerships
High-grade
common stock
Growth mutual
funds
Balanced mutual
funds
High-grade
preferred stock
High-grade convertible
securities
High-grade
municipal bonds
Money market
investments
HIgh-grade
corporate bonds
FDIC insured
checking &
savings accounts
Treasury bills,
notes & bonds
Insurance-based
investments
US Series EE &
HH bonds
FDIC insured CDs

There are more safe principal options than risky ones.

High-Risk Investors

People can be high-risk investors by choice, or, as in most cases, because they don't know enough about what they're doing.

High-risk investors generally are classified as those who can live with losing about a quarter of his or her investment portfolio in a year. They're willing to put that much of their investments on the line.

Let's say you have $10,000 to invest. If the thought of losing $2,500 of that doesn't make you break out in a cold sweat, you might qualify as a high-risk investor. If you think the high-risk investing personality fits you, it would be well worth your time to reconsider where and how you'll invest your money. While it's true that some high-risk investors make big bucks, many others have lost their shirts.

Let's say, for example, that you decide to invest all of your $10,000 in Internet stocks. You're not doing so because you've done your homework, researched carefully, and learned all about Internet stocks. You're doing so because you've heard that's where you can make big money fast. Investing without knowing what you're doing is called *speculating*.

If you get a hot tip about a stock at a cocktail party, and the next day go out and put down $5,000 on it, you're speculating. And speculating isn't smart. Not all high-risk investors are speculators, but a fair share of them are.

Taking Stock

Like gambling, **speculating** is taking chances and rolling the dice in hopes of making a killing in the market.

Some high-risk investors like the futures and commodities markets, while others prefer speculative stocks and bonds. Some get involved in the gold and silver markets, or invest in collectibles. High-risk investors often are people who have a considerable amount of money and they risk only a portion of their portfolios in higher-risk investments.

Investment clubs, which stress education and responsible investing, have no room for speculators and little room for high-risk investors.

Cashing In

There are some investors who invest all the time in high-stake stocks—and come out ahead. We're not saying that you should never take a risk when buying stock, just that you need to understand what you're buying and buy responsibly.

Moderate-Risk Investors

Moderate-risk investors are generally classified as those who figure they can live with losing up to 15 percent of that $10,000 in their portfolios. The thought of losing $1,500 doesn't exactly lower their blood pressure, but it doesn't send them to the hospital with chest pains, either.

Moderate-risk investors aren't reckless and they don't speculate. They normally invest their money in balanced mutual funds, high-grade preferred stock and convertible securities, high-grade common stock, and growth mutual funds. These are fairly dependable investments with histories of good returns. See Appendix A, "Glossary," for more information.

Conservative Investors

Conservative investors are the meat-and-potatoes people of the investment world. Keep your fancy appetizers, cream sauces, and puff pastry desserts. Just give these folks some good, solid investments that they can depend on. They're not looking to get rich quick and don't want to take chances with their investments. Many really conservative investors don't buy stocks at all, but invest their money in savings bonds, federally insured bank accounts, high-grade municipal or corporate bonds, money market accounts, or insurance-based investments.

Cashing In

Don't think you need to accept every person who shows an interest in joining your investment club. There are lots of clubs out there—if someone isn't a good fit for your club, he or she can probably find another club to join.

Just as people with different personalities can clash within a group, so can those with different investment personalities. An outspoken, high-risk investor in a room full of moderate or conservative types is sure to cause a stir.

When starting a club, it's a good idea to get a feeling for the investment philosophies of all prospective members. If it's clear that someone won't fit, simply explain the reason, and suggest that he or she look for another club in which members have similar philosophies.

Keeping an Eye Out for Slackers

We've already mentioned how important it is that each member of an investment club do his or her fair share to keep the club up and running.

Along with the researching of stocks, which is essential to a successful club, there are administrative tasks and organizational chores that will need to be done. Someone has got to keep records—both club records (like attendance) and financial records. You'll probably need to find and hire some professional help, choose a bank, and so forth.

Most groups assign each member one or more stocks, which the member is responsible for tracking. The member is expected to keep up with, and inform other members of, any developments that might affect the value of the stock. If the person in charge of a stock feels that it's time to sell—or to buy more—he should make that recommendation to the rest of the club.

In addition to the stock maintenance work, some clubs also assign research of new stocks on a rotating basis. If your club has 12 people, for instance, two people a month may be assigned to research various stocks and make recommendations of what might be good investments. Remember that members are contributing money to the club each month. That money must be used.

Be sure you explain the work that's involved to each prospective member. Researching companies and stocks takes time, and some people simply don't have the time that's necessary to belong to a club. Being very clear up front about what's expected from each member can make things much easier down the road. If you get the feeling that someone is balking at the thought of a couple of hours spent researching, or of helping out with organizational chores, a warning flag should appear in your mind.

Once the club is formed, anyone who doesn't contribute his or her fair share of work should be asked to resign.

Setting Expectations

Theoretically, all investment clubs work hard at making the best possible choices about where to put their money. In reality, however, that's not always the case.

Many investment clubs start as serious vehicles for people who want to make their money work for them, but degenerate into little more than social events.

Others turn into shouting matches, with members becoming discouraged and disillusioned.

Often, these problems occur because members have different expectations of what the club is to be. It's extremely important that everyone understands how the club will be run, and what its goals are.

Schedule a Get-Acquainted Meeting

Once you've rounded up a group of potential club members, it's a good idea to get everyone together for a get-acquainted session.

During that meeting, take time to explain the club's investing philosophy, which probably will be based on that of the person who started the club, and those of the members.

Then, explain the types and the amount of work involved with being a club member. Make sure that each person understands that he or she will be expected to research companies, investigate securities, and report back to the rest of the group.

Investment clubs can entail significant time and homework on the part of members, so make sure everyone understands that.

Also, make sure that everyone understands they're expected to work together, as part of a team. Make it very clear that members must be able to rely on one another for support and advice, and that all efforts should be for the good of the group.

Encourage Everyone to Participate

Once you've explained the club's philosophy and purpose, try to get all prospective members involved with discussion and planning.

It's very important to establish at the very beginning that everyone is expected to be involved and that everyone is welcome and encouraged to express their opinions and thoughts.

Keep your first meeting very casual so that prospective members feel comfortable, and give plenty of opportunity for everyone to greet others.

RSVP, Please

Once you're sure everyone has heard the club's philosophy and understands what will be required of each member, you can go ahead and arrange a follow-up meeting.

Everyone who decides to join the club should come to that meeting (unless there's a reason why you've decided you don't want someone to be a member), at which time you can establish ground rules, discuss administrative matters, and so forth. We'll cover all that information in Chapters 7, "Getting Your Investment Club off to a Good Start," and 8.

Be sure that you don't wait too long between your initial meeting and the follow-up meeting. People will lose interest—or perhaps find another club—if too much time passes.

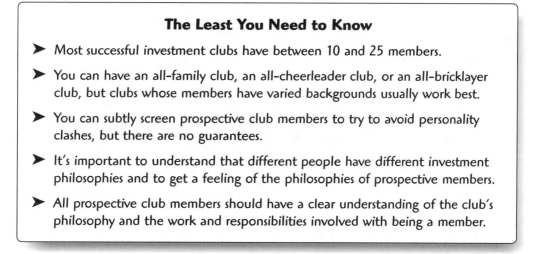

The Least You Need to Know

➤ Most successful investment clubs have between 10 and 25 members.

➤ You can have an all-family club, an all-cheerleader club, or an all-bricklayer club, but clubs whose members have varied backgrounds usually work best.

➤ You can subtly screen prospective club members to try to avoid personality clashes, but there are no guarantees.

➤ It's important to understand that different people have different investment philosophies and to get a feeling of the philosophies of prospective members.

➤ All prospective club members should have a clear understanding of the club's philosophy and the work and responsibilities involved with being a member.

Stock
Report:

So far,
so good...

Chapter 7

Getting Your Investment Club off to a Good Start

> ## In This Chapter
>
> ➤ Choosing a name for your investment club
>
> ➤ Finding a place for your club to meet
>
> ➤ Establishing guidelines and anticipating problems
>
> ➤ Selecting the right officers
>
> ➤ Remembering that fun *is* important, too

It's extremely important that your investment club is well organized—right from the beginning. Poor organization at the start is likely to lead to big problems later on.

While it's true that you'll be learning as you go—especially if you've never belonged to an investment club before—it's a good idea to have a plan in place for getting the club off to a great start.

If there's someone joining your group who has experience with investment clubs, by all means feel free to seek advice and ask for help. If you're all starting from scratch, don't worry. There are plenty of resources available to help you.

In this chapter, we'll deal with first things first. Your club needs a name, so we'll talk about what names might make sense for you. Remember that the name you choose will be representative of the club and all its members, so you shouldn't pick anything that's in poor taste or not indicative of what and who your are. You're going to need some officers, too, so we'll explore who might make the best officers and why.

Your club has to meet someplace, unless it's an online club, so we'll have a look at some logical meeting sites for you to consider. We'll also think about establishing some guidelines under which the club will operate.

We're also going to tell you in this chapter why it's important to not get *too* serious about your investment club. Sure, you want it to be successful and produce some benefits for its members. You've got to remember, though, that it's not a life-and-death situation. Like with most other things in life, everyone will be happier and more satisfied if you manage to have some fun along with all the work you'll be doing.

Okay, let's get started.

What's in a Name?

Check out the Internet and you'll find dozens of listings for investment clubs. Their names range from the predictable to the bizarre.

Some names state exactly what the group is, such as the Tallahassee Investment Club. Names of other groups, such as Witches of Wall Street are, let's just say, open to interpretation.

Heading for a Crash

Be careful about choosing a name for your club that might already be in use. If you live in Chicago, for instance, and name your club the Chicago Investment Club, chances are that another club (or possibly more than one) already uses that name. The National Association of Investors Corp. (NAIC) could tell you if such a group exists if it's registered with the NAIC, but if it's not, you'll have no way of knowing. Choose a name that's not likely to already be in use.

What you name your club is up to you and the other members. Family-based investment clubs often use the family name, while clubs in which all members share a common interest often base their name on that interest.

It's probably best to choose a name that lets people know what you are. We'd recommend using the words "investment club" in your name. Remember that you'll be using the name in your club agreement and when you register your club with the Internal Revenue Service (more about that in Chapter 12, "A Taxing Topic").

Just for fun, let's have a look at the names of some existing clubs. These were either taken from articles about investment clubs, names of clubs that we know about personally, or listed on the Internet:

➤ Travelers, Rottweilers and Aging Gentlemen Investment Club, Spalding, Lincolnshire, United Kingdom

➤ Iron Cross Investment Club, St. Louis, Missouri

➤ Cent Sational Stockers, Seattle, Washington

➤ The Sinbad Society, Chicago, Illinois

➤ Pfriends in Pfinance (PIP), Austin, Texas

➤ The Billionaires Club, Seattle, Washington

➤ Student Portfolio Analysis and Management (SPAM), the University of Missouri at Columbia

➤ Dow Dame$ Investment Club, LLC, Fayetteville, Arkansas

➤ Mad Dough Investments, Chicago, Illinois

➤ Bears and Bulls Investment Club, Springfield, Illinois

➤ Metropolitan Investing Club, Washington, D.C.

➤ The Elizabeth Swalocs Investment Club, Bedfordshire, England

➤ Buffalo Chip Investment Club, Cheyenne, Wyoming

➤ Flood City Investment Club, Johnstown, Pennsylvania

➤ Ladies Investment Portfolio Syndicate (LIPS), Queensland, Australia

➤ Rags to Riches Investment Club, Houston, Texas

➤ Buckeyes on Wall Street, Pickerington, Ohio

➤ Aquidneck Island Piggy Bank Club, Newport, Rhode Island

➤ Investmentclub MoneyMaker, Luebeck, Germany

➤ Ten-Seven Investment Club, Cincinnati, Ohio

➤ Angels and Assets Investment Club, Erie, Pennsylvania

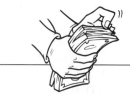

Cashing In

Where you meet can set the tone for your club's meeting, so consider carefully before choosing a location. Meeting in someone's home may indicate that your club will operate less formally than if you meet in a library or conference room. Meeting in a public place might cause club members to be more businesslike than they'd be in a member's home.

This is just a small sampling of the many names that groups have chosen for their clubs. Some groups try to be very clever and different, while others prefer traditional names that clearly state their purpose.

Just remember that, while one purpose of an investment club is the enjoyment of its members, you'll want people to take your club seriously. If your name is too offbeat, you may have trouble making that happen.

Where and When to Meet?

Unless you're operating online, your club will need a place to meet.

There are different schools of thought pertaining to this issue. Some clubs meet only in each other's homes, preferring a more personal setting than you'd find in a restaurant or other public building.

Others feel that meeting at home makes meetings too, well, homelike. They prefer a more businesslike setting.

Other options for meeting places might include:

➤ A public library

➤ A church, temple, or synagogue

➤ A retirement home

➤ A community center

➤ Your broker's house or office

In some areas, it's difficult to find a place to meet that's convenient to everyone, or that doesn't charge too much for meeting space. If that's the case, your best option might be to meet at members' homes, perhaps taking turns hosting the meetings.

If one club member's home is not large enough to hold the meeting, perhaps another member can take her turn, and she can provide the refreshments.

Most clubs meet once a month, with the understanding that all members will devote time to researching stocks between meetings.

Cashing In

It's a good idea to make an informal membership roster and distribute it to all club members. This gives members who don't know each other something to refer to during and between club meetings to help them know who's who. List the person's name, address, phone number, and perhaps his or her occupation. You can add a bit of personal information if you like, such as "Janet is married to so and so, and they have three children."

You could meet more often, but that would limit the in-between time that members have for "homework," and could make club work too cumbersome.

Meeting less than once a month probably isn't a good idea, either, because members tend to let club matters slide if the meetings are too far apart.

You might want to meet more than once a month while you're getting the club organized and off the ground. This gives members a chance to get to know each other a bit before they start working together and makes the first formal meetings more comfortable.

After the organizational meetings, plan to meet once a month, at least to start. If you find that you can't complete all the necessary business during monthly meetings, or if your meetings are going too long, you can always schedule an extra get-together to catch up. Or, if it turns out that all your members have a particularly busy month and many are unable to attend the regular meeting, you might skip a meeting.

Some clubs penalize members who don't show for meetings. Some require members with unexcused absences to pay fines, while others kick out those who miss too many meetings. Fewer members means the workload will be concentrated on the ones who attend, so make sure that everyone understands their attendance is important.

Be ready to be flexible, but do establish a regular meeting time and place. Have members vote on when and where you'll meet. Then, encourage them to adhere to the schedule as much as possible.

Because meetings tend to last longer than they need to, it's a good idea to limit the length of your club's get-togethers. You'll need to meet for at least an hour, but we'd advise not going longer than two hours. Attention tends to wane during long meetings, and they often become ineffective.

Some clubs hold their meetings over breakfast, lunch, or dinner, and it works just fine. Others, however, find that their meetings work better if they eat first, or if they meet without eating. Many groups conduct their meetings and have coffee and dessert afterward.

Your meeting format is up to you and your group. Just be sure that whatever you choose is effective for your club.

Building a Firm Foundation

We've already discussed how important it is to get your club off to a good start. The foundation you lay early on will allow your club to grow and prosper in the future.

Your foundation should be based on the goals of your club and the guidelines you establish.

Setting Goals

Successful investment clubs set goals and work toward meeting them. These goals should be general in nature, and members should be reminded of the goals often.

Goals vary from club to club, but education should always be among the list of goals you establish for your group. Investment clubs that stress education generally remain together much longer than clubs that are looking to get rich quick, and their members remain interested and committed to the group.

Other goals you might want to consider for your club:

Cashing In

Consider starting each club meeting by having a member read aloud your goals. This is a good way to keep the goals in the forefront, and remind members of what the club is trying to accomplish.

➤ Invest every month

➤ Keep every member involved

➤ Reinvest dividends

➤ Buy diverse stock

➤ Research all stock thoroughly

➤ Pool all club assets (experience, knowledge, money, and so on)

➤ Invest conservatively

➤ Be patient

➤ Have a good time as a group

➤ Look for growth companies

➤ Beat the S&P 500 Index average annual gain

Don't set too many goals at first. You can always add some later on. Make sure that everyone knows and understands the goals and refer to them often.

Establishing Guidelines

In the next chapter, we'll talk about your club's operating agreement and what it should include. Your operating agreement is the set of rules for the club, including the amount of money each member will contribute, how the club will be managed, what happens when a member leaves the club, and so forth.

Your club's guidelines are different and probably less formal than its operating agreement, but are still very important.

Some of the topics your club's guidelines might address include …

➤ The number of officers your club will have, and how often they'll be elected (we'll talk more about officers in the "Electing Officers" section, later in this chapter).

➤ The responsibilities of each club member between meetings. Each member could keep track of one or more of the club's investments, reporting the stocks' activity to other members during club meetings. This gives each member familiarity with a particular stock or stocks and eliminates the need for every member to keep up with every investment. The idea is to share the work, and this is a good way to do so.

➤ Voting rights and privileges. Some clubs allot votes based on the value of a member's account, while others give equal voting rights to every member. Voting is used to determine whether or not the club will buy or sell stock, elect officers, and conduct regular club business such as the meeting date and place. An argument against giving more votes to those members who have more money invested, or hold more membership shares, is that it tends to alienate new members, while giving members who've belonged to the club longer an unfair voting advantage. Some clubs, however, feel that long-time members with more money invested should have more say.

➤ National Association of Investors Corporation (NAIC) membership. We think it's a very good idea to get your club registered with the NAIC, but, for whatever reasons, there are clubs that don't join. You should at the very least explore the benefits of NAIC membership, and propose to other club members that you join. Check out www.better-investing.org for more information.

Anticipating Problems

Members of successful investment clubs and other organizations learn to anticipate problems and deal with them before or right after they occur.

Problems, such as friction between members, members getting discouraged and disinterested if the club doesn't see big (or any) financial returns right away, or certain members not doing their share of work, only get worse if they're not dealt with promptly. Club officers should be on the lookout for possible problems, and deal with them as soon as they become apparent.

Occasionally, an investment club will encounter far more serious problems than the ones mentioned earlier. For example, a member uses club assets for his own purposes or purchases a speculative stock with club funds without approval from other members.

These issues should be specifically mentioned in the club's operating rules, and procedures should be put in place to deal with serious problems. If problems crop up that are too serious to resolve within the club, you might have to consult a lawyer. We'll get into dealing with problems in a lot more detail in Part 5, "Keeping Track of Your Investments."

Heading for a Crash

Problems that aren't addressed and acted upon can be real morale-busters for your club. Keep an ear to the ground and be alert to signs of problems. Possible signs of trouble include members forming cliques, or two or more members who constantly clash on club issues. If you see these things happening in your club, act quickly to resolve the matter.

Electing Officers

As with any club, it's very important that your investment group elect good officers who are willing and able to put in the work necessary to keep the club running smoothly.

You should elect officers every year, giving many members the opportunity to serve if they desire. Don't think, however, that you necessarily need to elect new officers every year. If somebody is doing a great job as president and is willing to continue, thank your lucky stars and give him or her another term.

Most clubs have four officers:

➤ President

➤ Vice president

➤ Secretary

➤ Treasurer

Some clubs refer to their officers as partners. The president of the club would be called the senior partner and the vice president the junior partner. The secretary would be the recording partner, while the treasurer would be called the financial partner.

It really doesn't matter what you call your officers. The important thing is that they fully understand their duties, interact effectively with other members, and are faithful in doing their jobs.

The responsibilities of the various officers generally are as follows:

➤ **President.** The president conducts club meetings, sets the meeting dates and times, sets up various committees, and generally keeps an eye on all club proceedings. The president should have the respect and confidence of other club members. She or he should be organized, and have sufficient time to devote to club business.

➤ **Vice president.** The vice president takes over for the president if he or she is not available. Some clubs make the vice president responsible for a certain part of the meeting, such as an educational presentation.

➤ **Secretary.** The secretary is responsible for taking the minutes of the meeting and for distributing the minutes to each member *before* the next meeting. This is a very important job, because, through the writing of the minutes, the secretary effectively serves as your club historian. He or she also is responsible for receiving and distributing all club correspondence. Your secretary should be well organized and have sufficient time to devote to the job.

➤ **Treasurer.** The job of club treasurer is a very important one. Ideally, the treasurer should have some previous experience with investing and a good understanding of financial matters. The treasurer typically places orders with your club's broker to buy and sell stock. She or he gathers members' monthly contributions, keeps track of all the club's financial records, and is responsible for putting together a monthly statement of club receipts and disbursements and keeping track of each member's investments. Some clubs divide these duties among two members, and that's something you might want to consider. It not only spreads the work around, but gives more members a chance to learn. In some clubs, the treasurer, or another member designated and trained for the task, prepares yearly tax information for each member. Other clubs hire an outside person for that job.

Take This to the Bank

Meeting minutes are an integral part of a club's history and should be carefully preserved. Just for fun, consider the job of a secretary before the days of typewriters and word processors. Minutes—often pages and pages of them—had to be carefully copied by hand.

If your club is fairly large, consider appointing a nominating committee. The committee would come up with likely people to fill the positions of officers, contact those people to see if they're willing to serve, and bring the names to the club. All club members, of course, get to vote on the people nominated by the committee.

Keeping It Fun

One of the worst mistakes an investment club can make is to lose sight of its goal of creating and maintaining an enjoyable experience for its members.

Sure, you want club members to take their jobs of researching stocks seriously. Sure, you want your officers to be committed and fulfill their responsibilities. Sure, you want your club to make some money. If the club becomes too serious, however, or too focused on financial gain, it can quickly lose sight of one of its most important objectives— enjoyment.

Heading for a Crash

No club member should be allowed to intimidate another member by blaming him or her for recommending a poor stock choice. Nothing is more discouraging to a member than feeling that others hold him or her responsible for a poor recommendation. Make sure all members understand that responsibility is shared and no one member is to be blamed for bad choice. Everyone in the club gets a chance to vote on whether or not to buy the stock—it's a group decision.

A really important point for all club members to remember is that failure is not the end of the world. It's okay if your club occasionally buys a stock that turns out to be a real dog. It's not the end of the world, especially if members learn from the experience.

The National Association of Investors Corp. (NAIC) advises its clubs not to expect consistent, positive results until after they've been operating for five years. The first years are learning years and although you'll no doubt experience some successes, you're surely bound to have some failures, as well.

Some investment clubs hold social events that are separate from regular meetings. Members are encouraged to get to know each other outside of a meeting setting and to enjoy each other's company. Holiday parties are popular with many clubs.

Whether or not your club gets together at times other than its regular meetings, remember to have some fun whenever members are together. Set aside a little time at meetings for socializing and maintain an atmosphere that's friendly and inclusive.

The Least You Need to Know

➤ Your club's name should clearly indicate what and who it is.

➤ Meeting in a member's home tends to make the get-togethers a little more casual than those held in a public place.

➤ Monthly meetings work well for most groups.

➤ Setting reasonable goals and establishing good guidelines provides a sound foundation on which your investment club can grow.

➤ Most clubs elect a president, vice president, secretary, and treasurer each year.

➤ The duties of officers should be clearly defined, and officers should be chosen with care.

➤ Members may become discouraged and lose interest if the club becomes too serious.

 REF

Chapter 8

Establishing Operating Rules

In This Chapter

➤ Picking the right legal structure

➤ Finding a bank you can work with

➤ Writing an operating agreement that's right for your club

➤ Deciding if and when you need outside help

➤ Choosing lawyers, accountants, and the like

Once you've found members, chosen a name, and set a meeting time and place for your investment club, it's time to get down to business. Legal business, that is.

It's extremely important that you follow the necessary legal guidelines as you get your club organized and operating. Investment clubs must be registered either as partnerships or corporations and must comply with regulations of the U.S. Treasury Department.

Unless you have the necessary professionals among your club's membership, you'll probably need to consult some outside help to make sure that you're properly registered and that you're getting the best tax deal that you can. Some clubs do everything on their own, using the National Association of Investor's Corp. (NAIC) start-up materials as a guide. If you're confident enough and capable of doing so, go ahead. Just don't get stubborn and refuse to get some help if you get confused or run into problems.

You also need to make sure that you have the best operating agreement possible and that everyone in your club is familiar with the agreement and has some input into what it says.

In this chapter, we'll discuss choosing the best legal structure for your club; picking a bank that you're comfortable doing business with; finding good outside help, such as lawyers and accountants; and writing the best operating agreement possible.

You might think these things sound complicated, but don't worry. We'll guide you through each step, and we even include a sample operating agreement on which you can model your own agreement.

You'll be up and running—legally, that is—in no time.

Choosing a Legal Structure for Your Club

Basically, you have two choices when you form an investment club. You can make it a partnership, which is what most clubs do, or you can make it a corporation.

What's the difference, you ask? The biggest differences are in how your club will be taxed and the amount of hassle it will take to get your club up and running. Let's have a look.

Partnerships

Most investment clubs form as *partnerships*. A partnership is nothing more than a group of people who get together for a common purpose and agree as to how they'll conduct the club (or business) and how the profit, risks, liabilities, and losses will be distributed among them. Partnerships usually are pretty hassle-free to get going and as long as there's a good operating agreement, they generally work pretty well.

A big advantage of a partnership, as opposed to a corporation, has to do with taxes.

A Taxing Situation

Now, don't get excited and think you won't have to pay any taxes—good old Uncle Sam always seems to find us. In a partnership, however, you'll pay taxes only once, as opposed to twice, as you would within a corporation.

A corporation must pay corporate-level tax *and* its shareholders, or members, must pay individual income tax on their earnings. It's the same money, but it's taxed twice, at two different levels.

Taking Stock

A **partnership** is when two or more people get together to start a business or other group, such as an investment club. The partners agree on how the group or business will be conducted, including debts, assets, and liabilities.

A partnership is taxed differently from an S corporation, which is taxed differently from a C corporation. Let's have a look at how it works.

A partnership divides out the income and expenses evenly among the partners. Let's say that your club has 20 members, or partners. And let's say the club has earned $10,000 in dividends and interest in the past year. As a partner, your taxable portion of this income would be $500, or one twentieth of the earnings. You'd be required to report the earnings on your income tax return under Schedule B, Part I (interest), and Part II (dividends).

Expenses incurred by a partnership are divided among the club members the same way that income is apportioned. If the club spends $1,200 for an accountant or tax attorney to prepare its operating agreement and the initial tax return, each member would get to claim $60 in deductions on his or her income tax return.

Using an S corporation format for your club has very similar tax implications to those you have with a partnership. An S corporation divides the club's income out to the membership according to the number of shares each member earns. The advantage of an S corporation over a partnership is that the S corporation limits personal liability. Shareholders can only be liable for the value of the corporation's stock that they own.

C corporations also limit each member's liability, but they're taxed differently than S corporations. With a C corporation, the income (less deductions) is taxable to the corporation.

If your club is a C corporation, has 20 members, with each member owning 5 percent of the club's investments, and the club made $10,000 that year in interest and dividends, it would be taxed to the corporation. Then, after that tax is paid, the income could be distributed to the shareholders. At that point, you, as a partner, are required to pay tax on the distributions you receive.

As you can imagine, these different systems of taxation can really affect your bottom line when it comes to your income tax return.

If you as a club member are in the 15 percent tax bracket, you'll pay 15 percent tax on the income passed to you through the partnership (your club). If you're in the 31 percent bracket, you'll pay 31 percent on your income from the club.

To complicate matters, long-term capital gains are taxed differently than interest and dividends. Long-term capital gains are taxed either at 10 or 20 percent. If an investor is in the 15 percent tax bracket, the long-term capital gains are taxed at 10 percent. If he's in the 24 percent or higher bracket, the gains are taxed at 20 percent.

With a C corporation, the income is taxed to the corporation in the same manner as it is earned. Capital gains are taxed as gains, interest is taxed as interest, and dividends are taxed as dividends. After taxes and all expenses are paid, distributions are made to the shareholder. These are taxed to you as current income. If you are in the 15, 24, 31, 34, or 39.6 percent bracket, you'll pay your taxable rate on the income. That's why a C corporation isn't really a viable option for an investment club, and

Heading for a Crash

Don't assume anything when forming a partnership or corporation. Regulations can vary, not only from state to state, but from municipality to municipality. And don't assume that regulations never change. Not keeping up with regulations can cause serious problems for your club.

Taking Stock

Securities are investments that represent evidence of debt, ownership of a business, or the legal right to acquire or sell an ownership interest in a business.

why most clubs form as partnerships. You want capital gain treatment for the gains your club earns.

Setup and Maintenance

Another big advantage of a partnership over a corporation is that a partnership is much easier to establish and maintain.

Partnerships generally are only required to register with the county or state in which the group will operate. You'll probably need to pay a modest fee and provide a list of the members of your club.

Regulations concerning partnerships vary from state to state, so be sure you check with the proper agencies to find out about all applicable regulations.

Once your club is registered as a partnership, don't forget to find out what you'll need to do to keep its registration current. Just as you have to reapply for a driver's license and car registration, you'll need to apply periodically to renew your partnership status.

Sign on the Dotted Line

A third reason that most investment clubs are set up as partnerships is that the partnership format allows one or several members to transact business, execute trades, and write checks. These designated members can even transfer *securities* in and out of the club with the signature of just one partner, who serves as the club's agent.

Having one person designated to handle business for a partnership is a great boon to an investment club. It's far more convenient to need only the signature of the club's agent to transfer securities or perform other tasks, than to have all members make themselves available to sign.

Some club members get uneasy with the thought of one person being able to transfer securities, but there are safeguards you can take to assure that there's no misuse of funds. Make sure that all buying and selling records are available to club members at all times and pay attention to see that money is going to and coming from designated sources.

A few states require investment clubs to file with the Securities and Exchange Commission (SEC) if the club doesn't apply for and receive an exemption. We'll discuss the possible need for outside help a little later in this chapter. If you have a lawyer to advise your club, this is the type of thing you'll want to have him check on.

All in all, partnerships probably make more sense for investment clubs than corporations. Corporations, however, do have some advantages, so let's have a look.

Corporations

While we've pointed out several disadvantages of setting up and running your investment club as a corporation, there are some advantages, as well.

Who's Liable?

A primary advantage of a *corporation* is that it is something that's legally separate from its members. It limits the liability of each stockholder, or member, to the amount of his or her investment. If a corporation fails, or is found liable in a lawsuit, it's the corporation that's responsible, not the people who own it.

Taking Stock

A **corporation** is a legal entity that is separate from the people who are its members. The big advantage of a corporation is that it limits the liability of its members to the amount of their investment.

Types of Corporations

There are two basic types of corporations: C corporations and S corporations. The main difference between the two is the way that they're taxed—each one limits the liabilities of its members.

➤ **C corporations.** C corporations get a double whammy when it comes to paying federal income tax. Here's how it works. The corporation has to pay a tax on its earned profit and the people who get salaries or corporate dividends have to pay again. For obvious reasons, owners of C corporations don't like the way this tax structure is set up.

➤ **S corporations.** S corporations basically are corporations that get special tax status from the Internal Revenue Service (IRS) and don't pay tax on the corporate level. All profits and losses are passed along to members or shareholders, who have to include the income on their personal tax returns. If there's a loss, shareholders write it off on their personal taxes. Initially, an S corporation might sound more appealing than a C corporation, and in some ways it is. Although S corporations were created with small companies in mind, there are a lot of restrictions and regulations that go hand in hand with them.

Cashing In

If you're really interested in forming an S corporation for your club, you can get more information about S corporations from the IRS publication #589. You can order one by calling the IRS at 1-800-829-3676, or you can download the information off the Internet. Check out the IRS Web site at www.irs.ustreas. gov.

There aren't many investment clubs that bother even trying to get S corporation status, because it's a hassle and, as we said earlier, there are a lot of restrictions and regulations.

All members of an S corporation, for instance, must reside in the same state and all must be legal U.S. residents. The number of shareholders is limited and there are other restrictions, as well.

The type of legal structure you choose is entirely up to you and the other members of your club. Regardless, however, of whether you decide to form a partnership or a corporation, there are some legal things you've got to keep in mind.

Keeping It Legal

There are some things that your club will have to do to remain in compliance with local, state, and federal regulations.

Because these vary depending on where you live, you'll need to check carefully with a lawyer or financial advisor with experience working with investment clubs to make sure you're doing everything you need to do. See the "Looking for Outside Help" section later in this chapter for how to find this help.

One thing you'll certainly have to do is to get a tax identification number (we'll show you how in Chapter 12, "A Taxing Topic"). That's necessary in order to open a brokerage account. You'll also need to file financial reports with the IRS.

Remember that it's easier to get all the legal aspects of starting your club finished promptly—and do it right the first time around—than to try to straighten out a mess later on.

We know of a club that failed to file the appropriate initial tax return. The IRS caught up to them, eventually, and each member was billed by the IRS for $3,000. The matter got straightened out in time, but the club incurred some hefty fees with its accountant before the matter was resolved. It would have been much easier for the club—and less expensive—if the proper forms had been filed initially.

Choosing a Bank

Because you have to have a place to keep members' contributions until you're ready to purchase stocks, you'll need to choose a bank with which your club will be associated.

Presumably, everyone in your club is familiar with banks and how they work. Just in case a club member has been keeping her money under the mattress, however, here's a quick refresher.

Generally speaking, there are three types of financial institutions:

➤ Commercial banks

➤ Thrifts

➤ Credit unions

Commercial Banks

Banks handle about three quarters of the total amount of assets within the entire financial system. Commercial banks can have either a federal or state charter and are regulated according to which type they have. Those with federal charters must be members of the Federal Reserve system and the Federal Deposit Insurance Corporation (FDIC), which the bank pays to insure individual bank deposits up to $100,000.

Take This to the Bank

There are roughly 13,000 different commercial banks operating in the United States. In the banking heyday of the 1920s, there were about 31,000.

Commercial banks are permitted to take deposits, loan money, and provide other banking services. They vary greatly—from huge, national establishments to small, community banks.

Thrifts

These are financial institutions commonly known as savings and loans (S&Ls). First started in the 1930s, the original intent of S&Ls was to provide people with money with which they could buy homes. They accept deposits from and extend credit primarily to individuals. The collective reputation of S&Ls was damaged in the 1980s, when many of them failed and had to be bailed out by taxpayer (that means you) dollars. Those problems prompted recent legislative changes, which have improved the quality of thrifts. Thrifts are insured by the Savings & Loan Insurance Corp. (SLIC) for up to $100,000.

Cashing In

If you're interested in joining a credit union, first find out if you're eligible through work. If not, you might be able to join one that a family member is eligible for. Or, you might find one that you could join based on membership in a professional organization or club. For more information on joining a credit union, call the Credit Union National Association in Madison, Wisconsin, at 1-800-358-5710.

Cashing In

If you're wary about online banking, remember that it wasn't too many years ago that bank machines were introduced, and folks were plenty wary about them, too. If you're worried about online banking, take some time to look into it, and then decide. You'll definitely be hearing more and more about it as increasing numbers of people begin using it.

Credit Unions

Alternatives to commercial banks, credit unions are nonprofit organizations that provide many of the same services as banks. Generally, credit unions can offer better rates on loans and savings because they don't pay federal taxes.

Credit unions were first regulated in this country in the 1930s by the Federal Credit Union Act. That act limited membership to "groups having a common bond of occupation or association." Membership limits were expanded in the early 1980s, however, causing banks to protest that credit unions were taking their customers while enjoying unfair tax advantages.

The Supreme Court was called in to settle the dispute and ruled on the side of the banks. Depending on how the situation is resolved, this could mean that credit union membership will become more restrictive. If you join a credit union, make sure it's a member of the FDIC, which insures deposits. Some credit unions aren't members, which means that if they get into financial problems, your accounts aren't backed by the government—you could lose all your savings.

Online Accounts

Even though online accounts are commercial, thrifts, or credit unions, they're worth a special mention. Many people mistakenly think that online banking is only for clubs that operate online. That, however, isn't the case. Even if your club isn't an online investment club, you can still utilize an online account.

This could be a really good way to demonstrate the status of the club's account at meetings. You could have a laptop or computer at the meeting connected to the Internet, allowing individual club members to peruse the account online and actually see their investments and cash balances. This can be a great way to instill confidence in your officers and club members.

While many people still balk at the thought of handling their banking online, the practice is quickly gaining popularity.

Banks that offer online services promote them as being convenient, secure, and—this will get you interested—free.

The giant Bank of America, for example, formed recently from the merger of BankAmerica and NationsBank, offers online banking in every state. Online banking with this institution offers 24-hour, seven-day-a-week access to your personal accounts and your business checking account. It allows you to transfer funds between your accounts, and do things like check balances, order checks, ask technical questions, or request statements.

You need to have an account with a bank in order to set up an online account. Most banks provide a toll-free number on their Web sites, allowing you to call and set up an account over the phone.

Banks are very cautious about security, and you'll probably be asked to select more than one identification number or password that you'll need to gain access to your accounts.

Take This to the Bank

Banks that offer online services employ security measures to protect their customers' information. Some of those measures include displaying only a portion of a customer's account number on the screen, and automatic logoff if no action is taken within an account for a specified period of time (usually 10 or 15 minutes). Customers are required to use an I.D. and password for access to their accounts, and banks monitor their systems to prevent problems that could interfere with security.

Most people definitely can see the appeal of online banking. What would you rather do? Wait in line inside a bank or at a bank machine, or sit down at your desk with a cup of coffee and take care of business?

If your club hasn't checked out online banking, it's something to look into. The Bank of America Web site has a demonstration that tells you all about it, and you can find it at www.bankofamerica.com/onlinebanking. Most other major banks offer online services, as well, so you can check out individual Web sites. A few to get you started are …

➤ Chase Manhattan Bank at www.chase.com.

➤ Fleet Bank at www.fleet.com.

➤ Citibank at www.citibank.com.

➤ Sovereign Bank at www.sovereignbank.com.

Or, check out the Bank Web, a listing of hundreds of banks offering online services. Banks are listed by state, and you can connect to any of them from this site. Bank Web is located at www.bankweb.com.

Choosing an Account

Once you've decided what type of financial institution your investment club will use, you have to figure out what type of account you should stash your money with until you're ready to use it to buy investments.

Should you keep it in a checking account so that it's always available? Or should it be deposited into a savings account, a money market account (MMA), or even a short-term certificate of deposit (CD)?

The answer to those questions normally depends on how much money your club has and when you'll need it.

When first starting out, your club should have enough money to open a money market account. Money market accounts usually require a higher minimum balance than a savings account, but you get a higher return.

You could use a savings account if your club buys investments each month and leaves only very minimal amounts of money in the bank. If you maintain a balance, however, an MMA might be a better choice.

A good system for your club to look into is setting up a money market fund within the brokerage account. This will allow you to hold funds until stocks are purchased, unless you decide to only purchase shares through dividend reinvestment (don't worry—we'll get to all that in Chapter 19, "To Have and to Hold").

If you decide to go with a money market fund within your club's brokerage account, your club treasurer would deposit monthly club dues into the local money market fund account. After the deposit is made, a check would be mailed to the brokerage account for temporary investment (holding) until such time as securities are purchased.

Just don't assume that a savings or checking account is the only option for your club's money. You might be better off putting it in another kind of account, such as a money market or short-term certificate of deposit.

And don't forget to shop around for the best bank deal you can get. Fees and regulations vary greatly from bank to bank, so ask plenty of questions and get plenty of information before committing your club's money.

What to Include in Your Operating Agreement

Your club's *operating agreement,* or set of bylaws, is the set of rules and regulations by which you'll operate. You'll refer to the agreement often and use it to guide the club.

Because this agreement will be so important to your club, it should be carefully thought out, drafted, and executed.

Fortunately, there are some excellent examples of operating agreements around that you can model yours after. Don't, however, think that your agreement must be just like that of another group. Feel free to customize it to suit the members of your group.

And don't think that once your operating agreement is signed, sealed, and delivered it can't ever be changed. Successful investment clubs amend their operating agreements as their needs and circumstances change.

Normally, 75 percent of the membership must approve a proposed amendment to the operating agreement in order for it to be adopted.

Some important topics that your operating agreement should address …

> **Cashing In**
>
> Check out www.bankrate.com for information on the fees and rates of various banks. It's a great way to compare banks so you can get the best deal for your club.

> **Taking Stock**
>
> Your **operating agreement** is the set of rules and regulations under which your club will be formed and under which it will operate. It states clearly and definitively what your club and its members may and may not do.

➤ The name of your club.

➤ The purpose of your club.

➤ Matters relating to membership, such as a minimum and maximum number of members, responsibilities of each member, how members are admitted to the groups, how many members must be present at a meeting in order for business to be conducted, and so forth.

➤ Matters relating to officers, such as what offices will exist within the club, the duties of officers, how officers are elected, and the length of terms.

➤ Matters regarding club meetings, such as the frequency of meetings, at what meeting elections are conducted, and how and when special meetings will be called.

➤ Matters relating to capital contributions for investment, such as how much money each member contributes, how capital accounts are established within the club, how profits and losses are divided, who will deposit club funds, how capital is distributed if someone leaves the club, and so forth.

➤ Matters relating to the operating agreement, such as how and when it may be amended.

In the next section, we've included the Partnership Agreement of the Mutual Investment Club of Detroit, which was put together in 1940. Although you shouldn't feel like you have to use this exact agreement for your club, it will provide a good model and should help you get started with your own agreement.

Cashing In

Although your operating agreement will be the official document under which your club will run, don't be tempted to make it overly complicated or confusing. The best agreements are written simply and are easy to understand. They simply state what must be stated. Don't make your agreement more difficult than it needs to be.

A Sample Partnership Agreement

This partnership agreement is included in the National Association of Investors Association manual and is printed here with the permission of the NAIC. Complete notes about each section of this agreement can be found in the NAIC's manual.

**Sample Investment Club
Partnership Agreement**

Editor's Note:
The following text is the Partnership Agreement that appears in the NAIC Official Guide: Starting and Running a Profitable Investment Club. *If investment club members have questions about the agreement, they are advised to consult the detailed notes in the* Official Guide.

**Partnership Agreement
of the
Mutual Investment Club of Detroit**

THIS AGREEMENT OF PARTNERSHIP, effective as of ___(date)___ by and between the undersigned, to wit: (names of partners)

NOW, THEREFORE IT IS AGREED:

1. Formation. The undersigned hereby form a General Partnership in accordance with and subject to the laws of the State of Michigan.

2. Name. The name of the partnership shall be Mutual Investment Club of Detroit.

3. Term. The partnership shall begin on ___(date)___ and shall continue until December 31 of the same year and thereafter from year to year unless earlier terminated as hereinafter provided.

4. Purpose. The only purpose of the partnership is to invest the assets of the partnership solely in stocks, bonds, and other securities ("securities") for the education and benefit of the partners.

5. Meetings. Periodic meetings shall be held as determined by the partnership.

6. Capital Contributions. The partners may make capital contributions to the partnership on the date of each periodic meeting in such amounts as the partnership shall determine; provided, however, that no partner's capital account shall exceed twenty percent (20%) of the capital accounts of all partners.

7. Value of the Partnership. The current value of the assets of the partnership, less the current value of the liabilities of the partnership (hereinafter referred to as the "value of the partnership"), shall be determined as of a regularly scheduled date and time ("valuation date") preceding the date of each periodic meeting determined by the Club.

8. Capital Accounts. A capital account shall be maintained in the name of each partner. Any increase or decrease in the value of the partnership on any valuation date shall be credited or debited, respectively, to each partner's capital account on that date. Any other method of valuing each partner's capital account may be substituted for this method, provided the substituted method results in exactly the same valuation as previously provided herein. Each partner's contribution to, or capital withdrawal from, the partnership shall be credited, or debited, respectively, to that partner's capital account.

9. Management. Each partner shall participate in the management and conduct of the affairs of the partnership in proportion to his capital account. Except as otherwise determined, all decisions shall be made by the partners whose capital accounts total a majority of the value of the capital accounts of all the partners.

10. Sharing of Profits and Losses. Net profits and losses of the partnership shall inure to, and be borne by, the partners, in proportion to the value of each of their capital accounts.

11. Books of Account. Books of account of the transactions of the partnership shall be kept and at all times be available and open to inspection and examination by any partner.

continues

continued

12. Annual Accounting. Each calendar year, a full and complete account of the condition of the partnership shall be made to the partners.

13. Bank Account. The partnership may select a bank for the purpose of opening a bank account. Funds in the bank account shall be withdrawn by checks signed by any partner designated by the partnership.

14. Broker Account. None of the partners of this partnership shall be a broker. However, the partnership may select a broker and enter into such agreements with the broker as required for the purchase or sale of securities. Securities owned by the partnership shall be registered in the partnership name unless another name shall be designated by the partnership.

    Any corporation or transfer agent called upon to transfer any securities to or from the name of the partnership shall be entitled to rely on instructions or assignments signed by any partner without inquiry as to the authority of the person(s) signing such instructions or assignments, or as to the validity of any transfer to or from the name of the partnership.

    At the time of a transfer of securities, the corporation or transfer agent is entitled to assume (1) that the partnership is still in existence and (2) that this Agreement is in full force and effect and has not been amended unless the corporation has received written notice to the contrary.

15. No Compensation. No partner shall be compensated for services rendered to the partnership, except reimbursement for expenses.

16. Additional Partners. Additional partners may be admitted at any time, upon the unanimous consent of the partners, so long as the number of partners does not exceed twenty-five (25).

    16A. Transfers to a Trust. A partner may, after giving written notice to the other partners, transfer his interest in the partnership to a revocable living trust of which he is the grantor and sole trustee.

    16B. Removal of a Partner. Any partner may be removed by agreement of the partners whose capital accounts total a majority of the value of all partners' capital accounts. Written notice of a meeting where removal of a partner is to be considered shall include a specific reference to this matter. The removal shall become effective upon payment of the value of the removed partner's capital account, which shall be in accordance with the provisions on full withdrawal of a partner noted in paragraphs 18 and 20. The vote action shall be treated as receipt of request for withdrawal.

17. Termination of Partnership. The partnership may be terminated by agreement of the partners whose capital accounts total a majority in value of the capital accounts of all the partners. Written notice of a meeting where termination of the partnership is to be considered shall include a specific reference to this matter. The partnership shall terminate upon a majority vote of all partners' capital accounts. Written notice of the decision to terminate the partnership shall be

given to all the partners. Payment shall then be made of all the liabilities of the partnership and a final distribution of the remaining assets either in cash or in kind, shall promptly be made to the partners or their personal representatives in proportion to each partner's capital account.

18. Voluntary Withdrawal (Partial or Full) of a Partner. Any partner may withdraw a part or all of the value of his capital account in the partnership and the partnership shall continue as a taxable entity. The partner withdrawing a part or all of the value of his capital account shall give notice of such intention in writing to the Secretary. Written notice shall be deemed to be received as of the first meeting of the partnership at which it is presented. If written notice is received between meetings it will be treated as received at the first following meeting.

   In making payment, the value of the partnership as set forth in the valuation statement prepared for the first meeting following the meeting at which notice is received from a partner requesting a partial or full withdrawal, will be used to determine the value of the partner's account.

   The partnership shall pay the partner who is withdrawing a portion or all of the value of his capital account in the partnership in accordance with paragraph 20 of this Agreement.

19. Death or Incapacity of a Partner. In the event of the death or incapacity of a partner (or the death or incapacity of the grantor and sole trustee of a revocable living trust, if such trust is partner pursuant to Paragraph 16A hereof), receipt of notice shall be treated as a notice of full withdrawal.

20. Terms of Payment. In the case of a partial withdrawal, payment may be made in cash or securities of the partnership or a mix of each at the option of the partner making the partial withdrawal. In the case of a full withdrawal, payment may be made in cash or securities or a mix of each at the option of the remaining partners. In either case, where securities are to be distributed, the remaining partners select the securities.

   Where cash is transferred, the partnership shall transfer to the partner (or other appropriate entity) withdrawing a portion or all of his interest in the partnership, an amount equal to the lesser of (1) ninety-seven percent (97%) of the value of the capital account being withdrawn, or (2) the value of the capital account being withdrawn, less the actual cost to the partnership of selling securities to obtain cash to meet the withdrawal. The amount being withdrawn shall be paid within 10 days after the valuation date used in determining the withdrawal amount.

   If the partner withdrawing a portion or all of the value of his capital account in the partnership desires an immediate payment in cash, the partnership at its earliest convenience may pay eighty percent (80%) of the esti- mated value of his capital account and settle the balance in accordance with the valuation and payment procedures set forth in paragraphs 18 and 20.

continues

103

continued

> Where securities are transferred, the partnership shall select securities to transfer equal to the value of the capital account or a portion of the capital account being withdrawn (i.e., without a reduction for broker commissions). Securities shall be transferred as of the date of the club's valuation statement prepared to determine the value of that partner's capital account in the partnership. The Club's broker shall be advised that ownership of the securities has been transferred to the partner as of the valuation date used for the withdrawal.
>
> 21. Forbidden Acts. No partner shall:
>
>   a. Have the right or authority to bind or obligate the partnership to any extent whatsoever with regard to any matter outside the scope of the partnership purpose.
>
>   b. Except as provided in paragraph 16A, without the unanimous consent of all the other partners, assign, transfer, pledge, mortgage or sell all or part of his interest in the partnership to any other partner or other person whomsoever, or enter into any agreement as the result of which any person or persons not a partner shall become interested with him in the partnership.
>
>   c. Purchase an investment for the partnership where less than the full purchase price is paid for same.
>
>   d. Use the partnership name, credit, or property for other than partnership purposes.
>
>   e. Do any act detrimental to the interests of the partnership or which would make it impossible to carry on the business or affairs of the partnership.
>
> This Agreement of Partnership shall be binding upon the respective heirs, executors, administrators, and personal representatives of the partners.
>
> The partners have caused this Agreement of Partnership to be executed on the dates indicated below, effective as of the date indicated above.
>
>   Partners: (Signatures of partners)
>
> *Copyright © 1995–2000 National Association of Investors Corporation*

Looking for Outside Help

Until your club is up and running smoothly—and from time to time after that—you may need professional help.

We'll spend all of Chapter 13, "Going with a Broker—or Not," discussing matters relating to brokers, but there are other professionals from whom you might require help as well. If you have any lawyers and accountants within your investment club, you might consider asking them to review materials or suggest a trusted firm that can provide expertise.

Lawyers

Remember earlier in the chapter when we talked about choosing a legal structure for your club and making sure that all your legal affairs were in order?

There may be members of your group who are familiar with the various agencies you'll need to work with to get your club registered as either a partnership or corporation. If so, you might be able to set up a partnership (or whatever you decide to do for your club) quite nicely on your own.

You also can get help from the NAIC if your club chooses to join the organization.

If you don't have someone who's familiar with those agencies, or you're not a member of the NAIC, you should think about getting a lawyer to help.

Heading for a Crash

Don't risk getting your club off to a bad start by being too stubborn to hire the help that you need. Doing it yourself is great, but not if it puts your club at risk. Some people are reluctant to admit they need help, and in doing so they jeopardize themselves, other club members, and the club itself.

A lawyer also can help you make sure that your club is in compliance with all applicable federal, state, and local regulations. And legal matters may arise from time to time about which you'll want to consult an attorney.

There is no shortage of lawyers out there—that's for certain. Finding the lawyer who's best for your club, however, can take a bit of thought.

Many people hire a lawyer because he's a friend, or somebody they know from their synagogue, or their kid's scout group, or he's the cousin of your best friend. None of those is a good reason.

Your choice of legal representation should be based solely on the lawyer's qualifications and experience. You wouldn't, for instance, hire a divorce lawyer to help you get your investment club on the right legal track. While Brenda might get bigger divorce settlements for her clients than any other lawyer in town, she's likely to know little about legal structures for investment clubs.

With all due respect to Brenda, she's not the lawyer you want to hire.

Three things you'll need to consider when you choose a lawyer are these:

➤ Whether the lawyer will be available (within reason) when you need her

➤ Whether the lawyer has a consistent level of competency

➤ Whether the lawyer will represent your best interests

To find a lawyer who meets these criteria, talk to other investment club members. If you talk to members from 10 different clubs, 5 of them have the same lawyer and

Cashing In

A few directories to check out if you're looking for a lawyer are *Martindale-Hubbell Law Directory, Directory of the Legal Profession, Attorney's Register,* and *The Lawyer's Register by Specialty and Fields of Law.* These should be available in your local library. They include information about various lawyers and their credentials.

they all think she's the greatest thing around, you're probably on to something good.

If you find that five clubs had a particular lawyer and all fired her, however, you know to stay away.

Don't hire a lawyer because she represents a club member in other matters, unless she has the necessary experience to help your club. Sharon may have done a great job in settling the estate of Bob's parents, but if she doesn't have pertinent experience, you don't want her for your investment club.

Remember that lawyers don't work for nothing, and it will cost your club some money to get good legal help. Rates vary dramatically depending on the type of lawyer you hire and the area in which you're located. For a comparison of rates, call your local Bar Association and get the average hourly rate for the attorneys in your area. Ask if the Association has a general idea what a start-up fee for an investment club would be. Ask for the names of attorneys in your area who specialize in investment clubs or partnerships.

Accountants

Remember earlier in the chapter when we talked about tax regulations that affect investment clubs and the possibility that your club may be required to submit yearly filings or fees to your state or municipality? Again, maybe you have a club member who's well versed on all these matters. If so, feel free to seek his advice.

Tax preparers are cheaper than CPAs, who are cheaper than tax attorneys. You shouldn't need the services of a tax attorney to do the club's accounting work. Their specialty is complicated tax situations, and let's hope your club's situation is not complicated. Call a local accounting group and request information about the average cost of an investment club return in your area. Use this figure to gauge what your club will be paying for the accountant's work.

If nobody in the group is a financial expert, however, you should hire an accountant to help you.

An accountant also can help the club's financial partner, if necessary. Even if accounting services are not required consistently, it's nice to have somebody you can call when you need financial help.

Use the same techniques to find an accountant as you did when looking for a lawyer. Talk to members of other clubs and find out who's good. If a club has an accountant they really like, ask why. Resist the temptation to give your business to your buddy or relative—find someone with the experience you need.

We use professionals all the time to do the things that we can't do ourselves. We go to a dentist to clean and repair our teeth. We hire a professional roofer to fix leaks and replace faulty shingles. We hire professional movers to transport our possessions from one house to another. While your club may not need professional help often, don't assume that it never will. It's a good idea to know a good lawyer, accountant, and other necessary professionals whom you can call when necessary.

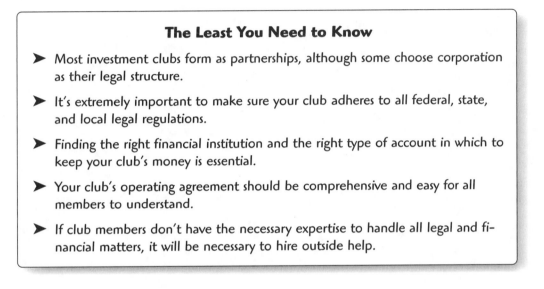

The Least You Need to Know

➤ Most investment clubs form as partnerships, although some choose corporation as their legal structure.

➤ It's extremely important to make sure your club adheres to all federal, state, and local legal regulations.

➤ Finding the right financial institution and the right type of account in which to keep your club's money is essential.

➤ Your club's operating agreement should be comprehensive and easy for all members to understand.

➤ If club members don't have the necessary expertise to handle all legal and financial matters, it will be necessary to hire outside help.

Chapter 9

Ensuring That the Club Runs Smoothly

> ### In This Chapter
>
> ➤ Keeping your club meetings interesting and fun
>
> ➤ Maintaining a level of enthusiasm among members
>
> ➤ Dealing with problems
>
> ➤ Joining the National Association of Investors Corporation
>
> ➤ Looking to other clubs for advice and help

You've taken a good deal of time and effort to get your club organized and ready to begin investing. You've rounded up friends and relatives and their friends and relatives to join the club.

You've drafted an operating agreement and made sure that all your members understand and sign it. You've selected a name for the club, set up meeting dates and times, registered your club, and found the outside help you might need.

After all that, how do you ensure that your meetings will be successful and that club members will remain enthused and happy about coming?

In this chapter, we'll look at how your club can operate successfully, so that members will remain enthusiastic. Remember, you've got to keep them ready and willing to do the work necessary to make your group a winner.

Many clubs—investment and otherwise—have failed unnecessarily. Failure occurs for many reasons, but often it's due to nothing more than poor organization, or not enough attention to details.

Perhaps certain members refuse to follow the club's regulations as stated on the operating agreement. This can cause resentment among other members and should be dealt with promptly to avoid bigger problems.

Remember that whenever there's a group of people together in an organized setting, even when they're working toward the same goal, there is the potential for conflict.

All club members should be prepared to deal with conflict quickly and effectively in order to keep the group operating smoothly. Let's have a look at what you can do to keep your group running like clockwork and make sure that its members are happy and working productively toward a common goal.

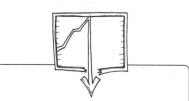

Heading for a Crash

If your meetings aren't going as well as you'd like, don't be too proud or stubborn to look for help. Ignoring the problem, or not taking steps to correct it, will only make things worse and can threaten the health of your club. Ask the other members what they'd like to change, or seek help from someone in another club.

Conducting Your Monthly Meetings

We talked in Chapter 7, "Getting Your Investment Club off to a Good Start," about where and when club meetings should be held and some of the things that should occur during meetings.

Because meetings are so vital to the health of an investment club, however, we're going to spend some more time discussing them here.

More than one club has failed because its meetings were so poorly run, or so disorganized, or just so darned boring that members simply stopped attending. We know of a club that ground to a halt after members got so disgusted with the way their president was running the meetings that they refused to come to them any more. They actually started trying to hold their own meetings—excluding the president. Needless to say, that club wasn't a good model.

Regular Attendance

Regular attendance by as many members as possible is very important to the health and ultimate success of your investment club. There are some really good reasons why attendance should be strongly encouraged—maybe even required.

Imagine that it's your turn to present information to your club regarding two stocks, then recommend which stock you think the club should buy.

You've spent weeks researching different companies and their stocks and stayed up really late last night fine-tuning your report and printing out some slick-looking fact sheets to distribute to other club members.

You choose your favorite outfit to wear to the club meeting and show up 10 minutes early to pass out your fact sheets so they're available when other members arrive for the 7 P.M. starting time.

People start to trickle in, but by 7:15 only 8 of 20 members are present. The president is upset because nobody called to be excused from attending. The treasurer is upset because the club's coffers are running low and monthly dues are needed to replenish them.

Nobody, however, is more upset than you are, because it's a club rule that 75 percent of all members must be present in order to vote on an investment. That means that all your hard work, your choice of clothing, and your fancy presentation are for naught—at least for tonight.

Lack of attendance at meetings can interrupt the continuity of a club and lessen the enthusiasm of members. It can make it impossible for a club to conduct any business, essentially making a meeting useless.

Cashing In

Some clubs fine members who miss more than the allowable number of meetings and add the money to the club's treasury. Other clubs—especially those with waiting lists—force a member who's missed too many meetings to resign.

Many clubs limit the number of meetings each member can miss, or stipulate in their operating agreements that all members must attend at least a certain percentage (usually 75 percent) of all meetings. And remember that all members—whether or not in attendance at the meetings—must contribute monthly dues.

Members who won't be at the monthly meeting should mail or drop off a check for the monthly dues to the club treasurer. Make sure the treasurer has it by the date of the meeting.

Increase Attendance

If your club is having trouble getting enough members to its meetings, you could try several things. For example:

➤ Designate someone to call each member a day or two before the meeting to remind him of the time and location at which it will be held.

➤ Set up a phone chain, where each member is responsible for calling one other member to remind her about the meeting.

➤ Assign certain tasks for each club member to perform at meetings, making it more difficult to beg off attending.

➤ Insist that anyone who can't attend notify the club secretary at least three days in advance. This prevents members from deciding at the last minute that they'd rather do something else.

Assuming you have enough members in attendance to conduct business, there are certain things that should happen at every meeting.

Cashing In

Some clubs conduct their business formally, closely adhering to an agenda and following rules of order. Others operate more informally, allowing greater flexibility and spontaneity. You'll need to find the style that best suits your club and modify that style as your club evolves. If you want to follow parliamentary procedures, you can find out everything you need to know in *Robert's Rules of Order*. It covers every topic you can think of related to meetings, bylaws, officers, and so forth.

Taking Stock

The **price-to-earnings ratio (P/E)** is a common stock analysis statistic in which the current price of stock is divided by the current earnings per share of the issuing firm.

Mandatory Meeting Minders

There are a number of things that have to happen at each meeting, for example:

➤ **Call to order.** The president calls the meeting to order, and the secretary notes who's in attendance.

➤ **Reading of the minutes.** The secretary should read the minutes from the previous meeting and ask club members if there are any changes necessary. If the minutes have been distributed previously and all members have read them, it's not necessary for the secretary to read them aloud.

➤ **The treasurer's report.** The treasurer should give a report at each meeting and be prepared to provide additional financial information to members if requested. It's a good idea to have a written financial report (it doesn't need to be fancy) to distribute.

➤ **Updating the stock information sheet.** Each member of your club should have a copy of the club's stock information sheet, which lists each stock the club owns, the number of shares owned, the cost per share when the stock was purchased, and the total cost to the club for each stock. The sheet is updated at each meeting, at which time members record current information regarding each stock. This information can include up-to-the-minute prices, industry rank, *price-to-earnings ratio (P/E)*, and so forth. One member should be responsible for gathering this sort of information on the day of the meeting and relating it to all members.

➤ **Stock reports.** In most clubs, each member is responsible for following one or two stocks in which the club has invested. Members should give brief reports of anything that has happened during the past month, or of upcoming events that could affect that stock. If a company in which you've invested has merged with another company, for instance, that's big news that should be reported.

➤ **Stock recommendations and selection.** This is normally everyone's favorite part of the club meeting (with perhaps the exception of refreshments). The person or people in charge of researching companies and recommending whether or not the club should buy their stock, give their report. They may, or may not, have prepared written reports. If so, each member should get a copy. If not, make sure that everyone can hear the report and provide wall space for charts, graphs, or other information that the presenter might have. At the end of the report, a recommendation is made to buy—or not buy—a particular stock, or more of a stock that the club already owns. Club members then vote on the recommendation.

Cashing In

Applications from people who want to join your club don't have to be formal. You could ask potential members to write a note expressing their interest in joining, or draft a simple application.

➤ **Business of the club.** Applications from potential members, correspondence, upcoming plans, and so forth should be reviewed and discussed at each meeting. All members should be kept up to date on club activities and anything that relates to the club. Avoid keeping any sort of information from members, even if you consider it to be trivial or insignificant. Club members like to know what's going on in their club—let them decide what's pertinent and what's not. Both old business and new should be discussed.

These are basic tasks and procedures that should occur at every meeting. They're the meat and potatoes of club business. Many clubs, however, have extra activities that keep things interesting and their members enthusiastic. We will cover some of these types of activities in the next section.

Heading for a Crash

Don't assume that everyone in your club has the same ideas concerning fun and entertainment. If you or another member of the club takes charge of scheduling all extra activities without consulting other members, you're running the risk of alienating members and causing resentment. Get some input from other members when planning events or activities.

113

Remembering to Keep It Fun

In these days of hectic schedules, too little time, and chronic high stress levels, we probably all could use a bit more fun.

Investing is serious business, but your investment club meetings don't need to be dry and boring. Once you've waded through the necessary agenda items, take time for your club to enjoy a little levity and diversion.

Some clubs take time for a brief educational segment, such as a report on a particular trend that analysts feel could affect the stock market. Many clubs set aside time for socializing—often with refreshments included.

A friend says her club takes advantage of opportunities offered by its broker. He occasionally provides dinners at nice restaurants for club members, with the understanding that they'll listen to a brief presentation concerning a certain investment vehicle that one of the broker's business associates is trying to sell. It's understood that the presentation is low pressure and club members are under no obligation to buy anything. Everyone enjoys the evening.

Some other ideas to keep meetings fun and interesting might include:

➤ Invite a business writer or editor from your local newspaper to address your club.

➤ Ask a faculty member from the business department of a local college or university to address your group on a pertinent issue.

➤ Invite members from other clubs to tell your group about how their club operates. You might get some great ideas for your own club.

There are lots of ways for your group to have a good time together, ensuring that members will become better acquainted and remain interested. Don't be afraid to throw out ideas for extra activities to the rest of your group.

Making Sure Members Remain Enthused

Even if you've done everything you can to keep your club's meetings interesting and enjoyable, there are times that members—at least some of them—might lose their enthusiasm.

This happens from time to time with nearly any group. It happens in classrooms, in the workplace, in families, and in social groups. Enthusiasm, like the moon, often seems to wax and wane in a cyclical fashion.

If club members seem less than enthusiastic for a meeting or two, don't be overly concerned, but don't ignore it, either. It could be that everyone is busy preparing for a holiday, preoccupied by approaching final exams or a particularly busy period at work, or that summer's coming and members' minds are drifting toward vacations instead of investments.

If your meetings are well run and well organized, you should assume that enthusiasm and interest will rebound before long. If they don't, and members seem to be losing interest, don't wait too long before you take steps to correct the problem. Consider these suggestions for keeping your club on track:

➤ Find out what's happening. If club members seem unenthusiastic and it lasts for more than a meeting or two, start asking questions. Don't wait for somebody to tell you what's going on; go ahead and find out.

➤ Determine if whatever is causing the lessened enthusiasm can be changed.

➤ Ask for, and listen to, suggestions for getting club members more involved and enthusiastic.

Cashing In

Enthusiasm is sort of like a cold in midwinter. Once a few people have it, everybody seems to get it. On the other hand, loss of enthusiasm also can be contagious.

➤ Try to recharge your group by planning some special activities. These can be club related, such as a special speaker, or unrelated. Some groups meet for golf, go out to dinner, or enjoy other activities at which no club business is conducted. This allows members to enjoy each other's company on a different level and adds a new dimension to the group.

If your club meetings are lively, well run, well organized, and leave members feeling that they've learned something, you should have little trouble with the enthusiasm level within your group.

Remember that enthusiasm is like fitness. It's a lot easier to maintain a level of it than it is to start at the bottom and build it up.

Dealing with Disagreements

As much as you may work to keep your meetings running smoothly and to keep your club's members happy and productive, you're likely from time to time to encounter disagreements.

People may disagree on which investments to buy. They might disagree on where or when the club should meet, or who should be admitted, or how capital should be dispersed when someone leaves the club.

Cashing In

When disagreements occur, always refer to your operating agreement to see if it addresses the matter at hand. Many problems can be solved in the early stages by following the rules and regulations stated in your agreement.

While some disagreements are petty, others can be serious enough to threaten the health of your investment club. The most serious disagreements—not surprisingly—seem to be about investments. Conservative investors may cringe at the suggestion from a less-conservative member that the club invest in technology stocks. Less-conservative club members might be frustrated at the thought of buying only very safe, not-so-exciting choices.

We talked about the possibility of disagreements and how to handle them earlier in this section, so refer to Chapter 6, "Bringing Club Members on Board," for a refresher, if you need to.

Many problems can be avoided by thinking carefully about who gets invited to join the club in the first place. Members with very different investing philosophies are more likely to clash than those with similar philosophies.

Investment clubs, however, are for learning, and differences of opinion can be great learning tools. Just try to learn to recognize and handle disagreements in the early stages, before they become major problems.

Affiliating Your Club with the NAIC

You can go it alone, but it's probably a good idea to get your club affiliated with the National Association of Investors Corporation. We've mentioned the NAIC extensively in earlier chapters, with good reason.

Founded in 1951 by the Mutual Investment Club of Detroit and three other investment clubs, the NAIC has consistently worked to make education the cornerstone of all investment clubs.

Take This to the Bank

Somewhere around 37,000 clubs across the United States belong to the NAIC. A recent survey of NAIC clubs showed that nearly 43 percent of them equaled or exceeded that return of the Standard & Poor's 500.

The cost of an annual NAIC membership is $40 per club, plus $14 per member. For your money, you'll get the organization's *Investor's Manual: The Handbook for Learning by Doing Investing* and *Better Investing* magazine. The handbook tells you how to set up a legal partnership, handle taxes, establish good record keeping, run a good meeting, and so forth. The magazine offers applicable information and advice for investors.

Membership also includes a low-cost dividend reinvestment plan in which 140 companies participate, a stock service plan in which dividend reinvestment plan stocks are all on one monthly transaction statement, and investor information reports on more than 120 companies. Regional chapters of the NAIC will help new clubs get started and hold useful workshops and seminars that NAIC members can attend.

NAIC members also get discounts on certain investment books and magazines.

The NAIC has a proven track record and is a good resource for most investment clubs. Using NAIC materials, such as its sample operating agreement, can save you hours of work.

Using Sound Advice from Successful Clubs

Let's face it. There's no point in reinventing the wheel.

Sure, you can draw up your operating agreement from scratch. You can chart a brand-new course for how you'll run your meetings, for your investment strategies, and for every other aspect of running an investment club.

You can, but why would you?

There are lots of successful investment clubs out there. Why not use some of their ideas, suggestions, and recommendations for setting up and running a good organization? Let's have a look at some of those things, so you can see which might apply to your club.

➤ The Beardstown Ladies wrote an entire book about their investment club and its experiences. The book, *The Beardstown Ladies' Common-Sense Investment Guide*, contains a sample operating agreement, tips on how to evaluate and select stock, how to read an annual report, and much more.

➤ The Moore Money Club, a family-based club in Georgia, offers some advice to other members of family clubs. The Moore group recommends that family clubs include some extras with their operating agreements, such as what happens in the event of a divorce within the club. Family clubs are great, Moore members say, but require extra attention in some areas.

➤ Members of the FORE! Investment Club in Washington, D.C., invest as much as possible in companies that offer dividend reinvestment plans. These plans use dividend payments to buy more stock with little or no transaction fees. They also try to buy stock as often as possible from local and socially responsible companies.

➤ Members of the West Chester Investment Club, located near Cincinnati, recommend that clubs remember they're investors, not traders. The best approach is to think long term, and to buy and hold stocks that you believe in, club members say.

➤ The Washtenaw Women's Investment Team in Ann Arbor, Michigan is committed to socially responsible investing, and it follows the guidelines of the Beardstown Ladies to determine what stocks it will buy. Club members avoid buying stock in any company that's involved in the tobacco, liquor, or gambling industries, and purchases no stock in the defense industry.

These, and many other ideas and suggestions from other clubs that are available in books, magazines, and articles can serve as a valuable guide for your club. You'll find all kinds of practical, useful advice by reading and talking to members of other clubs.

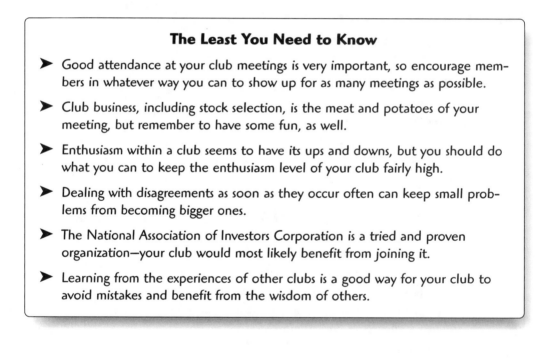

The Least You Need to Know

➤ Good attendance at your club meetings is very important, so encourage members in whatever way you can to show up for as many meetings as possible.

➤ Club business, including stock selection, is the meat and potatoes of your meeting, but remember to have some fun, as well.

➤ Enthusiasm within a club seems to have its ups and downs, but you should do what you can to keep the enthusiasm level of your club fairly high.

➤ Dealing with disagreements as soon as they occur often can keep small problems from becoming bigger ones.

➤ The National Association of Investors Corporation is a tried and proven organization—your club would most likely benefit from joining it.

➤ Learning from the experiences of other clubs is a good way for your club to avoid mistakes and benefit from the wisdom of others.

Part 3
Details, Details

Once you have the club organized, you'll need to attend to some important details.

Matters such as keeping proper records and reporting your profits for tax purposes are extremely important. This section will help you know exactly how to get those jobs done.

These are tasks that, if not done properly, can prevent your club from being successful.

Also, this part will examine how much your club members should invest, and how profits will be divided. It also will look at whether or not your club needs to work with a broker, and how to find the one who's right for you.

Being careful about keeping records and other matters will help your club operate smoothly and avoid potential pitfalls.

Chapter 10

Keeping Records the Right Way

In This Chapter

➤ Avoiding problems with good record keeping

➤ Keeping club minutes and financial records

➤ Resources to help with record keeping

➤ Finding the right people for the job

➤ Record keeping is everybody's job

If we were going to divide the world into two kinds of people, it wouldn't be good people and bad people, or tall people and short people. It wouldn't be liberals and conservatives, or even Republicans and Democrats.

If we were going to divide the world into two kinds of people, it would be those who enjoy, and are good at, keeping track of things (particularly when numbers are involved), and those who don't enjoy it and aren't good at it.

Maybe it's the right-brain-versus-left-brain thing that makes some people inclined toward keeping organized, accurate records, while others avoid record keeping at all costs. Or, maybe it's just personal preference.

Think about your friends and family members, and you'll probably see that they include both record keepers and nonrecord keepers. The two types normally are easy to distinguish.

Record keepers are the people whose checkbooks are carefully kept and always balanced. They keep track of all their receipts from the automatic teller machine and even remember to write down the amounts they withdraw. Examination of such a checkbook will reveal accurate dates, check numbers and amounts for each transaction. Record keepers also do things like keep the receipts when they go shopping until they're sure the portable CD player actually works, or the silk blouse actually fits.

They keep careful household records and can tell you without looking how much the quarterly water bill has been for the past two years, or how much they paid last year in property taxes.

Other people, however, are less fastidious when it comes to keeping track. ATM receipts, for instance, end up crumpled up in a pants pocket—completely unreadable after being washed, rinsed, and spun dry. It's not unheard of for nonrecord keepers to overdraw on their checking accounts—sometimes frequently.

Household records tend to be kept in a slipshod fashion—if at all. Shopping receipts end up in the washer with those from the ATM, or stuffed into a drawer and lost.

Nonrecord keepers are the folks who frequently are heard muttering phrases such as, "I know it's here somewhere," or "Geez, I just don't understand how that happened—again."

Households normally run better when they contain at least one good record keeper. There may be some tension between a record keeper and nonrecord keeper living in the same house, but at least there's someone keeping track of what's going on. A household without a record keeper can be a frightening place.

The same principle holds true for investment clubs. Not everyone in the group needs to be a record keeper, but it sure helps to have at least one or two.

In this chapter, we'll have a look at the importance of good record keeping for your club and who should be responsible for your club's records. We'll figure out how much record keeping actually is required, and we'll tell you why it's really important to keep everyone involved.

Understanding the Importance of Good Record Keeping

Keeping good records is important in many areas of our lives. Although we spoke lightly of it in the first section of this chapter, there are people who are better at record keeping than others.

While personal record keeping—like balancing your checkbook and keeping track of household expenses—is important, record keeping within a group is even more necessary.

If there are 15 members in your investment club, the way the records are kept directly affects 15 people. More people may be affected to a lesser degree.

In this section, we'll look at how good record keeping can get and keep your club on the right track. We'll also see how poor record keeping can derail your club.

Having a Good System Will Benefit Your Club

A good record-keeping system for an investment club is one that is accurate, easy for all club members to read and understand, and readily available for inspection at any time.

If your club's system has these properties, you're off to a good start. Record keeping shouldn't be a problem if the system is properly maintained.

It's important to understand that members of your investment club will rely heavily on whoever keeps the club's records.

Joe Jones, for instance, wants to be able to assume that the records are being kept properly, and that he can look at them whenever he wants to. Furthermore, Joe wants to be free to assume that, when he views the records, he'll be able to understand what he's seeing. He expects—and rightly so—that the records will make sense to him, to other club members, and anyone outside the club who may have cause to see them.

If Joe can assume that the records are accurate, available, and understandable, he'll have confidence in the person who keeps the records and in the club. He'll view the club as a well-run group and will likely be inspired about his membership in the club.

Cashing In

Clubs have disbanded in turmoil because of poor record keeping. If your club's record keeping isn't at the level it should be, don't wait to hire an accountant or bookkeeper to get it straightened out. Good record keeping, especially when it involves people's money, is essential.

Heading for a Crash

Warning bells should loudly sound if your club's record keepers are reluctant to let other members see their work. If that happens in your club, get to the bottom of it immediately. Don't assume there's something dishonest going on—the record keepers may just be overwhelmed or confused and don't want anyone to know it. Just don't wait to find out what the problem is.

A Poor System Causes All Kinds of Problems

If Joe Jones, on the other hand, is not confident about his investment club's record keeping, it can lead to all kinds of problems.

Suppose that Joe asks to see the records, only to find out when he gets them that they're not being kept properly. Joe, who has some record-keeping experience himself, notices that some of the numbers look wrong. He's sure that the club didn't pay the amount listed in the records for its PepsiCo stock. Furthermore, the club's recent purchase of Procter & Gamble stock isn't even included.

Or, suppose Joe asks to have a look at the records and the record keeper puts him off. She says she'll be glad to show Joe the records, but she doesn't have them with her right now. Or she says she'd really like to look over them first to make sure everything is up to date. Could Joe wait for just a day or two to see them?

Maybe Joe doesn't have any trouble getting the records, but once he does, he finds out it's impossible to understand what's there. The information isn't in any sort of order that makes sense and the reports are extremely difficult to read.

None of these situations give Joe much confidence in the club's record keeper. It can cause his confidence in the club to erode, as well.

Because Joe's upset about the problems with the records, he calls three other members to tell them about what's happened. He expresses his doubts about the club records and the other members also become concerned. Suddenly, there's a great deal of muttering about the records during meetings and many people start wondering what's going on.

Nobody wants to throw away his money, and members without confidence in how the club is being run are likely to be reluctant to hand over their dues.

How the records are kept is more important than who keeps them or what record-keeping method is used. Good record keeping is essential to the success of your club.

Cashing In

As with other matters regarding investment clubs, don't be tempted to reinvent the wheel when it comes to record keeping. Ask the treasurer of a successful club in your area to see her records, or to explain how she keeps them. You might improve on a good thing, but there's no point in starting from scratch to do what's already been done.

How Much Record Keeping Is Required?

Basically, there are two kinds of records that your club must have:

➤ Club minutes

➤ Financial records

These records can be kept in several ways. One member can be assigned to keep the club minutes and another to keep the financial records. Normally, the secretary keeps the minutes and the treasurer handles the financial records. It's not unusual, however, to have other members assigned to help with these tasks—many clubs have an assistant treasurer as well as a primary one. Keeping minutes and financial records can be done either by hand or electronically.

Many secretaries take notes by hand during meetings, then retype them on a computer afterward.

Take This to the Bank

Nearly any secretary who takes minutes during a meeting and rewrites them afterward will advise you to do so as soon after the meeting as possible. A topic that seemed very clear during a meeting can become fuzzy soon after.

If your club prefers, it can hire someone to keep its financial records. There are people who will do this, and it normally doesn't cost that much for the service, although prices will vary depending on who you get and the area in which your club is located.

Or, you can combine those methods and have club members keep some records, while your service does the rest of the work.

Some clubs keep very elaborate records, while others prefer more simple, to-the-point record keeping. All clubs, however, must have records concerning what happens at club meetings, and those that keep track of all financial business. Let's have a look at each area.

Club Minutes

Club minutes are simply a report of what happens during each meeting. They list the high points of what occurred and summarize any pertinent discussion.

Information that should be contained in the minutes includes:

➤ When and where the meeting was held

➤ Who called the meeting to order and at what time

➤ What members (and guests, if applicable) were present at the meeting

➤ Summaries of any reports such as the treasurer's report

➤ Summaries of any correspondence that was noted

➤ Summaries of any action that occurred during the meeting with notes on who made motions and who seconded them

➤ Summaries of pertinent discussions that occurred during the meeting

➤ Any changes in the club's membership, or membership on club committees

➤ Information about the next meeting

➤ At what time the meeting was adjourned

Cashing In

The secretary of a club serves as its historian, with the minutes serving as the official written record of what occurs. It's extremely important to be sure that your secretary is capable of this task before he or she is appointed. Don't assume that anyone can do it and give it to whoever agrees to take the job.

Cashing In

Remember that in a partnership each member is taxed according to his or her portion of the total value of the organization. That's why it's imperative to keep close track of every member's share of the overall value of the club.

Minutes normally are kept by the club secretary, with a copy distributed to each member. Minutes are extremely important, for they serve as an official record of club business. Your club might consider setting up a Web site, on which it could post minutes and other pertinent club information. Or, a club member might have a Web site the club could use.

While the minutes are a very important aspect of record keeping for your club, they are no more important than the financial records.

Financial Records

Financial records are the heart and soul of an investment club. Without finances, there's little point to the club. You're not there—presumably—for the cake and coffee served at the end of the meetings. Your financial records will be referred to again and again and are important to all members. Without financial records there would be no club minutes, because there would be no point in holding meetings.

Your financial records must do two things:

➤ Keep track of every member's share of the entire value of the club

➤ Record every cash transaction that occurs

Once again, there's no reason to invent your own system for doing either of these chores. The National Association of Investors Corporation (NAIC) has developed a unit value system, which is a method for keeping track of the investments of each partner within a club, and the share of the total value of the club that each member holds.

Because the value of the stocks in which your club has invested will fluctuate, your club's value will not remain steady. As a result, neither will the assets of any one member of the club.

It's a good idea to have someone tabulate your club's assets on a regular basis. It always should be done before a club meeting.

The NAIC's unit value system is explained in its *Investor's Manual,* which your club will receive when it joins the association.

Your club's financial records also must indicate all its cash transactions. You'll need to be meticulous in the detail you pay when recording the cost and amount of a particular stock your club has purchased or sold. You'll need to keep records for tax purposes.

Cashing In

The NAIC is a great resource for investment clubs, but don't forget about other sources of help. Check out www.investorama.com for more information about investment clubs and lots of ideas about running one.

If all this sounds more complicated than you'd prefer, don't worry. There's no need to despair. Let's have a look at what sort of record-keeping help is available to your club.

Resources Available to Help with Record Keeping

We've already mentioned the NAIC's Investors Manual as a source of help for your club's record keeping. The NAIC offers other sources of assistance, as well.

Some other means of help available include:

➤ **NAIC Club Accounting Manual.** This manual explains club accounting step by step, and gives record keepers the tools they need to be successful in their tasks.

➤ **NAIC Club Accounting Software.** Designed to work in conjunction with the accounting manual, this popular software program is available in separate versions for Windows and Macintosh computers. It features full data interchange between them. The software can help new clubs get started with computerized accounting and allows established clubs to easily transfer their existing manual books to computerized accounting. More than 32,000 copies of the software have been sold to NAIC-member investment clubs.

Heading for a Crash

The NAIC software package isn't cheap. It costs about $170 for NAIC members and about $200 for nonmembers. While it can be well worth the price, don't rush out and buy it before you're sure whoever will be keeping your records wants it—and will be able to use it. Otherwise, you could be wasting your club's money.

➤ *Better Investing* **magazine.** In addition to general information that can help your club with its record keeping, *Better Investing,* a publication of the NAIC, runs ads of services that will keep your club's books. If you decide to go with outside help, this might be the place to find someone.

As you can see, yours isn't the only club that's ever set up a record-keeping system. There is help available if you need it. Remember that the chore of record keeping—either minutes or financial—should never belong exclusively to one person. While one person will most likely be primarily responsible for keeping the minutes and another for keeping financial records, help should be available to these people whenever it's needed.

Choosing the Right Person—or People—for the Job

Because good record keeping is so important to your club, it's imperative that you have the right people for the job.

If you're going to choose record keepers from your club's membership, take some time to consider who the best choices are. Just because Linda was secretary of her school's parent-teacher group for two years doesn't mean that she's the only person capable of taking minutes for your investment club.

Heading for a Crash

Some club presidents and members allow incompetent record keepers to stay in office because they don't want to cause hard feelings by asking them to step down. Doing so could adversely affect your investment club. If your club has someone who's not doing his job, the best thing to do is find someone to replace him.

Make sure you choose members who have sufficient knowledge for keeping good records—especially those who will be keeping financial records.

Also, be sure you choose members with enough time to devote to the tasks. It won't do your club any good if the person appointed to keep financial records discovers the chore takes more time than he anticipated and lets the process slide.

If you're hiring outside help, be sure that the person you choose has good credentials. Don't be afraid to ask for references and to check out those references before you hire. Consider checking with your local Chamber of Commerce for recommendations. If you find that the person appointed or hired to keep your club's records isn't doing an adequate job, don't hesitate to replace her with someone who's more willing or better qualified.

Remember that your club belongs to all its members, not just the officers, or the founder, or the people who've been in it the longest. Everyone deserves to be represented by the best people available.

On the other hand, the people who keep your club's records shouldn't be loaded with so much work that they become overwhelmed by their jobs. All members should be willing to help the record keepers in whatever ways possible and should express appreciation for their work.

Keeping Everyone Involved in Record Keeping

We've already mentioned how important it is for members to have access to all club records at any time. Doing so benefits both members and the club treasurer and keeps members involved in a very important part of club business.

Most clubs appoint an audit committee, which periodically reviews the books to make sure everything is in order and the bookkeeping is on track.

This should in no way be offensive to the treasurer, or whoever is keeping the books. Hopefully, the bookkeeper will welcome the support and help of the audit committee, and the audit committee will offer its help in the proper spirit.

If a club is concerned about the way its records are being kept, or simply very cautious, it can obtain insurance bonding. Insurance bonding will cover the assets of a club in the event that a member finds a way to take off with the club's money.

Mind you, this isn't something that happens often, and it's probably nothing that you need to worry about. Strange things do happen, however. If it's the feeling of your club that bonding is needed, go ahead and find out about it. The NAIC can provide bonding to its members.

Having everyone involved with the bookkeeping process, however, limits the chances of somebody absconding with club funds. It also makes it less likely that the records will be inaccurate or just plain wrong.

Make sure that the books are opened often, and everyone is familiar with the record-keeping process.

Some people thoroughly enjoy record keeping. If that describes any of your club members, be sure to get them involved. Don't, on the other hand, force someone who doesn't enjoy keeping records to do so. Chances are that he'll be unenthusiastic about the chore and his work will reflect the lack of interest.

Also, be sure to take advantage of the professional experience of any of your members. If somebody in your club is an accountant, for instance, you may have a ready-made treasurer. If she's unable, or unwilling to be the club treasurer, maybe she'll at least be willing to work with whoever is appointed to the post.

The Least You Need to Know

➤ A good record-keeping system is accurate to read and understand and readily available for inspection.

➤ Poor record keeping can result in distrust and lack of confidence among members of your investment club.

➤ Club minutes and financial records are required records for an investment club.

➤ Record keeping can seem confusing, but there are resources available to help.

➤ Choosing the right people as your club's record keepers is extremely important.

➤ Everyone—not just the club secretary and treasurer—should be involved with record keeping.

Chapter 11

Exactly How Does an Investment Club Operate?

In This Chapter

➤ Understanding why your club will need an initial contribution

➤ Deciding how much members should pay for initial and monthly contributions

➤ Keeping investments equal makes it easier to track

➤ Understanding how club ownership works

➤ Dividing up profits and paying departing members

Now that you've come up with an operating agreement, chosen the first officers of your club, and decided where and when you'll meet, it's time to talk about money.

The manner in which your club deals with and makes decisions concerning money and finances will largely depend on the type of members you have.

If all 15 members of your club are high-level professionals making over six figures a year, your monthly dues probably will be a lot steeper than a club of 20-somethings just getting started in their careers.

Maybe you and the rest of the members of your club are college students, or teenagers, or retired persons with fixed incomes who have little money to spare. That doesn't mean you can't have a great investment club, or make sound decisions for your club.

You'll just be doing so with less money than some other investment clubs. Remember that no matter how modest your investments are, you'll still benefit from the education a club offers. And, even modest investments can add up over time.

Determining an Initial Investment

Some investment clubs require that members pay a fairly high initial investment, while others ask for a minimum from each member. Clubs that ask for hefty initial contributions often are trying to get enough money together to begin investing immediately.

Other clubs ask for an initial contribution to cover their start-up costs, then wait until they've collected enough monthly contributions to start buying stock.

Take This to the Bank

Even social agencies who work with people with very limited incomes often charge a small amount for the services or products they provide. Why? They say that people are much more serious about something they have to pay for and are much more likely to follow through on, and so forth.

Cashing In

Consider holding a combined yard sale or garage sale to raise money for your club's start-up expenses. Everyone could bring their "stuff" to one person's home, from which it would be sold. In addition to raising some money to offset expenses, an activity of this sort would give members a chance to get to know each other.

Operating Expenses

A club doesn't need a great deal of money to get off the ground, but it will need some. Let's look at the types of expenses your club may encounter either as it starts up, or a little further down the road.

➤ **Start-up expenses.** These can include things like software that you'll use for record keeping, attorney's fees if you use a lawyer to help you set up a partnership agreement or for other reasons, office supplies, notebooks for members, NAIC membership, and so forth. For example:

Initial Expense	Cost	Reason
Bookkeeping Software	$200	Create the financial records of the investment club.
Attorney Fees	$500	Establish the liability partnership/corporation, operating rules, tax documents.
Office Supplies	$100	Printer paper, pens, legal notepads, index cards, voting ballots, and so on.
Internet Setup	$100	Establish a Web site and e-mail account.
Membership Dues	$250	Membership for club and 15 individual members in NAIC.
Miscellaneous	$100	Initial meeting refreshments.

➤ **Ongoing expenses.** Maybe your club consults regularly with a bookkeeper. The initial investment you ask for from each member could be used to offset the accountant's fees. For example:

Monthly Expense	Cost	Reason
Bookkeeping Fees	$75	Maintain the financial records of the investment club.
Office Supplies	$25	Printer paper, pens, legal notepads, index cards, voting ballots, and so on.
Internet Services	$20/month	Maintain an email account and a Web site for club information.
Miscellaneous	$20	Meeting refreshments.

➤ **Speakers or training for members.** There are some very good speakers around, some of whom charge to speak to a group and some who don't. Or maybe your club wants to send some members to an educational meeting sponsored by the National Association of Investors Corp.—there would be some expenses involved. Initial contributions also could be used for these types of expenses. For example:

Expense	Cost	Reason
Speaker Fund	$300	To pay for guest investment speakers.
Attorney Fund	$250	To pay for any out-of-the-ordinary legal fees.
NAIC Fund	$300	To pay for educational meetings.
Miscellaneous	$200	To pay for any out-of-the-ordinary club fees.

Let's Get Serious

Requiring an initial deposit from each member also ensures that members who join your club are committed to the process. People tend to be more serious about and committed to something that they've paid for. If you've ever seen a child who's just spent his birthday money to buy a toy, you'll probably notice that he's much more interested in taking care of the toy than he'd be if someone had handed it to him. Why? Because he used his own money to buy the toy; it's given him a sense of ownership.

It can be very discouraging for the founders of an investment club to wade through the entire process of setting up the club, putting together their operating agreement, establishing meeting times and places, and on and on, only to have half of the people who said they were going to join change their minds. All of a sudden, you have 7 or 8 members, instead of the 15 you were counting on.

Sure, you can still have an investment club with only seven or eight members. What that means, however, is that each member will have to contribute more initially to cover start-up costs and other expenses. Also, having a very small group makes it difficult to cover all the work involved with maintaining an investment club. Each member would need to assume more responsibility in order to keep the club running smoothly.

As we discussed previously, people move away, have babies, retire, or whatever. Life is full of changes and surprises, many of which we can do little about. Since members do leave clubs over time, it's not a good idea to start with too small a group. You could be forced to scramble for new members in the years ahead.

Take This to the Bank

Members of investment clubs also invest outside their clubs. The average portfolio of investments held by club members, outside their holdings in the club, is greater than $110,000. See what a little education and confidence can do?

Financial Commitments

So you want a financial commitment initially from club members, but you don't want to scare them away by making it too high. After all, the members of your group may not have a lot of money to spare. You'll have to decide how much you need to start the club and maybe get a little money stashed away for expenses down the road, or to use to buy your early investments. And you'll need to evaluate how much you can ask each member to contribute, without scaring anyone away.

Some clubs start off with a $200 contribution from each member. Others require $500, and some clubs require even more.

It's great if you can ask each of your 15 members to contribute $750—giving your club $11,250 to use as needed. Many people, however, can't afford to lay out that much money at one time.

If the prospective members of your club can afford a larger contribution, it's nice to get the money up front. As the months roll by and the contributed funds aren't needed for expenses, the excess money can be invested in stock, or added to the other stocks already in the membership's portfolio.

We've known of clubs that started with initial contributions of as little as $50 a member. This is okay, too, although members might be required to kick in more money later, as unexpected expenses crop up.

Heading for a Crash

Many people join investment clubs because they want to begin investing, but have little money with which to do so. Pooling their money with others allows them to invest, without spending more than they have. If you ask members for too large an initial contribution, they might feel that you're violating the spirit of investment clubs, and decide not to join.

Depending on your membership, asking for additional funds down the road may, or may not, cause a problem. For many investment club members, coming up with the monthly dues is enough of a challenge. It might be better to collect a little more from each person at the beginning, than have to hit up your members for more money once the club is up and running.

Just remember that making the initial contribution too high could keep people from joining your club, while making it too small could mean trouble down the road, should you have to ask for more money to cover expenses or unexpected costs.

Make your own charts, similar to the ones above, and try to anticipate any expenses you might have, either immediately or within the next six months or so. That will give you an idea of how much money you'll need. Then, determine if you want to have additional money to invest right away, or you'll invest only the monthly dues of your members. That will give you an indication of how much you'll need, and what you should require for the initial member contribution.

Discuss the contribution issue with the members of your club and get their feelings about what would be a reasonable amount. Maybe nobody will come out and admit they can't afford more than $100, but you'll notice if there's reluctance or hesitation when you mention a certain amount.

Just be sensitive to the discussion and don't let anybody pressure another member.

After you've discussed the matter, you can do one of two things. We recommend that you vote on the matter immediately and move on to other business at hand. You can, however, hold off on voting until your next meeting, giving members a chance to think about how much they can comfortably handle. Just remember, the sooner the decision is made the better.

Determining a Monthly Investment

Once you've figured out how much each member will be asked to contribute initially, you'll need to think about monthly contributions.

Just as with initial investments, the amount that members are able to contribute monthly will vary from group to group and among members of the same club. Establishing an amount that members will hand over to the club each month can be challenging, so we thought we'd first discuss average contributions, then look at how to decide what's right for your club.

Cashing In

Don't let the initial investment issue sit on the table for too long. It's best to discuss the matter, take a vote to find out what club members think is best, and move along. Letting it sit can be setting yourself up for extended debate, which can be distracting when there's other business to take care of.

The Average Investment

The average monthly investment among investment club members is $20 to $25. If you multiply the monthly contribution amount by the number of club members, you'll know what your club will have to invest every month.

> 10 members @ $25 a month = $250 for your club to invest

> 15 members @ $20 a month = $300 for your club to invest

> 18 members @ $22.50 a month = $405 for your club to invest

If you have 10 members, for example, your club will have $200 to $250 per month (plus dividends earned) to invest each month. We'll discuss more about the dividends later in the book (see Chapter 19, "To Have and to Hold"). Just know for now that the more money members have invested in your club, the more money you'll earn as dividends and interest. This income can be reinvested in additional stock.

Many clubs take their previous month's income, add it to the current month's dues, and invest that money.

If you have 15 members instead of 10, of course, you'll have more to invest. With 15 members, your club would have $300 to $375 per month, depending on whether the amount you have chosen as the monthly contribution amount is $20 or $25. If your club has 25 members, you'd have even more to invest each month.

Remember that the $20 to $25 monthly contribution figure is an average. There are clubs that have been around for a long time, in which the contribution amount was $10 per month for years. Some of these clubs have gotten to have so much money ($1 million or more in value) that the membership has decided that monthly dues are not necessary. The fund yields enough income so that there are sufficient funds for additional investment.

That's any investment club's dream, and, hopefully, it will happen eventually to your club. When you first start out, however, you'll need money to invest, which will come from monthly contributions from your members.

What's Right for Your Club

You probably should decide how much each member contributes monthly at the same meeting that you establish the initial contribution. This keeps money as the focus of discussion at a particular meeting, allowing members to consider both contributions at once.

Many people don't like to talk about money—especially money they're required to part with. The discussion your club has concerning monthly contributions, however, is extremely important. Having enough money for your club to purchase stock each month reminds your members that belonging to the club is worthwhile.

Understanding that there's a required monthly contribution for an investment club is different

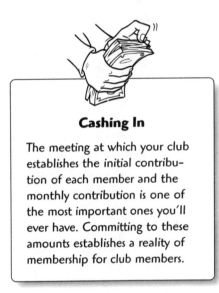

Cashing In

The meeting at which your club establishes the initial contribution of each member and the monthly contribution is one of the most important ones you'll ever have. Committing to these amounts establishes a reality of membership for club members.

than knowing that the contribution will be $30. Knowing that the contribution is $30 forces members to determine where the money will come from, what they may have to give up in order to have the money available, and lets everyone know how much money the club will have each month to invest. It helps members to realize that their commitments to the club are real.

It's important for everyone to understand early on their financial responsibility to the club. It would be unfortunate for people to join your club, only to have to leave in eight or nine months because the financial commitment was too great.

We recommend that you ask members to contribute $50 a month. That's significantly more than the average investment—true. But, when you think about the significance of what you're doing with that money, it becomes very desirable to contribute as much as you can.

Remember that many of the clubs that ask for $20 a month have been around for a long time, and have a lot of money accumulated. Remember, too, that $20 was worth a lot more in 1964 than it is today. Members who have been paying $20 a month for 35 years made their sacrifices early on.

Cashing In

Investing $50 per month means you'll have contributed $600 at the end of the year. It means that you'll be putting out $1.65 per day, less than the cost of a bagel and a large cup of coffee.

Some people simply won't be able to afford $50 a month, and that's okay. A lesser amount is fine. If somebody's maxing out her 401(k) plan at work, paying off hefty college loans, and has a huge mortgage, chances are there's not $50 left at the end of the month to stash in an investment club.

Finding That $50

Many people, however, spend way more than $50 a month on things they don't really need, and have nothing to show for their money at the end of the month. There are lots of ways you can save money, many of which you'll hardly notice. Let's have a look at some easy ways to save $50 or more every month.

➤ Carry your lunch to work a couple times a week instead of dropping $4.95 for a sandwich and Coke at the corner deli.

➤ Cut your grocery bills. Buy store brands instead of national brands and cut down on prepared foods such as Lean Cuisine or Hot Pockets. Use less meat and look for specials.

➤ Buy in quantity when it makes sense. When bread is on sale, buy a couple of extra loaves and put them in the freezer—same goes with meat and vegetables.

➤ Wash your car yourself, rather than going to a full-service car wash. If you have access to a hose, you can do this at home. If not, use a self-service car wash.

➤ Give up your daily soda from the machine at work or the cappuccino from the downstairs coffee bar. Buy cases of soda at the grocery store and bring one to work.

➤ Rent videos instead of going to the movies. Paying to see just one first-run movie—plus popcorn—every week can cost more than the $1.65 per day you're trying to save.

Every time you pass by the coffee counter without plunking down $1.05, put the money you might have spent there into an envelope earmarked for your investment club dues. Put it in the front of your sock drawer, add to it every day, and don't take it out for any other purpose.

Don't borrow from yourself to go to Burger King the day before payday, or give your money to the kids for a movie. Once it's gone, it's hard to replace. This money is every bit as important as your other savings. Make it a priority.

Take This to the Bank

We know of one club member who saved for her investment club dues by keeping a bowl on her kitchen table. She, and eventually her family members, would put their loose change, or extra bills into the bowl, and enjoy watching it fill up between club meetings. This not only funded Mom's monthly dues, but it also served to get the whole family interested in her club and the investments it made.

# Equal Contributions—or Not?

It's strongly recommended, at least for the first year, that each member of the club contributes the same initial funding, and that each member pays the same monthly dues.

Some members may feel that they want to contribute more to the group. It's important, however, that everybody is equal as the club works through the learning process. Group dynamics are interesting and you don't want one member to have a bigger say in the process just because he owns more of the club's fund than someone else.

Eventually, due to members dropping out of the club and new members coming in, the amount of ownership each member has won't be the same. You'll learn all about what happens when members leave the club in Chapter 24, "The Ebbs and Flows of an Investment Club." Some people will have much more money invested in the club than others. At that point, it might work out for your group to allow varying contributions. Be aware, however, that varying contributions causes a lot more work for your treasurer, who has to keep track of each member's contributions and share of ownership.

While your club is getting started, however, it's best that everyone contribute equally.

Cashing In

It is strongly recommended that all members have an equal share of the investment club for at least the first year. We feel that to not set up your club this way could be inviting trouble. It's best to have everyone on equal footing until your club has established a routine and members are familiar with each other and the buying and selling processes.

Understanding Club Ownership

There are two ways in which members can own portions of their investment clubs. The first way is to own a share of the club. When members join, each one contributes an equal amount. Ownership equates to the value of the club's assets (the account) divided by the number of members in the club.

Okay, in English, please. The way most clubs work, is that if there are 20 members, each member owns one twentieth of the club, or 5 percent of the total portfolio. Here is another example:

100 (% of portfolio) ÷ 20 (# of members) = 5 percent

Thus, if the portfolio is worth $10,000, and each member has an equal 5 percent, each member would own $500 of the portfolio.

As long as the contributions (dues) are made equally by each member, the ownership will continue to be calculated based on the number of members, each owning an equal share. As the account grows in value, each member will have the same percentage of the club's growth.

That sounds fairly simple, and it is. If your club is a corporation, rather than a partnership, the members will have stock in the club instead of shares, and they'll be called *shareholders*. As with a partnership, it's important that each shareholder have only one share of stock for at least the first year, as the club gets started.

Taking Stock

A **shareholder** is a person who owns shares in a corporation.

Cashing In

If your club allows varying contributions and you haven't purchased the National Association of Investment Corp.'s accounting software, you really should check it out. Go to the NAIC's Web site at www.better-investing.org for more information.

How Can You Have More?

So, how can a member own more than another member? There are two ways. Members can either buy another member's share when she leaves the club, or they can contribute more than the allotted dues each month.

Many clubs do not permit more than the stated monthly dues, because, as we mentioned previously, it can cause big problems with record keeping. If the monthly dues are $50, and one member invests $100 per month, how does the treasurer keep track of the additional contributions?

What the treasurer must do is keep track of the additional calculations and each member's ownership percentage changes with each additional payment.

If your club has equal member ownership, it's easy to determine your share of the club's fund. If there are 20 members and each member owns one twentieth, you just divide the monthly fund value by 20 to determine your share of ownership.

With unequal contributions, the treasurer will be required, monthly or quarterly, to report what percentage of the club each member owns. A particular member could own 5 percent of the club's fund one month and, because of unequal dues, have 5.5 percent of it the following month.

Another way that club ownership becomes unequal is through a member leaving the club and another member buying her out. This is accomplished when somebody pays the club the value of a share of the exiting member, then that sum is distributed out to the member who is leaving.

Your club has 20 members and a fund worth $10,000. Each member's share is worth $500. When a member decides to leave, her share is purchased by another member. Now there are 19 members, with one member owning 10 percent of the club, while the others still own 5 percent.

When each member owns an equal share, this extra report isn't required. Each member, knowing they own one share, can take the monthly value of the account, divide it by the number of members and know what his share is worth.

What If Somebody Leaves?

When a member decides to leave the club, regardless of the reason, he is entitled to his share of the club ownership.

Figuring out how much the departing member is due can be done in several ways. Your club will need to decide what it's most comfortable with. Basically, you need to decide at what point the departing member's share of the club's value will be established. You can:

➤ Use the prior month's-end value of the account

➤ Use the date on which the departing member's letter of intent to leave the club arrived to the treasurer

➤ Use the date on which assets are sold to fund the buyout

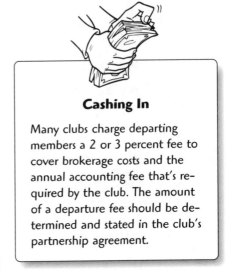

Cashing In

Many clubs charge departing members a 2 or 3 percent fee to cover brokerage costs and the annual accounting fee that's required by the club. The amount of a departure fee should be determined and stated in the club's partnership agreement.

Each method has pros and cons. If you use last month's ending value, for instance, and the market drops before you get to sell the stock, the remaining members will have to make up the difference. Using the date on which club assets are sold to fund the buyout of the departing member seems to be the most equitable solution.

Can You Own Too Much?

Investment clubs have been known on occasion to get out of balance because one— or several—members obtain too much ownership.

Not to worry, however; it's easy to prevent this from happening. The thing to do is establish limits of ownership in your operating agreement. State in the agreement that no member may own more than 25 percent (or whatever percentage your club chooses) of the club. The agreement should state that members can own one share, two shares, or whatever, but never more than the specified percentage.

Ownership can and should be limited if the member is contributing additional monthly dues, or purchasing additional shares over the years.

While it's not necessarily bad for the amount of ownership to vary among club members, it's been known on occasion to cause some problems. When each member owns one share of the club, all decisions by the club are equal.

If one member owns 25 percent of the club's account, however, it can make decision-making unequal. Those who own more of the club's account than other members may feel that they should have greater control.

Taking Stock

Unrealized profits, or **unrealized losses,** are the difference between what the club paid for a stock, and the amount it's worth on any given day. Profit doesn't become realized until the stock is sold and the money earned is taken by club members.

Who Gets the Profits?

Realizing a profit probably is an important consideration to your investment club—as it should be. After all, nobody makes investments while hoping to lose money.

If, over the years, you put $1,800 into the club, and your share of the club increases to $5,000 because the stocks purchased have increased in value, you've made a $3,200 profit. Profits are shown each month when the treasurer reports the holdings of the club.

If club members contribute $20,000 over a period of time, during which the value of the account reaches $32,000, the club has $12,000 in *unrealized profit.*

Unrealized profit (or *unrealized loss*) occurs when the stock is still held and the profits are only on paper.

The unrealized profits are just part of the value of each member's share of the club. A member who owns one twentieth of the club will be apportioned one twentieth of the profits.

Each member's share is valued by dividing the total worth of the club by the owner-ship shares. The profits then are allocated to each member according to how much ownership each person has. For example:

$10,000 (portfolio total) ÷ 20 (# of members) = $500 each

If ownership is unequal and based on percentages, then profits are allocated according to those percentages. A member who owns 8 percent of the club, for instance, gets 8 percent of the profits.

You'll learn in Chapter 24 exactly how assets are sold or distributed when a member leaves your club. Basically, the outgoing member will receive the value of the stock on a particular day that should be specified in your club's operating agreement. It might be the last day of the month, or the date that the club received notice that the member was leaving. Whatever the value of the investment fund is that day, that's the value used to determine the amount given to the departing member. If a stock plummets in value or skyrockets after that date, it's unfortunate either for the departing member or the remaining club members.

If there are holdings within the fund with large capital gains, the member who is leaving can create a problem for the remaining members. The remaining club members should have the choice of which assets are to be sold. This should be decided at the first meeting after the notification of termination has been received.

If all your stocks are at huge gains and a member is leaving, your club must sell enough to pay off the leaving member, or each member must contribute additional funds (equally) to pay off the member. This rarely happens. The sale usually occurs, and gains are forced to be taken.

When actual profits are realized, or taken, they're totaled at the end of the year, then distributed to each member according to their ownership in the club. If your club has 20 members, and you own one share, you get one twentieth of the actual profits taken.

The same theory also is true for dividends and interest. The interest for the year should be totaled, then allocated to each member according to ownership. Total dividends earned are allocated to each member, also according to their ownership.

While this all may sound rather confusing, it really isn't. Basically, every club member is entitled to a share of the club, because he or she owns a share of the club. Some members may be entitled to a larger share than others, depending on how much money they've contributed.

As long as all members understand the process for paying off members, dividing profits, and other procedures, you should have few problems.

The Least You Need to Know

➤ It's important to establish an initial contribution that's reasonable for all members, while giving the club the money it needs to get started.

➤ The average investment club monthly contribution is about $25, but your club may want to ask for more.

➤ Many clubs allow members to invest varying amounts, but be ready to face some accounting challenges if you do.

➤ A member's ownership in the club is based on how much he or she contributes.

➤ Profits and losses are distributed according to ownership, meaning how much money you have contributed and what portion you own if you are in a partnership, or how many shares you have purchased if you are in a corporation.

Chapter 12

A Taxing Topic

In This Chapter

➤ Getting a tax identification number for your club

➤ To file or not to file?

➤ Reporting individual income for tax purposes

➤ Taxes, taxes, and more taxes

➤ The tax consequences of capital gains

➤ Finding professional help for your club's tax returns

Hardly anybody likes to talk about taxes. Heck, most people don't even like to *think* about taxes. Well, before you decide to skip this chapter and move ahead to a more palatable topic, there are a few things you have to know.

Up until now, you've been learning about different kinds of investment clubs—setting up your club and running the monthly meetings, how much to invest, and so forth.

We've told you that investment clubs are intended to help you learn, to be a good source of enjoyment and socializing, and, hopefully, a means of making some money.

Well, guess what? The income and profit you realize from your investment club are taxable. The good old Internal Revenue Service (IRS) wants its share of your club's action—just as it does with the rest of your yearly earnings.

Under your partnership agreement (we're assuming that's what your club has, because the great majority of clubs do), members are taxed on their proportionate share of the club's income. You might think that it would be better if the club could pay all the taxes resulting from the income it generates, but that's not how it works under the partnership agreement.

Unless you're earning money under the table, which we'll go on record right now as saying is *not* a good idea, the IRS will get you.

Actually, you might be earning some tax-deferred money in a retirement plan or other investment. All that means is that the income you're earning in those accounts will be neither received nor taxed until a later date when you withdraw the funds or they mature. Generally, however, the IRS requires you to pay taxes on what you earn—including any income your club realized through its investments.

Okay, you're going to have to pay taxes. But how do you go about doing so? Who's responsible for reporting the income on the assets you own in the club's portfolio this year? How does the club report the income so its members can declare their share of it on their personal tax returns?

When you finish reading this chapter, you'll know more about taxes than you ever thought you'd need to. You'll have the information that you need to make sure that your club, and each of its members, is able to properly report taxable income to the IRS. After all, if we have to pay taxes, we might as well understand what we're doing about it. Here we go!

Getting Your Club a Tax ID Number

As discussed in Chapter 8, "Establishing Operating Rules," an investment club can be set up either as a partnership or a corporation.

Regardless of the format your club chooses, it will need its own tax identification number from the IRS. This is necessary so that the club can file a tax return each year, reporting earned income to the IRS.

Take This to the Bank

The IRS isn't the most popular government agency, but it's trying to make it easier for taxpayers to get the necessary forms and information. Check out the agency's Web site at www.irs.ustreas.gov. The IRS also offers a CD-ROM with over 2,000 tax products to help you with filing. The CD can be ordered from the superintendent of documents by calling 202-512-1800, or by connecting to www.access.gpo.gov/su_docs.

While it's true that belonging to an investment club adds one more tax situation to your life, it's nothing to get too excited about. Filing for your club earnings isn't as troublesome as you might think.

For the club to file an income tax return, it needs a tax number, known as an Employer Identification Number (EI#). This number is for tax filing and reporting purposes. Your broker and bankers also need this number to identify your club. You can apply to the IRS for your club's EI# by using Form SS-4. The form is shown here.

Form **SS-4**
(Rev. February 1998)
Department of the Treasury
Internal Revenue Service

Application for Employer Identification Number
(For use by employers, corporations, partnerships, trusts, estates, churches, government agencies, certain individuals, and others. See instructions.)
▶ **Keep a copy for your records.**

EIN
OMB No. 1545-0003

Please type or print clearly.

1 Name of applicant (legal name) (see instructions)
2 Trade name of business (if different from name on line 1)
3 Executor, trustee, "care of" name
4a Mailing address (street address) (room, apt., or suite no.)
5a Business address (if different from address on lines 4a and 4b)
4b City, state, and ZIP code
5b City, state, and ZIP code
6 County and state where principal business is located
7 Name of principal officer, general partner, grantor, owner, or trustor—SSN or ITIN may be required (see instructions) ▶

8a Type of entity (Check only one box.) (see instructions)
Caution: *If applicant is a limited liability company, see the instructions for line 8a.*

- ☐ Sole proprietor (SSN)
- ☐ Partnership
- ☐ REMIC
- ☐ State/local government
- ☐ Church or church-controlled organization
- ☐ Other nonprofit organization (specify) ▶ ______ (enter GEN if applicable)
- ☐ Other (specify) ▶
- ☐ Personal service corp.
- ☐ National Guard
- ☐ Farmers' cooperative
- ☐ Estate (SSN of decedent)
- ☐ Plan administrator (SSN)
- ☐ Other corporation (specify) ▶
- ☐ Trust
- ☐ Federal government/military

8b If a corporation, name the state or foreign country (if applicable) where incorporated | State | Foreign country

9 Reason for applying (Check only one box.) (see instructions)
- ☐ Started new business (specify type) ▶
- ☐ Hired employees (Check the box and see line 12.)
- ☐ Created a pension plan (specify type) ▶
- ☐ Banking purpose (specify purpose) ▶
- ☐ Changed type of organization (specify new type) ▶
- ☐ Purchased going business
- ☐ Created a trust (specify type) ▶
- ☐ Other (specify) ▶

10 Date business started or acquired (month, day, year) (see instructions)
11 Closing month of accounting year (see instructions)

12 First date wages or annuities were paid or will be paid (month, day, year). **Note:** *If applicant is a withholding agent, enter date income will first be paid to nonresident alien. (month, day, year)* . . . . ▶

13 Highest number of employees expected in the next 12 months. **Note:** *If the applicant does not expect to have any employees during the period, enter -0-. (see instructions)* . . . . ▶ | Nonagricultural | Agricultural | Household

14 Principal activity (see instructions) ▶

15 Is the principal business activity manufacturing? . . . . ☐ Yes ☐ No
If "Yes," principal product and raw material used ▶

16 To whom are most of the products or services sold? Please check one box. ☐ Business (wholesale)
☐ Public (retail) ☐ Other (specify) ▶ ☐ N/A

17a Has the applicant ever applied for an employer identification number for this or any other business? . . . . ☐ Yes ☐ No
Note: *If "Yes," please complete lines 17b and 17c.*

17b If you checked "Yes" on line 17a, give applicant's legal name and trade name shown on prior application, if different from line 1 or 2 above.
Legal name ▶ Trade name ▶

17c Approximate date when and city and state where the application was filed. Enter previous employer identification number if known.
Approximate date when filed (mo., day, year) | City and state where filed | Previous EIN

Under penalties of perjury, I declare that I have examined this application, and to the best of my knowledge and belief, it is true, correct, and complete.
Business telephone number (include area code)
Fax telephone number (include area code)

Name and title (Please type or print clearly.) ▶

Signature ▶ Date ▶

Note: *Do not write below this line. For official use only.*

Please leave blank ▶	Geo.	Ind.	Class	Size	Reason for applying

For Paperwork Reduction Act Notice, see page 4. Cat. No. 16055N Form **SS-4** (Rev. 2-98)

Use Form SS-4 to apply for a tax number, known as an Employer Identification Number (EI#).

Cashing In

The address, fax, and phone number information for the IRS will be on Page 2 of the SS-4 form. Make sure you have the proper address, phone, or fax number before trying to submit your application.

You can get the necessary SS-4 form with instructions by calling the IRS at 1-800-TAX-FORM (1-800-829-3676). You should receive the form in one to two weeks.

After you get the form and provide the necessary information to the IRS, your club will receive its tax identification number. Some of the information you'll need to provide includes:

➤ The name and address of the club

➤ The name of the person applying for the number (usually the treasurer or another officer of the club)

➤ The legal structure of your club (partnership or corporation)

➤ When your club was formed

Obtaining a tax identification number isn't difficult, it's just something that needs to be done. Like a Social Security number, the tax ID number will be unique to your club.

The IRS makes it really easy these days to get a tax identification number. You can do so over the phone after you've obtained the SS-4 form and filled it in. That's right—a simple phone call will do the trick. Call toll-free at 1-800-TAX-FORM (that translates to 1-800-829-3676).

If you have all the necessary information available when you call, you can obtain the number immediately.

The person who calls the IRS to request the number must be authorized to sign the application. This probably would be your club's treasurer, or another officer.

When the applicant receives the club's tax identification number from the IRS, he or she should write it in the upper right-hand corner of the form. Then, the form must be signed and mailed back to the IRS office, as specified on the form.

The form has to be sent back within 24 hours, so don't be tempted to stick it in a desk drawer and forget about it for a while. The IRS will send your club written confirmation of its tax number.

If you don't need the tax number immediately, or you're reluctant for some reason to talk with an IRS representative, you can fax your completed application. Written confirmation and your assigned number should be mailed to you within a day or two.

Snail mail is another option. If you mail your application to the IRS, you should receive your club's tax identification number within four to five weeks.

Tax Reporting

Remember way back in Chapter 8 when we discussed the different legal structures under which your club could operate? We told you about the two types of corporations—C corporations and S corporations—and talked about partnerships, the structure that most investment clubs choose.

A major consideration when deciding to form a partnership or a corporation has to do with how each organization is taxed. Let's refresh your memory.

➤ C corporations get hit twice when it comes to paying taxes. They have to pay tax on their earned profits, and people who get salaries or corporate dividends have to pay again because they're taxed on their earnings. The money is taxed twice at two different levels. What this means to your investment club is that the club would pay taxes on the income earned, and then the money left would either be paid out to you as a member, or reinvested in new stock. Either way, the funds are taxed twice. If your investment club's portfolio earned $10,000 (income and capital gains), and your club is a C corporation, the corporation would pay tax on the earnings. After the expenses of the club are paid, the members (shareholders) would receive taxable distributions on which they would pay more tax. The same money is taxed two times—once at the corporate level, and once at the personal level—that's you!

➤ S corporations basically are corporations that get special tax status from the Internal Revenue Service (IRS) and don't have to pay tax on the corporate level. All profits and losses are passed along to members or shareholders, who have to include the income on their personal tax returns. This means the tax is only paid once, instead of twice as with a C corporation. Club members would still have to pay taxes on money earned, but the club itself, as an S corporation, would not. S corporations sound good as far as taxes are concerned, but they can be a hassle to set up and carry a lot of restrictions and regulations.

➤ Partnerships are groups in which each member must report and pay income tax on his or her share of the partnership's earnings, but the partnership is not taxed. Money earned by a partnership is taxed only once, instead of twice, as with a C corporation. So this means that each member of the investment club (who is a partner) is taxed on investment dividends and earnings, but the club itself is not taxed.

Partnership Taxation

A partnership acts and is known as a conduit, or a middleman, of sorts. All the interest and dividends a partnership earns, as well as the capital gains and losses, flow through the partnership to each member. The allocation of earnings is based on each member's ownership in the group.

149

Taking Stock

Dividends are a portion, or share, of a company's net profits that are distributed by the company to a class of its stockholders. Dividends are paid in fixed amounts for each share of stock held. **Interest** is the cost for the use of borrowed money. **Capital gains** are profits from the sale of investments or assets.

Cashing In

Partnerships file tax returns by using Form 1065. You can pick up the form wherever tax forms are distributed in your area. Corporations and trusts must use different forms, so check with your tax adviser if your club is something other than a partnership. You can download IRS tax information off the Internet, or order it by calling the IRS at 1-800-829-3676.

For example, if your club has 20 members and each member owns one share, everybody will receive one twentieth of the interest that the club earns.

If your club earns $1,000 on its investments for the year 2000, each member will need to report $50 (or one twentieth of $1,000) of interest when he files his individual income tax return for the year.

Because the partnership is a conduit, the income earned within the club is distributed to the members in the same format as it's earned. Interest earned must be reported as *interest* by members, taxable dividends that members receive must be reported as taxable *dividends,* and *capital gains* that are passed through to members must be reported as capital gains. We talk more about taxable income later in this chapter (see the "Tax Consequences of Short-Term and Long-Term Capital Gains" section).

The topic of this section, however, isn't paying taxes; it's about reporting taxes. Rules concerning tax reporting also vary from legal structure to legal structure.

Since the great majority of investment clubs are partnerships, we're going to tell you all about tax reporting (or not) for investment clubs formed under that legal structure. If your club is formed as a corporation, consult a tax adviser about filing tax returns.

Filing a Return for Your Club

There's some confusion among investment clubs regarding tax returns, so be sure to read this section carefully.

Investment clubs are required to file tax returns for their first year of operation. If you form your club in January of 2000, for instance, your club will need to file for the year ending December 31, 2000. If you form in June of 2000, you'll still need to file for the year ending December 31. Even if you form your club in November or December, you'll need to file for the year ending December 31. On the form, you'll report whatever income the club has made and other pertinent information. It's just like if you open a savings account on December 20. You need to report the interest you earn as taxable income for the year in which you opened the account. Although you need not report income earned that is less than $10, any income you earn is taxable to you.

After the first year, however, your club can decide whether or not to file a tax return. The only catch is that you need to inform the IRS if you choose not to file.

If you choose not to file tax returns after your first year, you need to stipulate that in your first-year tax return. Once you do, that's it. If you don't tell the IRS on your first-year return, however, that you won't be filing any more returns, you're obligated to file.

The obvious question that may have come to mind is "Why would any investment club file a tax return if it's not required to?" Let's get real. Most people don't relish the thought of sitting down to fill out tax returns, or paying somebody else to do it.

Whether or not your club files a return after its first year is a decision you'll have to make as a club. We'll tell you, however, that it's something you should consider carefully. Don't dismiss the possibility of filing, because there are some important advantages to doing so.

To File or Not To File

Let's consider some of the pros and cons of filing—or not filing—tax returns:

➤ **Filing returns provides records for the club.** Filing tax returns forces you to find out and record exactly what earnings your club had for a given year. The returns serve as documentation that can be used to show new members what the club has done. They also are handy to have, just in case the IRS has any questions concerning your club's taxes.

➤ **Filing tax returns takes time and can be a hassle.** As we mentioned earlier, filling out tax returns ranks at about the same level as going to the dentist for most folks. Not filing definitely is simpler.

➤ **Not filing can save your club money.** If your treasurer or another club member is not comfortable filling out tax returns, the club would have to hire someone to do the job. Not filing would save the money you'd have to pay somebody to do the work.

The IRS doesn't require investment clubs to file tax returns, but your club must decide whether or not it thinks it's a good idea not to do so. If you're having trouble deciding, consult a tax advisor or a good accountant for help.

Heading for a Crash

Don't make a decision about filing tax returns, then fail to document it in your club minutes. Club membership changes, which can cause a lot of confusion and trouble for new members if previous members didn't bother to record when, why, and by whom a decision to either file or not file was made.

Cashing In

Club members might not prepare their own tax returns, opting instead to pay a professional to do so. They should, however, understand how their club investments affect their personal taxes. To keep members informed, invite an accountant at least once a year to talk about this topic as a guest speaker for your club.

Filing for Each Member

Regardless of whether or not you choose to file returns as a club, each member of the club is responsible for reporting club income on his or her individual tax return.

Your treasurer should gather all relevant tax information for club members, whether or not the club will be filing a partnership return.

Members need to accurately report all income that's earned and distributed to them through the club. In order for members to be able to do that, the treasurer needs to provide individual information for each one.

The IRS has a special form on which members of partnerships report their share of income, credits, deductions, and so forth. This form is known as a K-1 (see the following form). It instructs partners about what income needs to be reported on their individual tax returns, both at the federal and state levels.

Your club treasurer may want or be willing to prepare a K-1 for each member. Even if she doesn't actually prepare the form, she'll need to supply members with the information they need in order to fill out the form. Or members may choose to hand that information over to an accountant who will prepare their tax returns.

We recommend that the club treasurer provide an informal accounting to the membership each year, especially if the club doesn't file a tax return. This should be distributed along with each member's tax information sheet. An informal accounting allows members to see how the club's income was calculated.

It doesn't need to be anything fancy. Something like the example that follows would be fine.

1999 Dividends

Amount of Company Dividend	
200 shares EMC Corp.	$100
100 shares Ford Motor Co.	200
200 shares Exxon	400
200 shares PP&L Resources	300
	$1,000 for the year

With 20 club members and $1,000 in dividends, each member would earn $50 in dividends ($1,000 ÷ 20 = $50).

SCHEDULE K-1 (Form 1065)	Partner's Share of Income, Credits, Deductions, etc.	OMB No. 1545-0099
Department of the Treasury Internal Revenue Service	▶ See separate instructions. For calendar year 1999 or tax year beginning , 1999, and ending ,	1999

Partner's identifying number ▶	Partnership's identifying number ▶
Partner's name, address, and ZIP code	Partnership's name, address, and ZIP code
SARAH YOUNG FISHER *15 WEST main St.* *YORKTOWNE, PA*	*XYZ INVESTMENT CLUB* *15 WEST main Street* *YORKTOWNE, PA*

A This partner is a ☐ general partner ☐ limited partner
  ☐ limited liability company member
B What type of entity is this partner? ▶ ....
C Is this partner a ☐ domestic or a ☐ foreign partner?
D Enter partner's percentage of: (i) Before change or termination (ii) End of year
  Profit sharing . . . . % . . . . . . %
  Loss sharing . . . . % . . . . . . %
  Ownership of capital . . . . . % . . . . . . %
E IRS Center where partnership filed return:

F Partner's share of liabilities (see instructions):
  Nonrecourse . . . . $ ....
  Qualified nonrecourse financing . $ ....
  Other . . . . $ ....
G Tax shelter registration number . ▶ ....
H Check here if this partnership is a publicly traded partnership as defined in section 469(k)(2) . . . . . ☐
I Check applicable boxes: (1) ☐ Final K-1 (2) ☐ Amended K-1

J   Analysis of partner's capital account:

(a) Capital account at beginning of year	(b) Capital contributed during year	(c) Partner's share of lines 3, 4, and 7, Form 1065, Schedule M-2	(d) Withdrawals and distributions	(e) Capital account at end of year (combine columns (a) through (d))
		( )	( )	

(a) Distributive share item			(b) Amount	(c) 1040 filers enter the amount in column (b) on:
Income (Loss)	1	Ordinary income (loss) from trade or business activities . . .	1	See page 6 of Partner's Instructions for Schedule K-1 (Form 1065).
	2	Net income (loss) from rental real estate activities	2	
	3	Net income (loss) from other rental activities	3	
	4	Portfolio income (loss):		
	a	Interest	4a *175*	Sch. B, Part I, line 1
	b	Ordinary dividends	4b *280*	Sch. B, Part II, line 5
	c	Royalties	4c	Sch. E, Part I, line 4
	d	Net short-term capital gain (loss)	4d	Sch. D, line 5, col. (f)
	e	Net long-term capital gain (loss):		
		(1) 28% rate gain (loss)	e(1)	Sch. D, line 12, col. (g)
		(2) Total for year.	e(2) *800*	Sch. D, line 12, col. (f)
	f	Other portfolio income (loss) *(attach schedule)*	4f	Enter on applicable line of your return.
	5	Guaranteed payments to partner	5	See page 6 of Partner's Instructions for Schedule K-1 (Form 1065).
	6	Net section 1231 gain (loss) (other than due to casualty or theft) .	6	
	7	Other income (loss) *(attach schedule)*	7	Enter on applicable line of your return.
Deductions	8	Charitable contributions (see instructions) *(attach schedule)* . .	8	Sch. A, line 15 or 16
	9	Section 179 expense deduction	9	See pages 7 and 8 of Partner's Instructions for Schedule K-1 (Form 1065).
	10	Deductions related to portfolio income *(attach schedule)* . . .	10	
	11	Other deductions *(attach schedule)*	11	
Credits	12a	Low-income housing credit:		
		(1) From section 42(j)(5) partnerships for property placed in service before 1990	a(1)	
		(2) Other than on line 12a(1) for property placed in service before 1990	a(2)	Form 8586, line 5
		(3) From section 42(j)(5) partnerships for property placed in service after 1989	a(3)	
		(4) Other than on line 12a(3) for property placed in service after 1989	a(4)	
	b	Qualified rehabilitation expenditures related to rental real estate activities	12b	See page 8 of Partner's Instructions for Schedule K-1 (Form 1065).
	c	Credits (other than credits shown on lines 12a and 12b) related to rental real estate activities.	12c	
	d	Credits related to other rental activities	12d	
	13	Other credits	13	

For Paperwork Reduction Act Notice, see Instructions for Form 1065.   Cat. No. 11394R   Schedule K-1 (Form 1065) 1999

Use Form K-1 to report the partnership's share of income, credits, deductions, and so on.

Exactly What Can You Be Taxed On?

The IRS taxes income. Its definition of income is "everything that increases wealth, which isn't excluded from being taxed." There you have it.

Income isn't the same as an increase in the value of your club's portfolio. You don't have to pay tax on that increase unless you sell securities and take the money.

This can be confusing to new investors. Let's look at an example. Say that you contribute $500 to your investment club during the year and the club uses that money to buy stock. At the end of the year, the value of the stock has increased, and your $500 is worth $750. If you leave the stock alone, you don't have to pay income tax on your gain.

Why not? Because that $250 isn't income. You didn't sell the stock and realize gain, or profit.

Take This to the Bank

While you need to pay tax on capital gains, you get to deduct capital losses from your taxable income. This is sometimes a consideration when deciding whether or not to sell a security.

You only pay tax on income that is *paid* on your investments (dividends and interest). Also, you're responsible for tax if you realize gain. That happens when you sell a security and make a profit.

Conversely, if you sell a security at a loss, you can deduct the loss on your income tax. It's sort of a consolation prize for the money you lost.

If you pay $1,000 for stock and sell it for $1,500, you have a $500 capital gain. If you buy a stock for $1,500 and sell it for $1,000, you've realized a $500 capital loss. You must report the $500 gain or loss and you'll be responsible for the tax that is due for the gain. A loss will help you pay less tax money on your return.

If your club treasurer isn't comfortable with figuring out tax returns (either for the club or individual members), be sure to consult a professional. Filing incorrect or improper returns can cause a lot of hassle. It's worth the money it costs to hire a professional to do the job properly. Of course, if your treasurer has a financial background and can do the returns himself, so much the better for the club.

Tax Consequences of Short-Term and Long-Term Capital Gains

If you looked at this heading and were tempted to close the book altogether and go for a sandwich or something, just hold on a little bit longer. The heading might sound a bit daunting, but the content isn't really all that difficult or confusing.

First of all, let's clearly define a capital gain and explain how it can affect you. Then, we'll get into the differences between long-term and short-term gains and why tax consequences vary between the two.

A capital gain, as mentioned earlier in this chapter, is the profit realized from the sale of an investment or asset. If you sell a house for more than you bought it, you realize a capital gain. If you sell a stock for more than you bought it, you realize a capital gain. As we told you earlier, capital gains are taxable.

There are several types of capital gains, but the two we're most interested in are *long-term gains* and *short-term gains:*

Taking Stock

Short-term capital gains are profits that come from the sale of investments that you've held for less than a year. **Long-term capital gains** are profits from the sale of investments that you've held for more than a year.

➤ Short-term capital gain occurs when you sell a security that you've owned for less than one year. They are taxed differently than long-term capital gains.

➤ Long-term capital gains are those realized from the sale of an investment you've had for more than a year.

Short-term gains are taxed at your regular tax rate. If you're in the 28 percent tax bracket, for instance, any short-term gains you realize will be taxed at 28 percent. If you have a short-term capital gain of $300, for example, you'd have to pay $84 in taxes. A $2,000 short-term capital gain would cost you $560 in taxes.

Consider your tax bracket if you're thinking about selling securities for short-term gain. If you're in the 15 percent bracket, you'd pay only $150 on a $1,000 gain. Someone in the 39.6 percent bracket, however, would lose nearly 40 percent of the $1,000. There's a big difference in how much tax you'll pay, depending on the rate at which you're taxed.

You should never invest with only taxes in mind, but it's considered wise to keep the long-term nature of a gain in mind when a trade is made. How does one do that?

Long-term gains, on the other hand, are not taxed at the same rate as your other income. If you're in the lowest tax bracket, which at this time is 15 percent, you pay 10 percent tax for long-term capital gains. If you're in a higher tax bracket (28 or 39.6 percent), you pay 20 percent on long-term gains.

All this information can be confusing. If you've realized capital gains through your club's investments, you might want to discuss the matter with an accountant or tax adviser.

Take This to the Bank

Tax on capital gains usually is only due when the asset resulting in the gain is sold. Your club's portfolio can grow tenfold without tax liability because all the growth has occurred without any actual shares being sold. Remember that every time an asset is sold at a gain, the capital gain liability will pass to the member at next year's tax time.

Getting Professional Help with the Club's Tax Needs

If you look in the Yellow Pages, you'll see the names of a bunch of people who will be happy to—for a fee—prepare your club's tax information. It can be a little confusing, however, because they call themselves different things. Your phone book is likely to contain listings for tax preparers, enrolled agents, certified public accountants, and tax attorneys.

How do you know which of these professionals you need?

Each of the categories listed above has a different level of expertise. A tax preparer typically has the least amount of expertise, and a tax attorney the most. The more expertise someone has, the higher his or her rate generally will be. If you need answers to standard questions concerning your club's income, there's no reason in the world that you need a tax attorney.

On the other hand, if, for some reason, your tax situation is very complicated, you might want to step up from a tax preparer. Let's have a look at each category.

➤ **Tax preparers.** As a group, tax preparers have the least amount of training. They don't need to be licensed and many of them work part time.

Cashing In

If you're thinking about selling securities on which you'll realize a capital gain, don't ignore the timing. If you've held the security for almost a year and there's no reason to think the value will decrease dramatically before the year is up, it might be worth your while (and your taxes) to hang on to the security until you've had it for a full year.

H&R Block is a well-known company that prepares taxes. The people that work for H&R Block are tax preparers. Preparers are normally reliable if your tax return is fairly straightforward. They won't break your budget either. They usually charge about $200 for a basic investment club return. The actual amount depends on how many members are in the club and possibly other factors.

➤ **Enrolled agents.** Enrolled agents are licensed. They can represent clients in front of the IRS in the event of an audit. Enrolled agents generally have more training than tax preparers, and are required to participate in continuing education. As a group, they charge more than tax preparers.

➤ **Certified public accountants (CPAs).** CPAs undergo a great deal of training and must pass an exam to receive their credentials. They have to complete continuing education courses each year in order to remain certified. If your club's taxes are complicated because of business interests or partnership income, you might need a CPA. CPAs usually charge about $125 an hour, so be prepared for a hefty bill.

➤ **Tax attorneys.** You probably will never need a tax attorney to complete your tax return, unless the club's financial situation gets incredibly complicated. If you do, be prepared to pay—big time! Many tax attorneys charge a minimum of $300 an hour.

If you need a professional to help your club with its taxes, follow the guidelines for hiring outside help mentioned in Chapter 8. Find someone with whom you're comfortable, and is recommended by other investment clubs. Be sure you ask about rates before agreeing to hire.

The Least You Need to Know

➤ Every investment club needs to get a tax identification number from the Internal Revenue Service.

➤ All clubs must file a tax return for their first year, after which filing is optional.

➤ Investment club members must include club income and loss on their personal tax returns.

➤ You'll be taxed on any profit you make as a result of your membership in the investment club.

➤ Long-term and short-term capital gains are taxed at different rates, which can make a big difference in what you'll pay.

➤ There are several categories of professionals to help with your tax returns, if necessary.

Chapter 13

Going with a Broker—or Not

In This Chapter

➤ Understanding the role of a broker

➤ Deciding whether your club needs a broker or not

➤ Choosing the type of broker you'll need

➤ Determining if your broker is a good one

➤ Making a deal with the broker that makes sense for your club

---

Hopefully, it's very clear in your mind by now that the primary purposes of your investment club should be to provide education for members, to be an enjoyable social experience, and to make some money.

You probably can take care of the social aspects of the club yourself. You might, however, need some help with the education and making-money parts. Finding the right person to guide you through the sometimes thorny world of investments can be a real blessing for your club.

Historically, stockbrokers have guided investment clubs through the learning and investing processes. Some clubs, however, especially ones that have been around for a while and attained a good level of education and experience, invest without the aid of a broker.

Also, online trading has prompted some clubs to go it alone—making their own decisions about their investments.

In this chapter, we'll look at whether your club would be better off working with a stockbroker, or if it might be feasible to operate without one. We'll also discuss the different types of brokers and tell you how to find a good one. To start out, however, let's look at exactly what a broker is and what he or she does.

Just What Do Brokers Do?

A *broker,* short for stockbroker, is a person who earns a commission or fee for acting as an agent in making contracts or sales.

In plain English, a broker will help you select and buy stocks, then charge you for his trouble.

Taking Stock

A **broker,** or stockbroker, is a person who buys and sells stock for you, or for your investment club. He earns a commission or fee for his trouble.

Cashing In

Take a minute to think about all the service providers you use from time to time. Travel agents, doctors, tennis instructors, car mechanics, insurance agents, and delivery people all give you a particular service in exchange for money. A stockbroker is no different.

The real job of a broker is to buy and sell the securities within your investment club's account. He'll set up a stock brokerage account for your club. All your investment transactions will be done within that account.

A stockbroker provides a service to his customers—that is, he buys and sells stock as the customer requests. And he gets paid for providing that service. Just as a dentist expects to be paid for filling a cavity, or a waiter expects to be paid for taking orders and delivering dinners, or a carpet cleaner expects to be paid for cleaning a rug, stockbrokers expect to be paid for buying and selling your investments.

Brokers work for companies, or sometimes through another broker. They have bosses who demand productivity. The first thing that investors should know and remember about brokers is that brokers are working to earn money and make a living.

If you don't like your broker, or don't feel that he's doing what you want him to do, you're free to find someone else to work with. You're not bound to a broker any more than you are to a particular dentist or dry cleaner.

Brokers work for individuals, clubs, and businesses. Ideally, a symbiotic relationship develops between a broker and his client in which both parties benefit.

If your investment club decides to go with a broker, the broker will buy and sell investments for the club. The really important thing to remember is that brokers only are authorized to buy and sell what and when their clients tell them to. Your club will decide at its monthly meeting what it wants to buy or sell. Then your broker will make the trades.

Brokers may or may not be investment *financial advisers*. An investment adviser is a person who gives investment advice. She'll sit down with clients and explain and discuss various investment options. When the clients and the adviser have reached common ground on investment options, the final decision of when to make a trade is left up to the adviser. Advisers will buy and sell, depending on the market at the time the transaction is made, their judgment about a stock, and so forth.

A broker must pass a Series 7 test, given by the National Association of Securities Dealers (NASD). This permits him to dispense investment advice and execute *authorized* trades, as directed by a client. An investment advisor may or may not have a Series 7 authorization, but will have received authorization to be an adviser through the Securities and Exchange Commission (SEC) in Washington, D.C., or through his or her state SEC.

Taking Stock

A **financial adviser** is permitted to advise clients concerning their investments and has authority to make decisions regarding those investments on his clients' behalf. A broker is authorized only to execute trades as directed by a customer.

A broker can be, but is not necessarily, an investment adviser. Make sure to ask about the credentials of the person you choose to work with your club. Most brokers who work with investment clubs are brokers—not financial advisers. They will buy and sell stock for your club according to instructions from club members. Brokers, in effect, take and place orders. Just as a waiter will come to your table, take your order for what you want to eat, and go back to the kitchen to place your order, a broker will come to your investment club meeting, listen to what you want to buy, and then place your order.

If your club decides to buy AT&T stock at $55 a share, your broker will put in the order to buy AT&T at $55. Or he'll buy the stock *at the market,* if instructed. That means that he'll purchase the stock at whatever price he can get for you at the time of the trade. If you tell your broker to sell the stock a week later, he'll put in that order.

Obviously, brokers don't commute daily from Peoria to Wall Street in New York City. They don't make their trades on the actual floor of the New York Stock Exchange.

Taking Stock

At the market refers to a security transaction that occurs at whatever price the broker can get for you at the time of the trade. You either buy or sell a stock at a set price, or you give an order to buy the security at whatever price the security happens to be when the order is placed.

Cashing In

If you ever get the opportunity to be on the floor of the New York Stock Exchange, go for it. It's an awesome experience to be on the floor, following around a trader as he sells shares of IBM, Coke, and MMM (3M).

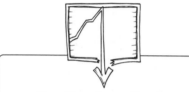

Heading for a Crash

Whatever you do, don't make the mistake of thinking that your club can go without a broker if you don't have the necessary expertise. Navigating the stock market can be tricky business, and trying to do it if you're qualified can be setting your club up for disaster.

What happens is that either by phone or by computer, a broker will place a trade order to someone at the main office of the brokerage house, who, in turn, gives an order to an actual trader on the floor of the exchange.

The trader makes the trades as directed from the brokerage house and the order is sent back to the trading desk, where your broker is given the price of the trade.

In short, your broker is someone who will make the transaction for you. When the trade is completed, the broker gets a commission of about one percent of the value of the traded stock.

That explains basically what brokers do, but it's important to understand that there are numerous types of brokers who perform different tasks and services. We'll get to that discussion later in the chapter.

Deciding Whether Your Club Needs a Broker or Not

As we said earlier in this chapter, some clubs wouldn't dream of operating without a broker. Others do just fine without the benefit of a broker.

Maybe your club is lucky enough to have some well-versed financial types with good investment experience among its membership. If you are lucky enough to have one in your club who is willing to educate and lead the club, you probably don't need a broker. Most clubs, however, don't find themselves in that enviable position.

Some clubs are reluctant to use a broker because they feel that it detracts from their learning process. They think that if their broker is providing information and advice about stocks, members will be less inclined to go out and research and learn on their own. True? It could be, theoretically. Hopefully, however, your members are motivated and eager to learn and will use any advice from a broker as a backup to their own educational efforts.

We'll later talk about the use of online brokers. They require you, as members of an investment club, to do all the research. Online brokers just consummate trades.

A broker's expertise is especially useful during your club's early months or years, when your experience is at a low point.

If you decide that your club needs a broker—and most clubs do—you should understand the different types that are available. After that, you can choose the one that makes the most sense for your club.

Full-Service or Discount?

There are many kinds of brokers, but basically, they can be broken down into two categories:

➤ Full-service brokers

➤ Discount brokers

The difference between a full-service broker and a discount broker is sort of like the difference between self-serve and full-serve gas stations.

Sure, you can get gas at either kind of station. You probably can get three or four different grades of gas at either one. And if it's only gas that you need, then a self-serve station is just fine.

If you need somebody to check your oil and tire pressure, however, you might just be out of luck at a self-serve station. And if your windshield is covered with bugs, don't count on anybody offering to clean it for you.

Full-service brokers are the gas stations at which attendants will pump your gas, check your oil, clean your windshield, and give your kid a lollipop. Discount brokers can offer you gas, but don't count on too much else. Let's have a closer look.

Full-Service Brokers

A *full-service broker* normally works for a major brokerage firm. She receives commissions on the trades an individual makes, or she gets a fee based on the value of funds within an account.

Let's say, for instance, that your club wants to buy 100 shares of the hot Cisco stock. If your broker is full-service and works on a commission basis, she'll sit down with you and discuss whether or not Cisco is a good idea for your club. Perhaps she'll recommend that you wait and see if the price drops, or suggest an alternative stock that she thinks makes more sense for your club.

Taking Stock

A **full-service broker,** who works on a commission basis, gets money every time you buy or sell a stock. One who is fee-based gets a percentage of the value of her client's account.

If you decide to go ahead and buy Cisco or another stock, she'll take a commission based on the cost of the transaction. It could cost you hundreds of dollars for your club to buy or sell a stock, depending on the value of the security.

A fee-based full-service broker receives—instead of a commission based on a trade—a percentage of the assets within her client's brokerage account, usually around 1 percent. If your account is worth $200,000, for instance, the broker gets $2,000 a year from your account. In return, you get to make a specified number of trades per year at no cost or minimal cost. You're not charged a commission on the trades that your broker makes on your behalf.

If the value of your account is very low, you'll probably have to pay a minimum fee that's greater than 1 percent of your account. A full-service broker won't be thrilled to do a lot of work and get 1 percent of $2,000 at the end of the year.

The problem is that the minimum fee might seem like a maximum one to a just-starting-out investment club. A minimum fee could be $1,000 a year. If your club requires that each of its 10 members contribute $300, totaling $3,000 as an initial investment, paying that minimum fee could wipe out one third of your club's nest egg. That's not such a good arrangement for your club.

Take This to the Bank

Your broker doesn't get the full amount of the commission he charges on a brokerage trade. If the broker works for a major house, like Merrill Lynch or Morgan Stanley Dean Witter, he'll get 40 percent of the fee. The other 60 percent goes to his company to cover the costs of the office, the trader in New York, computer expenses, and other costs of doing business.

Because of that, if you choose to work with a full-service broker, you'll likely begin your relationship on a fee-for-service (transaction) arrangement.

If you hire a full-service broker, he should come to your meetings—or at least be willing to come as often as possible. He'll discuss your investments with you and guide you toward certain investments.

Every investment club has its own personality. A club that has a strong leader will either use its broker to lead only a part of the meeting, or as a co-leader. This type of club will have little problem continuing if its broker leaves the business or is promoted to another city.

Other clubs, however, are guided by their brokers. The broker directs the meeting, sets the tone for the day, and so forth. Assuming that you have a good broker, this is okay. Just be aware that if your broker decides to move to a warmer climate, your club might need to find someone else.

There's a club in our area that has had the same broker for more than 20 years. The rapport between the broker and club members is terrific. At each meeting, the broker spends 10 minutes teaching the club about some aspect of investing. Club members say he's been invaluable to them over the years and that he's an integral part of their club.

The information a broker possesses is invaluable to beginning investors. His firm also serves as a resource to your club because your broker can get additional information from his firm if necessary.

Heading for a Crash

Make sure that club members, officers, and your broker understand the role that your broker will play. Will he be a resource or a leader? Many problems have occurred because people had very different expectations concerning the role of their broker.

Discount Brokers

Discount brokers serve primarily to take and place orders for investments. They most likely will not come to your monthly meetings. There aren't very many local discount brokerage houses, and the discount broker you work with is likely to be located in a completely different area from where you live.

Although some discount firms will provide investment information, it won't be delivered personally. Information will either be mailed, e-mailed, or faxed to a club member, who will bring it along to the meeting.

Discount brokers won't guide you through the investment process, as a full-service broker will. If your club uses a discount broker, members will need to do nearly all the research for their proposed investments. After the research has been completed and the club has voted to buy a stock, a designated club member—usually the treasurer—will call the broker to make the transactions. Trades are made over the phone or by computer.

A discount broker will—or at least should—provide information to your club if requested. He won't spend a great deal of time with you, but should provide basic information. Basically, his role is that of an order taker.

In addition to full-service and discount brokers, there's a category of brokers known as deep discount brokers. These are like discount brokers, only more so. With a deep discount broker, you call, make the trade, and receive confirmation of the trade over the phone.

Cashing In

Having an online account set up is handy because you can check it out at any time. You can find out your account's market value just by logging on and accessing the proper site. You may never trade online, but the account is available whenever you want to look at it.

Deep discount brokers were established as competition to other sorts of brokers before the advent of online trading. They won't give you any advice. They simply take, place, and confirm your order.

Online trading, obviously, is done via computer. If your club chooses to trade online, it would set up an online account by which transactions are made via the Internet.

Online brokers are great if your club has voted and knows ahead of time what you are investing in. Like deep discount brokers, online brokers offer no advice. A designated member of the club contacts the online broker, make the trade, and the transaction is completed. What is particularly awesome about online trading is the ability to go online and see the market value of your account, make the transaction, and see that it has been made.

Getting the Best Deal (and Broker) for Your Club

To get the type of broker that makes the most sense for your club, you'll need to assess and evaluate your needs.

Is there someone in your club who can provide direction and help make investment decisions? Is your club looking for someone to help educate its members and provide information about various investments? Or do club members prefer to do all the research themselves and only need someone to take and place their orders?

When your club is just getting started, there aren't all that many investment decisions. Members, for instance, might agree that the first stock your club should buy is Microsoft. If your club has only minimal money stockpiled, the amount of Microsoft you'll be able to buy at $110 a share is pretty much predetermined. You can't buy more shares than your club has money to pay for.

If you feel your club's decisions at this point are minimal and you don't need a full-service broker, then hire the discount broker and begin learning about investing and the investment process on your own.

On the other hand, if you want a broker who can teach you about investing, make the trades, and help you invest in stocks that make sense for your club, then go ahead and find a good, full-service broker.

A fairly new investment club in our area has gone online. The members decided to do all the work (stock research) themselves, and they make the trades online. Club members enjoy getting on their computers in the evenings and checking on the club's account.

Being lead by an experienced broker is important for many club members. Remember, although the fee is higher than online or using a discount broker, the full-service broker can bring experience and knowledge to the table.

New club members want to learn (that's why they are with your group) and don't know where to find someone to help them. To begin the process of finding someone to help your group, besides word of mouth, call every brokerage house in town and ask for a broker who is interested in guiding your club.

Of course, that's usually the new man in the office. Second thought might be to call the NAIC and ask for the names of other investment clubs in your area. Call and find out who they are using, if they are happy with their adviser, and where they would go for their next adviser. Nothing like asking experience where they would turn if they could begin the process again.

Not All Brokers Are Created Equal

Let's face it. Not everybody is really good at what they do. This doesn't apply just to the financial area—it's pretty much universal. There are some doctors, for instance, whom you would choose to perform open-heart surgery on you, rather than others.

You'd much rather take your car for repairs to a competent repairman, than to somebody who calls himself a repairman but really knows little about cars and engines. And you'd really like your kids to get the best teachers in the school, rather than the ones that stopped caring about teaching a long time ago and are just hanging around until they can retire. The same principle is true with brokers. There are some out there that are better than others. It's just the way it is.

To be fair to brokers, we've got to tell you that a broker doesn't agree to work with an investment club because she plans on making a fortune on the trades within the club's account.

Most clubs don't trade a lot. It's often difficult for club members to agree on when and what to sell. As we'll talk about later, members hate to take capital gains.

So, why would a broker agree to work for your investment club? Maybe because she enjoys the company of your club's members. Maybe because she wants to become known to club members and handle their personal accounts, as well.

Getting business outside of the club should be a natural progression for a broker who does a good job. There's nothing wrong with a broker looking for outside business, as long as it doesn't interfere with the work she does for your club.

Many experienced brokers won't be interested in working with your club on a full-service basis. They have enough clients, aren't looking for new business, and don't want to put in the time and work that your club might require.

Take This to the Bank

The average investment club meets 10 to 12 times a year, for at least an hour each month. That's a fair amount of time for a broker who's busy trying to make a living. You should understand that your club takes a broker's time away from either his office or his family, and appreciate what he brings to the table.

Following is a list of questions to help your club decide what type of broker would be best for you. Review it with your club members and use it as a guide when choosing a broker.

Yes	No	1.	Do you want an investment expert at each meeting?
Yes	No	2.	Do you want an individual to provide all or most of the investment research for your club?
Yes	No	3.	Are you looking for the lowest price commission on every trade?
Yes	No	4.	Are you interested in the availability of online trading and having 24-hour access to our account?
Yes	No	5.	Do you want to talk with an investment person throughout the month concerning your account?
Yes	No	6.	Is there a person within the club who has enough experience to deal with a discount broker and who agrees to guide the club through its beginning investing?
Yes	No	7.	Is the club interested in having guest speakers attend monthly meetings to teach about their areas of expertise, instead of having the same person at each meeting?

If you want an expert at your meeting every month, you want an in-house full-service broker as your adviser. Does your club want each member to do extensive research of company financial information, or do you want someone to guide you through the process? If you, as a club, want to do the work, think about using a discount broker. If you don't need help, a discount broker seems like the way to go.

If cost is more important than the work involved, use a discount broker. If you think your ideas, as a club, are as good as the ideas of someone with experience, use a discount broker. As I tell my clients, I can clean my own house or do my own taxes; it's called the ag factor. Is it easier to pay someone else to do the work for you, or do you want to do the work (whether to learn or to save money) yourselves?

Use this questionnaire as a guide to what's best for your club. Then, make your decision. Talk to members of other clubs, if necessary. Once you decide what kind of broker you want, and find one that you like, breathe a big sigh of relief. Do, however, remember that the needs of your club may change, and you may at some point need a different type of broker.

The Least You Need to Know

➤ Unless your club is blessed with financial types who are willing to help the club get started, you'll probably need a broker—at least early on.

➤ Brokers are people who help you select, buy, and sell stock, charging you either a commission on the transaction or a fee.

➤ The two main groups of brokers are full-service and discount. It's important to understand the difference.

➤ Some clubs will need full-service brokers, while others will do quite well with discount brokers.

➤ As in any profession, there are some brokers who are better than others.

Part 4

It's Time to Do Some Homework

Certainly, one of the primary purposes of your club is to invest money and, hopefully, make a profit. Before you can do that, however, you'll need to do your homework.

In this section, we give you an overview of the stock market and how it works. This will help you understand the market and make it less daunting when you begin investing.

We'll also have a look at mutual funds, and explain why your club might want to consider looking at them as investments.

Most important, we'll tell you how to get information about the stock your club might consider buying, and how to research companies that offer their stock for sale.

The more information you have before you start buying investments, the more intelligent and informed your investment decisions will be.

BUY!!!! SELL!! BUY!!!!

Chapter 14

Understanding the Stock Market Before You Jump In

In This Chapter

➤ Understanding what it means to invest

➤ Going public and raising capital

➤ Stock market exchanges and indexes

➤ Looking at the bond market

➤ Different investments carry different levels of risk

And now, the moment you've all been waiting for—it's time to talk about the actual process of investing your club's money.

You have a broker lined up. Club members have contributed initial investments and maybe a month or two of monthly dues. You have your tax identification number and someone capable—either a club member or outside help—is standing by, ready to start keeping accurate records of your club's transactions.

Before you pick up the phone and instruct your broker to buy 50 shares of your favorite stock, however, you have to read this chapter. It's important because it will give you an overview of the stock market.

This chapter will help you understand how the market's performance is evaluated and why a company offers its stock for sale, in the first place.

We'll tell you about the three major exchanges and the different kinds of investments that are available.

So, although your club is very close to beginning to invest, don't start quite yet. A little homework is in order first.

What Does It Mean to Make an Investment?

Investing is the process of purchasing securities or property, for which stability of value and the level of expected return are somewhat predictable.

Taking Stock

Investing is buying something with the expectation of making a profit. You're able to—within reason—predict the rate of return you'll get from the investment.

That means that you buy something like stocks, bonds, an apartment building, or whatever. You know the value of your investment, and you're able to—within reason—predict what your return from the investment should be.

Of course, sometimes your expectations go up in smoke, along with your investment. You don't always make money on investments, but you can reasonably expect to realize some kind of return.

If you aren't investing, you're speculating, which is really gambling. Speculating is taking above-average risks with the hope of achieving above-average returns. When you speculate, you buy something on the basis of its potential selling price, not on the basis of its actual value.

A client told us recently that her son "invested" heavily in one stock in 1999 and ended up losing $400,000. His brokerage commissions for the year were $70,000. We pointed out that her son had not so much invested, as he had speculated—or gambled.

Your club needs to learn about investing—not speculating.

Investments fall into two broad categories: tangible and intangible.

➤ **Tangible property.** Also known as real or personal property, tangible property is something you can see. You can touch it. Often, you can live in it. Tangible property includes your home and the 12-acre lot in the mountains that you plan to eventually build on and retire to. Your car or truck is tangible property. The jewelry you own, your coin collection—even that complete set of Beanie Babies that you were so proud of a couple of years ago—all are tangible property. The value of tangible property is in the item that you have.

➤ **Intangible property.** Intangible property is something that you can't see or touch. You can't drive it or live in it. Intangible items are stocks and bonds. The value is in what the paper represents—maybe 100 shares of Microsoft stock—not the paper itself.

Neither type of investment is better than the other. Plenty of people have done very well investing in real estate. But, because your club most likely will be buying intangibles—such as stocks and bonds—that's where we'll focus our discussion. Let's look, first of all, at exactly what stock is and why a company offers it.

Why Does a Company Offer Its Stock for Sale?

Imagine this: You start a small company making computer games. It's just you and two buddies. Your product takes off and you need to expand the business big time to keep up with your orders. You borrow some money, acquire more manufacturing space, and hire a bunch of employees.

As your company grows, you need to expand more and more. To do that, you need more money. You've already borrowed as much as the bank is going to loan you, so you need to find other investors. You hook up with some investors who are looking to back a promising up-and-coming company and you form a corporation. Each investor puts some money into your company, and in return, gets to own a certain amount of it.

As the company keeps growing, you need even more money to grow it. So, you start thinking about taking your company public, which is a means of raising capital. Taking your company from private to public means that you offer shares, or little pieces of the company for sale to anyone who wants to buy them.

Any interested party can buy your company's stock through federally registered and underwritten sales. You're no longer confining your company's stock to partners, family members, maybe some employees, and friends, as you probably did when it was a privately held company. Now your stock is available to anyone who has the cash and inclination to buy it.

Going public means that you publicly offer shares of stock in your company. The stock of the company that's going public is listed at a particular price per share at which the public can buy shares. Offering your shares for sale is called an *initial public offering,* or IPO.

Cashing In

If you're interested in reading about what it's like to take a company public, check out *The Complete Idiot's Guide to Being a Successful Entrepreneur,* by John Sortino. Sortino, who founded the Vermont Teddy Bear Company, has a great story about taking his company public, along with lots of other good information.

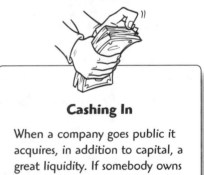

Cashing In

When a company goes public it acquires, in addition to capital, a great liquidity. If somebody owns stock in a public company and wants to sell it, it's no big deal for the company. Ownership of the company can move freely from one person to another.

The company gets a large percentage of the initial offering price. The underwriter, lawyers, and everyone else who worked to make the IPO happen get paid, too. The people who invested become part owners of the company.

Once the stock is purchased initially, it gets traded, and hopefully increases in value.

This is a very simplified explanation of why and how companies go public. Generally, a company offers its stock for sale to the public in order to raise capital. Once it has this capital, it can expand, and it has better borrowing power than it did previously.

What Exactly Is the Stock Market?

We hear an awful lot of talk about the stock market. The stock market is up—the stock market is down. We invest in the stock market and we pin our hopes on the stock market. What, exactly is the stock market?

The *stock market* is a generic term that encompasses the trading of securities.

Trading within the stock market takes place in stock exchanges. There are three major exchanges in the United States:

Taking Stock

The **stock market** is the organized securities exchange for stock and bond transactions.

➤ **The New York Stock Exchange (NYSE).** This is the largest equities marketplace in the world, located on Broad Street in New York City (not Wall Street). 3,025 companies are listed on the exchange. Companies are listed on the NYSE if they have at least 2,000 shareholders, a minimum of one million shares of publicly held stock, and many other criteria. Trading is done on the floor via an auction system. For more information about the NYSE, check out its Web site at www.nyse.com.

➤ **The National Association of Securities Dealers Automated Quotation System (NASDAQ).** The NASDAQ is a major stock exchange, linked with the purchasers and sellers of securities through computers. Computers provide up-to-date bid and ask prices on thousands of selected, highly active over-the-counter securities. There isn't a physical floor of the exchange for NASDAQ, as there is with the NYSE and AMEX. Trades are made entirely through computers. You can get a synopsis of every stock on the exchange on the NASDAQ Web site at www.nasdaq.com.

➤ **The American Stock Exchange (AMEX).** The AMEX was at one time the second largest organized security exchange. Its organization and procedures are quite similar to those of the New York Stock Exchange, except that its listing requirements are not as stringent as those of the NYSE. For that reason, it attracts smaller companies. AMEX recently was purchased by the National Association of Securities Dealers Automated Quotation System (NASDAQ), but both exchanges currently stand on their own. You can check out the AMEX Web site at www.amex.com.

The stock market works on the premise that a willing buyer buys shares of stock from a willing seller. An auction process is used to accomplish that. The seller asks a certain price, and the buyer offers a certain price. The buyer and seller come to an agreement, and a transaction occurs.

Performance Evaluation

Performance is a fundamental process used to compare how the stocks in your club's portfolio have done compared to the market as a whole. Performance, or return, is the level of profit from an investment. It's the reward you get for investing.

Performance of the stock market is measured against the Dow Jones Industrial Average (DJIA), the S&P 500, and numerous other indices. The Dow Jones has a utilities index, an industrial index, and a transportation index. That means that it includes averages for utilities, industrial, and transportation stocks.

The DJIA is a composite, or group, of 30 stocks with a daily average. Tomorrow, if the stocks as an average go up in price, the DJIA goes up. If the average value of those 30 stocks goes down, the DJIA goes down.

The S&P 500 Index is a measure against the performance of the 500 largest companies in America.

There are two kinds of investment returns: *total return* and yield. Total return on an investment is the current income, plus the capital gain or loss. Yield is the amount of dividends or interest paid on an investment. These returns can be very different, but they're both important when you look at the total picture for your portfolio.

There are formulas for figuring out your total returns, both with and without dividends. Your accountant or financial adviser can help you do that. Remember that you also could have a negative return.

Taking Stock

The **performance** of a particular investment is the level of profit you make from it. Performance is measured for a period of time by a quarter, half year, or annual rate of return.

Taking Stock

Total return is the current dividend or interest income, plus any capital gain or loss on an investment for the year. It's considered a better measure of an investment's return than just the dividend or interest alone.

If your club purchases a $1,000 certificate of deposit on January 15 that pays 6 percent ($60 in interest per year), the CD is said to yield the investor 6 percent a year. The total return for the investment is 6 percent.

However, if your club decides to put $1,000 into a stock that pays 6 percent, on January 15, and at year end, the value of the stock is $1,200. That means that the club received the dividends totaling $60, the total return for the investment is the $60 plus the $200 increase in value ($260), or a 25 percent total return for the year.

Your club should do a total return evaluation for each stock in the portfolio and then a total return for the portfolio.

Comparing Indices

Once you've figured out your return, you can compare it to any of a number of indices. Most money managers compare their returns to the S&P 500 Index. Other indices, however, are set up for particular types of stock. You should find the index that matches the type of stock you have. Some of the indices are ...

➤ **NASDAQ composite.** All stocks listed on the NASDAQ exchange.

➤ **Russell 3000.** 3,000 largest cap stocks in the United States.

➤ **NYSE composite.** All stocks listed on the New York Stock Exchange.

➤ **Russell 2000.** The lowest capitalization stocks in the Russell 3000.

➤ **S&P 500 composite.** The leading companies in leading industries.

➤ **S&P 100 composite.** 100 blue chip stocks.

The Many Flavors of Stock

Stocks are simply investments that represent a piece of ownership in a company. The more stock you own, the bigger the piece of the company you have. The word "stock" is commonly used interchangeably with the phrase "common stock."

All stock, however, is not created equal. The following is a rundown of some of the different kinds of stock:

➤ **Blue chip stock.** This is the common phrase for stock of well-established companies that historically pay dividends in good years and bad. Some examples of blue chip stock are General Motors, Exxon, and IBM.

➤ **Growth stock.** Companies that have sales, earnings, and market share that are growing at rates higher than the average company or the general economy issue this stock. They do not typically pay large dividends and any appreciation goes untaxed until a gain is realized. These would include stocks like Micron Technology, General Motors H, and Safeguard Scientifics.

➤ **Emerging market stock.** These are smaller and younger versions of growth stock. For example, Republic of Brazil FRN, Aracruz Celilose, SA, ADS, and Quinenio SA companies. The problem with the stocks in this category is that you've probably never heard of them.

➤ **Income stock.** These are stocks that historically pay regular and steady dividends and usually appreciate in value to keep up with inflation. They're popular among older, income-oriented investors. Utility stocks are an example of income stocks.

➤ **Cyclical stock.** These tend to prosper and grow when the economy expands, but perform poorly when the economy suffers. Types of companies that offer cyclical stocks are automobile, paper, airlines, steel, and cement.

➤ **Defensive stock.** This is stock that's relatively unaffected by general fluctuations in the economy. They're not Raytheon and other companies that prepare weapons for war. Examples of defensive stocks are Coca-Cola and Pepsi.

➤ **Interest-sensitive stock.** The performance of the company is largely affected by changes in the interest rate, and the stock value will react accordingly. Examples are bank and insurance company stock.

➤ **International stock.** This is stock for companies located outside the United States, for example, Nestle, Glaxo, and Gucci companies.

Taking Stock

Diversification is acquiring a group of assets in which returns on the different assets are not directly related over time. Proper investment diversification, requiring a sufficient number of different assets, is intended to minimize the risk associated with investing.

If you do buy stocks, say in the Disney Corp., you're buying a tiny piece of a huge company. Regardless of whether you buy 10 shares of Disney stock or 10,000, owning stock makes you a shareholder in the company. As long as the company makes a profit, you're entitled, as a shareholder, to share and benefit from it.

Shares of stock of stock usually are sold in groups of 100—called round lots. Groups of less than 100 shares are called odd lots. If you buy 100 shares of stock from a company that has one million shares of stock outstanding, you can figure that you own one 1,000th of the company.

Taking Stock

Asset allocation is the process of assigning investment funds to categories of assets based on financial objectives and risk tolerance. Your club may allocate funds to common stocks representing various industries.

You'll get annual dividends (income paid by investments). And hopefully, the price of the stock will increase, so that if you wanted to, you could sell your stock for more than what you bought it for and make a profit.

Dividends usually are paid four times a year to shareholders on specified dates. Let's use, for example, Fulton Financial, a regional bank in Central Pennsylvania. Fulton pays its quarterly dividend on the 15th day of every January, April, July, and October. This payment is made to all shareholders who owned the stock on the 20th day of the month prior to the dividend date. If you didn't own the shares on that date, you won't receive the dividend.

It's important to have a variety of stocks in your portfolio. This is called *diversification*. Diversification limits the chances of your entire portfolio devaluing at the same time. It minimizes your risk. To achieve diversification, you use *asset allocation,* which is the process of determining the assignment of investment funds to broad categories of assets.

If your club decides it wants to own Intel, or other technology stock, then it might also want to consider an oil stock; a cyclical stock, such as Ford; some defensive stock; some international exposure; and so forth. The allocation is an important part of the investment process for diversification.

And Then There's the Bond Market

In today's stock market, bonds have acquired a sort of "poor sister" image. With phenomenal returns occurring in the stock market, why would anyone consider earning a boring 6.5 percent return by investing in bonds?

Especially, why would an investment club that's looking to learn about stocks consider buying bonds?

Bonds are held for security. Individual bonds give a stated payout for a stated time period. Your original funds are almost guaranteed if you purchase a good bond.

Bonds are debt instruments, or lending investments. When you buy stock, you own the stock. When you buy a bond, you're really loaning your money, with the understanding that you'll get it back—with interest—after a specified period of time. The bond issuer promises to pay the investor a specific amount of interest for a period of time and to repay the principal at maturity.

Let's say that General Motors issues a $10,000 bond that will pay 6.5 percent interest and is due June 15, 2003. If you invest in the bond, you're lending General Motors $10,000 until June 15, 2003. In the meantime, they promise to pay you 6.5 percent on your $10,000.

General Motors is paying less interest to use your money than it would have had to pay to borrow the money from a bank or other type of institutional lender.

At the same time, General Motors is paying you more to use your money than you'd get if you put your $10,000 in your local bank or in a certificate of deposit.

It's a good situation for everybody but the bank, as long as the company can pay the interest rate as agreed throughout the term of the "loan," and can pay you the funds in full when the bond is due (at maturity).

You'll get the interest payment twice a year—$325 each payment. On June 15, 2003, you'll get your $10,000 back.

So, you're earning money on your loan. Not as much as you might realize in the stock market, but it's a sure thing. You can count on getting that $325 twice a year.

Bonds are the most widely used lending investment. There are different kinds of bonds, including municipal bonds, general obligation bonds, revenue bonds, corporate bonds, savings bonds, and government agency bonds. Certificates of deposit, treasury bills, and notes also are lending investments.

While certificates of deposit are generally administered by banks, bonds are offered by corporations, the government, or a mortgage holder, for purposes of generating income. Most bonds offer a fixed rate of interest and the value of a bond is based on changes in interest rates.

Take This to the Bank

An important thing to remember about bonds is that when interest rates go up, the value of your bond goes down. When interest rates go down, the value of your bond increases.

If you're holding a bond that pays 6 percent interest and the interest rate jumps to 8 percent, you lose on the value of your bonds. But, if you're earning 8 percent interest on your bond and the interest rates drops to 7, you're still entitled to 8 percent—the agreed upon rate. In that case, your bond would have increased in value, compared to new bonds being issued.

We all saw interest rates plummet in the mid-1990s. Investors saw the rates paid on their CDs drop in half. Banks were only offering 4.5 percent CDs. Interest rates on notes and bonds were only slightly higher.

Companies that had issued the higher interest rates knew that if they could "call in" their higher-interest-paying notes, they could reissue them at a lower rate, sometimes only having to pay half of the interest that was required on the original bonds. While this was a huge advantage to the company, it was an equally big disadvantage to the investor. A company that can pay less to borrow money can use the difference to increase research and development within the firm, pay off some of the debt, and so forth.

Bonds are pretty safe, but even they come with some risk. Just as with stocks, it's important to do your homework and try to make sure that the bond you're considering is a good one.

Understanding Stock Market Risks

You already know that the stock market can be risky. You can, however, minimize your risk by making smart choices and getting advice when you need it. Basically, there are two types of stock market risk. There's *systematic risk,* which affects the market overall, and there's *unsystematic risk,* which affects only a particular business or industry within the market. Understanding the market the best you can, and knowing what sorts of things affect it will help you minimize your risk.

Some reasons that people run into trouble with the stock market include:

➤ They invest in a company that they know very little about.

➤ They take advice from a friend or relative who claims—often without foundation—to have made huge profits on this or that stock.

➤ They think they can trade themselves, without the benefit of brokers or advisers.

Everyone knows that investing money is never risk free. The goal is for you to find the investments that offer the best chance for a good return, with the least amount of risk.

Taking Stock

The type of risk that affects the entire market is called **systematic risk.** The kind of risk that affects only a single business or industry is called **unsystematic risk.**

Meeting your goal takes some know-how. First of all, there are all kinds of investment risk. Some of the different types are …

➤ **Business risk.** Risk that results from the way in which the business that issued the security is managed.

➤ **Financial risk.** Risk associated with the finances of the company.

➤ **Purchasing power risk.** The effect that inflation might have on the value of your holding.

➤ **Interest rate risk.** How changes in interest rates may affect your investment.

➤ **Market risk.** The tendency for stock to move with the market.

➤ **Default risk.** The chance that the company you've invested in will be unable to service the risk.

➤ **Foreign currency risk.** The risk that a change in the relationship between the value of the U.S. dollar and the value of the currency of the country in which your investment is held will affect your holding.

Reading all those possibilities for risk can be scary, but it's important for you to understand as much about this subject as possible.

The stock market is subject to some pretty significant fluctuations and many possibilities for risk. It's been shown, however, that if you invest your money for the long haul, you'll probably do okay. If you have a limited period in which you want to, or are able to leave your money in stocks, you risk having to take it out at a time when the market is down. If that happens, you'll lose money. Investments in real estate carry similar risks. The real estate market can be great—or it can drop pretty dramatically.

We'll discuss more about risks in some of the later chapters.

Safe, but Not Exciting

Some investments carry decidedly less risk than others. But, if you invest in something really safe, you're almost sure to get a lower return. It's just one of those things.

If it's feasible for you to have your money invested for a long time, then stocks are probably a better investment than low-risk, low-yield bonds. Take a look at the statistics below. They'll show the chances of the returns on stocks beating the returns on bonds at different lengths of time after the initial investment.

➤ If you hold an investment for one year, there's a 60 percent chance that stocks will give you a better return than bonds.

➤ If you hold an investment for five years, there's a 70 percent chance that stocks will give you a better return than bonds.

➤ If you hold an investment for 10 years, there's an 80 percent chance that stocks will give you a better return than bonds.

➤ If you hold an investment for 20 years, there's a 90 percent chance that stocks will give you a better return than bonds.

➤ And, if you hold an investment for 30 years, there's nearly a 100 percent chance that stocks will give you a better return than bonds.

Probably the best way of controlling risk, as far as your investments are concerned, is through diversification. When you diversify, you put your money into different investments, so that if the value of some of them decreases, the value of the others is likely to be high enough to keep your investments stable.

183

Exciting, but Just How Safe?

We've told you repeatedly that stocks keep your blood pumping with their potential for payoffs. They also can be an incredible, wake-you-up-at-night headache.

It's important to remember that there are different types of stocks, with different degrees of risk.

➤ **Growth stocks.** These are reputed to be one of the easiest ways to make money, because they're issued by companies that have higher-than-average earnings and profits. However, they're volatile, and can decrease in value, too. Be prepared to hold onto growth stocks in order to ride out any ups and downs.

➤ **Income stocks.** True to their name, these stocks pay dividends, or income, on a regular basis. They're not the flashy investments that growth stocks are, but they're more dependable, and easier on the blood pressure.

➤ **Growth and income stocks.** These offer the best of the two previous types of stocks. You can get capital gains from growth stocks, as well as some dividends from the income stocks. Unfortunately, you might not get all the growth benefits that you would from pure growth stock.

When you're just getting started in investing, the best thing to do is get a good understanding of investment options and the associated benefits and risks. Factor in your investment timetable and how much risk you're willing—and able—to take. Then, do what feels right for you.

The Least You Need to Know

➤ To invest is to purchase securities or property for which you understand the value and have a reasonable expectation for return.

➤ A company offers its stock for sale in order to raise capital.

➤ The stock market has three major exchanges: the New York Stock Exchange (NYSE), the American Stock Exchange (AMEX), and the National Association of Securities Dealers Automated Quotation System (NASDAQ).

➤ There are many kinds of stock, some of which carry more risk than others.

➤ Bonds are generally safe, predictable investments.

➤ A stock on which an investor has the opportunity to realize great profit almost always carries significant risk.

Chapter 15

Considering Mutual Funds as Investments for Your Club

In This Chapter

➤ Understanding the concept of mutual funds

➤ The many flavors of mutual funds

➤ Load funds versus no-load funds

➤ Hidden fees to watch for

➤ How mutual funds can benefit your club

➤ Some fund families to consider

Now that you may be thoroughly confused by all this discussion of total return, performance, the stock and bond markets, and all other topics that have been mentioned up to this point, it's time to really start concentrating on the process of investing.

After all, that's what your club was formed to do, right? We don't think you decided to go through all the work of forming a club just to get a night out of the house once a month.

When investment clubs start talking about where to put their money, they tend to look primarily at buying stock of particular companies. That's fine. There's nothing wrong with it. In fact, we're going to go on at length about it in the next chapter.

Don't think, however, that buying individual stocks is the only investment option for your club. In this chapter, we'll tell you all about mutual funds, and how they can be a valuable addition to your club's portfolio.

When you buy mutual funds, your money is pooled with that of many other people and used to buy groups of stocks, bonds, and other holdings. Many people don't fully understand this.

We know a woman who asked her financial adviser to sell all the stocks in her portfolio and put her money into mutual funds. She felt she could get better returns with mutual funds than she could with the stock she owned.

What she didn't realize was that some mutual funds are comprised of stocks, and by reinvesting her money into mutual funds, she actually would be buying more stock.

It works the other way around, too. Many people buy mutual funds because they think their money is safer in funds than it is in individual stocks. If your mutual funds are stock funds, chances are they'll be subject to the same ups and downs as the stock market.

What Are Mutual Funds and How Do They Work?

Mutual funds are investments that combine the money of many investors and place the cash into stocks, bonds, and other holdings.

Taking Stock

A **portfolio manager**, sometimes called a money manager, is a professional who decides where to invest the money you hand over for mutual funds. You benefit from the expertise of the portfolio manager and his team.

Most mutual funds are worth hundreds of millions of dollars. The largest funds are worth a billion dollars or more. Needless to say that when you own shares in one of these mega-funds, you own a very, very small piece of the total fund.

To better understand what mutual funds are, think of a mutual fund as a pie. When you plunk down your money for mutual funds, you're purchasing a slice of the pie.

The size of the slice you get depends on the value of the total pie at the time you buy the fund. If the value of your mutual fund goes down, the pie (and your piece of it) gets smaller. If the value of the total fund increases, the pie (and your slice) gets bigger.

These pooled funds are managed by *portfolio managers*. Portfolio managers, aided by analysts, are responsible for finding the best places to invest your money.

Mutual fund managers are required to follow a *prospectus*, which describes the key aspects of the fund. It's a formal written document that directs the fund managers and apprises the investors of the type of funds they purchase.

It's very important for perspective mutual fund owners to read the prospectus so they know what they are buying. Incredibly, many people don't bother to read the prospectus and actually have little idea where their money is invested.

Know What You Are Purchasing

Taking Stock

A **prospectus** is a document that describes in detail the key aspects of a mutual fund, its management and financial position, the operations of the fund, its investment objectives, and other key matters.

When you call a broker and tell him you want to buy 100 shares of stock in Dell Computers, you can be pretty darned sure that you're buying a stake in a computer company.

When you buy shares of Windsor II, however, a mutual fund within the scope of the Vanguard Group's mutual fund family, you'll need to do your homework to find out exactly where your money is going.

We have a client who invested in a mutual fund called the Alliance North American Government fund. She thought it was a safe investment, because her broker told her that it was. She was in her late 60s and had previously lost a great deal of money in another type of investment. She didn't want to take any more chances.

Unfortunately, shortly after she invested, the Alliance North American Government fund lost 30 percent of its value overnight. It seems that it was heavily invested in Mexican government bonds. The value of the peso dropped and the fund dropped along with it.

The client was hysterical and we greatly sympathized with her. She made a very serious mistake, however, by not reading the prospectus when she purchased the fund. She relied on the advice of her broker and never took the time to learn what the fund entailed.

She assumed, because of the name of the fund, that it was government insured. Wrong!

Make sure that you pay close attention to the advertising literature you get when you invest in a fund.

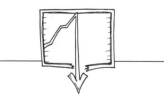

Heading for a Crash

Remember that a name is only a name. Mutual funds can be called anything. You have to read the material carefully to make sure that your investment is what you think it is. If you don't, you could be putting your money into something that isn't stable.

Cashing In

Seventy-nine percent of total mutual-fund assets were in stock funds at the beginning of 2000, compared to only 50 percent 10 years ago. That's despite the fact that only one stock fund has outperformed the S&P 500 Index for the past nine years. Investors are changing how they invest their funds.

The situation has improved, but there's still some shamelessly misleading information going around out there. Okay, enough of these dire warnings. Let's have a look at the different types of mutual funds.

Different Types of Mutual Funds

Not all mutual funds are created equal. Mutual fund companies offer different types of funds for different types of investors. As with stocks and bonds, some types involve more risk than others. The most common types of mutual funds are …

➤ Stock funds

➤ Bond funds

➤ Money market funds

Stock funds—duh—are those that invest in stocks. There are different kinds of stock funds. Some are higher risk than others.

Bond funds are those mutual funds that invest in bonds (see how easy this is?), and they're usually less risky than stock funds. Furthermore, some of them are tax-free. Bond funds contain large groups of bonds, which normally are planned so they'll mature at about the same time.

Money market funds are those in which the value of your original investment doesn't change. They're not much different from savings accounts, in fact, but they have some distinct advantages. Many money market funds offer check-writing privileges and pay a higher yield than savings accounts. They're the safest type of mutual fund. If you invest $1 per share, you'll get $1 per share back—plus interest.

Don't confuse money market funds with the money market accounts at your neighborhood bank.

The money market account at your local bank takes your funds and invests them in loans, certificates of deposit, and so forth. You get interest on the money you invested.

Mutual money market funds are set up by mutual fund companies and aren't backed by any institution. They're usually put into short-term investments.

Other types of mutual funds include:

➤ **Hybrid funds.** As the name implies, these are funds that invest in a mixture of securities—mostly stocks and bonds.

➤ **Global and international funds.** These are funds that invest money internationally. Global funds can include companies within the United States, but international funds can't.

➤ **Index funds.** These funds are invested in the same stocks that make up a particular index and in the same ratio; for instance, Vanguard's Index 500 fund has the same makeup of stock as the S&P 500 composite.

Take This to the Bank

There are innumerable index funds available to investors. You can invest in the Russell 5000 Index, the NASDAQ Index, the EAFE Index, and so forth.

➤ **Sector funds.** These funds invest in only one type of investment, such as a health care fund, or a telecommunication fund. Using sector funds is one of the riskier methods of investing in a mutual fund, since the funds aren't diversified. They are invested in only one industry.

➤ **Balanced funds.** These are funds in which similar portions of common stocks and bonds are held together. They focus more on income than growth and have a lower risk factor than other common stock funds.

➤ **Tax-managed funds.** These funds are designed to minimize capital gains for the investor. The fund manager sells losses and gains to offset each other within the fund to minimize the tax impact of the fund on the investor.

Hopefully, this gives you an idea of some of the types of mutual funds that are out there. Check the additional resources listing in Appendix B, "Resources," to find some sources from which you can learn more about mutual funds.

Choosing a Load or No-Load Fund

Now that you've got an idea of some of the different kinds of mutual funds, we're going to throw in another concept or two.

Mutual funds can be either load funds or no-load funds, which means you either pay a sales commission when you buy the fund or you don't. Let's have a look at which one is which.

No-Load Funds

No-load mutual funds are those that you can buy without paying a sales commission to a broker, financial adviser, or whoever you might buy the fund from. No-load funds usually are offered directly through the mutual fund company.

Heading for a Crash

Be sure you know what fees will be charged before you agree to buy a mutual fund. Some fees may be no-load, but you could be charged for marketing and promotional costs, for reinvesting your dividends, and other hidden costs. You could end up paying more than you want to if you don't check it out carefully.

You save money with no-load funds because there are no commissioned salespeople or financial advisers working on an hourly basis. For that reason, no-load funds have been gaining in popularity. Just over 50 percent of total mutual funds assets were invested in no-load funds at the start of 2000, as compared to just 33 percent 10 years ago.

Companies that offer no-load funds have toll-free phone numbers that you can call for recommendations of what funds to buy. A customer service representative will answer questions and provide information.

If you want to buy shares of a no-load mutual fund, you send your money directly to the mutual fund company. An account will be set up in your name and your money deposited into a fund.

A word to the wise: Be careful when you buy from one of these mutual fund companies. Some of them sell load funds (for which you pay a sales commission) as well as no-load funds. It's your responsibility to know if the fund you're ready to invest in has a load or not.

Mutual funds, even no-loads, can have some pesky fees associated with them. A new phenomenon is something called "redemption fees." Several fund companies are setting up redemption fees, which are charged if an investor sells the funds within a certain time period. An example of this is Vanguard's gold and precious metal fund. This fund has a 1 percent redemption fee if the shares are sold within one year of purchase. Vanguard's health care fund has a five-year redemption period.

The redemption fee isn't paid to Vanguard; it's paid to the fund itself to reward shareholders that stay in it for the long term. The redemption fee is to prevent people from investing in the fund for only a short-term basis. Fund managers want long-term investors.

Load Funds

If no-load funds are those on which you pay no sales commission, it makes sense that load funds are those that come with a fee for the commission. The commission goes to the person who sells you the fund, whether it's a broker, financial adviser, or whoever.

If you buy a fund that has a load, it's your job as an investor to find out how much the fee is and how you pay it.

Different Kinds of Load Funds

Just when you think you've gotten the hang of the difference between no-load and load mutual funds, we're going to go and take it a step further by explaining the different kinds of load funds.

It's important to understand that the scope of investment choices is always changing. The investment community comes up with new investments as quickly as it can dream them up. Most are beyond the scope of this book.

These different kinds of load funds, however, are a result of the investment community's attempts to make load-funds painless for investors, while still generating the money needed to pay investment advisers fees for services rendered. In other words, investors are made to believe they're getting something (service) for nothing.

Cashing In

We believe that all people should be compensated for their work. It's a problem, however, when fees are hidden and investors don't even know they're paying them—much less know how much their advisers are getting paid to make investments for them.

Many advisers receive a percentage of the value of the investment they've sold from the mutual fund company. If you're buying from a broker or financial adviser, make sure you know how much he's being compensated. This would include both the commission that you're paying and the money he might be getting from the investment company.

If the broker or adviser is evasive about what he's making, find somebody else to help you.

Many investors are unaware of the fees associated with mutual funds. You might be paying an annual management fee for being in the fund, or a sales charge when you purchase the fund.

Having said all that, let's explore the different kinds of load funds.

Front-End Load Funds

These are mutual funds in which the fees are paid up front. Investors can pretty much see what fees are involved when they buy the funds, and the costs will be included on their statements.

Cashing In

If you buy a loaded fund, make sure your investment is within a Family of Funds. A Family of Funds is a group of mutual funds that permit an investor to trade within the group, without incurring another sales charge. If you buy a front-end load in the Merrill Lynch gold fund, for instance, keep it a short time, then reinvest in a Merrill Lynch international fund, you won't be assessed a second sales charge.

If you invest in a $10,000 mutual fund with a 5 percent front-end load, for instance, you'll really only be investing $9,500. The other $500 is the sales charge (the load), that will be going to the investment adviser and his company.

Since the fee is paid up front in a front-end load, you're free to move your money out of the fund at any time. There are no time parameters with a front-end load fund.

Deferred Sales Charge Funds

With this type of fund, the load can be postponed, or deferred. The sales charges usually begin at a high rate, then gradually decline over a period of years until they reach zero.

A 5 percent deferred sales charge on a $10,000 investment works this way. The broker or financial adviser gets $500 on the sale. You, as the investor, don't pay the charge, unless you withdraw the investment within the first year. During the second year that you hold the investment, the deferral drops to 4 percent, which you don't pay unless you withdraw the funds. During the third year, the charge drops to 3 percent, only to be paid if you withdraw the funds during that year, and so forth.

If you're willing to keep your money in the fund for six years, you don't have to pay the sales charge.

This method can be a painless way to invest. Remember, though, if you need the money within the specified deferral period, you'll need to pay the fee.

Again, the only way we recommend that you buy a deferred sales charge fund is if you buy one within a Family of Funds.

Take This to the Bank

Mutual funds are listed as A and B shares, depending on how you've chosen to purchase the fund. Class A shares are the front-end load funds. B shares are the deferral sales charge funds.

Six years is too long to risk investing in a deferred sales charge for just one fund. If you can move from fund to fund within a Family of Funds, however, the deferral option might make sense.

Back-End Load Funds

A back-end fund means that you pay a fee when you sell the fund. You may be charged a back-end fee, for example, if you purchase and then sell a fund within too short a time period. Back-end load funds used to be more common than they are today.

One thing to know about mutual funds is that the sales charges are not assessed on the dividends and capital gains invested within a fund. New deposits will be assessed on the sales charge. All reinvested funds, however, are not assessed that charge.

Fund loads and fees should always be reviewed by the salesperson and stated in the prospectus sent from the company.

Open-End Mutual Funds

Open-end mutual funds are big—really big. These are the really huge funds that can issue an unlimited number of shares to investors.

This allows the funds to continue to grow as long as investors are willing to keep putting their money into them. These funds start out with an amount of invested money. As more and more people invest, their value keeps growing.

Fidelity Magellan, one of the largest funds in America, is now worth $1,060,000,000. It has performed well enough over the years to keep investors plowing their money into the fund, and to keep the fund growing.

Some fund managers limit the size of their funds, closing them down for a period of time when they get too large. Windsor, of the Vanguard Fund, decided several years ago to close to all new investors.

Cashing In

When an investor buys and sells shares of an open-end mutual fund, the transactions are always conducted with the mutual fund company, not with another investor.

Taking Stock

Net asset value is the value at which you purchase a mutual fund. It's calculated by taking the total of all securities in a mutual fund, less any liabilities, divided by the number of shares outstanding.

Closed-End Mutual Funds

While the term "mutual fund" is supposed to be used only in reference to open-end funds, it is regularly used to specify closed-end funds, as well. Closed-end funds operate with a fixed number of shares outstanding and don't regularly issue new shares of stock. The number of shares available to investors are limited in closed-end funds. The shares are sold like stocks and bonds.

While open-end fund shares are bought and sold through the mutual fund company, closed-end funds are sold on the stock market. Shares of these mutual funds are listed for sale in *The Wall Street Journal*, right there with other common stocks. A well-known closed-end fund is the Japan Fund.

The share prices of closed-end funds are determined not only by their net asset value, but also by general supply and demand in the stock market. Closed-end funds sometimes trade for less than their *net asset value*, known as a discounted share.

If the shares sell for more than the net asset value of the fund, those shares are said to be sold at a premium.

How Mutual Funds Can Be Beneficial to Investment Clubs

We know, we know. You joined an investment club because you wanted to learn about investing in the stock market. You want to know why you should buy Nortel stock rather than Lucent, and what the heck somebody means when she starts talking about a stock split.

You might be wondering about now just why we've spent all this time telling you about mutual funds. It's because mutual funds can be a proper and beneficial investment for your club.

International Exposure

Mutual funds are a great way to invest in international funds, for instance, which give your portfolio some desirable international exposure.

International exposure provides diversification to your portfolio. The theory is that stocks may do well abroad even if we are having a downturn in the U.S. markets. Another reason is that the economies of many third-world countries are growing at a faster pace than our economy. They have so much catching up to do. That helps emerging market companies to grow faster than many well-developed companies in the U.S.

A problem is that it's difficult to acquire information about stocks from other countries. Reporting information isn't always available and the methods aren't always synonymous with the American system of accounting.

For those reasons, a mutual fund that includes international investments can be a great way to invest without taking as many risks as you would by investing in individual stocks.

Diversification

Another reason for your investment club to invest in a mutual fund is for diversification. We've talked about diversification in other parts of this book, but it comes up again in connection with mutual funds.

Let's say that your club has decided to invest in a biotechnology stock. Biotechnology stocks are stocks of companies that develop genetic engineering, enzyme reproduction, and so forth.

These stocks are very volatile, and investing in one of these companies is much riskier than investing in, say, Coca-Cola.

Your club, however, feels that there's great opportunity in this area. You could buy stock from one or two companies in this field and risk having the value of your stock take a nose dive. Worse still, you could risk having the companies whose stock you bought go bankrupt (yikes!).

Or, you could buy a biotech mutual fund. That would mean that your money is invested in a lot of biotech companies, not just one or two. It's spread out, giving you the security of knowing that if one or two companies fail, you'll lose only a portion of your money—not the whole amount.

As we discussed earlier, a fund that invests in only one sector of the market is called a sector fund. A sector fund portfolio manager and fund analysts spend their time looking only at companies within that sector—in this case, the biotech sector. You'll benefit from the attention they give to their particular sector.

Finding and Buying the Funds You Want to Be In

If all this talk about mutual funds has you thinking that maybe your club should be buying some, you might be wondering how exactly you go about doing so.

Cashing In

It takes a while to achieve diversity in a portfolio when you're buying individual stocks. Buying mutual funds gives you instant diversity.

Cashing In

Morningstar provides an incredible amount of information on one small report—everything from the fees associated with a mutual fund to what percentages of the fund are invested in which sectors of the market. It may tell you, for instance, that 46.1 percent of the fund is invested in technology stocks, 13.9 percent in health stocks, 9.4 percent in services, 8.3 percent in consumer durables, 6.9 percent in retail, 5.4 percent in energy, and so forth. Knowing this not only gives you a better understanding of your mutual fund, but makes it more interesting to follow the market because you know where your money's invested.

How do you find and buy the funds that you want to be in?

We already discussed the importance of reading the prospectus, an important step in picking a mutual fund. Take it back a step further, however, and you might ask how the heck you even know which fund's prospectus you want to read. Where do you start?

Well, let's say that your club is interested in investing in an international fund. You've read (a page or two back) that international exposure is desirable and you think it would be good for your portfolio.

To find out more about international funds, you can head for your local library, or jump on line to access the Morningstar reports.

Morningstar, Inc., is a Chicago company that publishes Morningstar Mutual Funds, a twice-monthly newsletter that rates mutual funds. Morningstar can be found online at www.morningstar.com. There are other services that do the same thing, but the industry preference seems to be Morningstar.

Morningstar starts by breaking funds into two categories: domestic equity and international equity. The domestic equity funds are then broken down into at least 12 subgroups.

The international funds are broken down into nine subgroups. Of the nine, only three are nonsector funds. If you decide you want a nonsector fund, then you've narrowed your choices to a more manageable field.

Your next step would be to review the analysis sections report to see if one of these three categories suits your club more than another. Maybe you're only interested in a global fund, as opposed to a foreign fund, because you want to include U.S. investment.

Once you've narrowed it down further by deciding on issues such as global versus international, your next step is to look at the star ratings of funds within the fund group you're interested in.

Morningstar uses stars to rate fund performance against similar competitors, taking into account the risks associated with each fund.

The star rating is a starting point, not a conclusion. The star rating is a great way to identify funds that have provided the best balance of risk and return within their asset classes—this balance may continue in the future.

Stars are not buy-and-sell recommendations, or market-timing devices, or any other sort of prediction. An investor should also consider the style of the portfolio manager, the portfolio holdings, the fund objective, fund expenses, risk, and so forth.

As you can see from the sample sheet on Brandywine, the report tells you about the top holdings, how the fund has performed, and which category the fund is evaluated; information about the portfolio manager, an analysis of the fund, a rating of the category, and, very important, the fees associated with the fund.

Brandywine — Morningstar Mutual Funds sample report. Ticker BRWIX, Load None, NAV $28.61, Yield 0.0%, Assets $4489.7 mil, Objective Growth.

© 1996 Morningstar, Inc. All rights reserved. 225 W. Wacker Dr., Chicago, IL 60606, 312-696-6000. Although data are gathered from reliable sources, Morningstar cannot guarantee completeness and accuracy.

MORNINGSTAR Mutual Funds   183

197

If you're interested in buying a mutual fund, call the fund's 1-800 number, or go on-line and get a prospectus. The prospectus will tell you how much the fund costs, the fees associated with it, and so forth.

Once you've read the prospectus and decided to buy, call your broker or the fund directly, and state the amount you want to invest. At the end of the day, the fund has a net asset value. That's the price at which you'll buy shares of the fund.

Some Mutual Funds to Consider

Following is a list of large family of funds that have performed well over the years. Remember that this is a guideline, but you'll still need to do your homework and check them out. There are lots of other good funds besides these, and not all the funds within these fund families are great funds.

➤ **Baron Funds.** Contact at 1-800-992-2766, or on the Web at www.baronfunds.com.

➤ **Brandywine Funds.** Contact at 1-800-656-3017, or on the Web at www.brandywinefunds.com.

➤ **The Kaufmann Funds.** Contact at 1-800-261-0555, or on the Web at www.kaufmann.com.

➤ **Oakmark Funds.** Contact at 1-800-625-6275, or on the Web at www.oakmark.com.

➤ **The Vanguard Group.** Contact at 1-800-871-3879, or on the Web at www.vanguard.com.

➤ **Fidelity Investments.** Contact at 1-800-544-6666, or on the Web at www.fidelity.com.

➤ **T. Rowe Price.** Contact at 1-800-225-5132, or on the Web at www.troweprice.com.

➤ **Nicholas Funds.** Contact at 1-800-227-5987, or on the Web at www.nicholasfunds.com.

➤ **Lindner Funds.** Contact at 1-800-995-7777, or on the Web at www.linderfunds.com.

You can ask your broker about other funds, or check Morningstar for recommendations.

The Least You Need to Know

➤ Mutual funds are investments in which your money is pooled with that of many other people.

➤ The three most common types of mutual funds are stock funds, bond funds, and money market funds.

➤ Load funds are those on which you pay a sales commission, and no-load funds are those on which you don't pay a commission.

➤ It's important to watch for hidden fees when buying mutual funds.

➤ Mutual funds can give your club international exposure and help to diversify its portfolio.

➤ Morningstar reports can help you choose mutual funds that are right for your club.

Chapter 16

Targeting Companies from Which to Buy Stock

In This Chapter

➤ Identifying the companies in which you want to invest

➤ Diversification is the only way to go

➤ Looking for industries and companies that are bound to grow

➤ Gathering information about the companies you target

➤ Knowing how to use annual reports to screen and evaluate companies

Investing is a very interesting process. It's exciting when your investments keep increasing in value—when you pick a home run. By home run, we mean a stock doubling or tripling in value overnight due to a buyout, merger, or other unforeseen event.

Although the news media and the man on the street seem to feel that investing is as easy as washing one's car, it takes hard work, knowledge acquired through research, a little guesswork, and a little of lady luck.

Peter Lynch, the famous Fidelity Magellan portfolio manager, in his book *One Up On Wall Street: How to Use What You Already Know to Make Money In the Market* explains how he purchases equities. Mr. Lynch uses ideas acquired by noticing that his daughter and her friends bought their clothes at Gap, and that his wife purchased L'eggs nylons. These facts lead him to look into the manufacturers of these items. He did the research, liked what he saw, and subsequently purchased the shares—and made a nice profit.

The first place to look at a company is to purchase something you know. Should it be Exxon Mobil, IBM, Ford Motor Corp., or Cisco? Ask members of your investment club to come to your next meeting with ideas and the search begins.

The S&P 500 Index has had a 28.46 percent annualized rate of return for the past five years. Think what that means. If you had invested $10,000 in 1994, today it would be worth $34,981.

You make this money by investing. You didn't have to get up and be at work on time, you didn't have to work when you or your children were ill, you didn't have to deal with office politics or pleasing other people. You just sat back and watched your money make money.

Take This to the Bank

In January 2000, the Vanguard 500 Index Fund passed the Fidelity Magellan Fund as the largest mutual fund in the world.

What Kind of Companies Should You Look For?

The flippant answer would be to invest in whatever stock will go up in value and stay up as soon as you buy it. Okay, but what kind of company is that? In the last chapter, we talked about the various types of stocks. The question that all investors need to decide is in which direction they want to go. It all depends on risk.

Although there are innumerable IPOs (initial public offerings) coming to market almost daily, it seems important that your investment club invest in companies that are stable, that have a good earnings history. The stock prices may not increase three-fold over night, but they will not drop as quickly either.

Your club is in for the long term, and because of the investment club format, decisions are not easily rendered during the year. Changes can only be made monthly. Your club meets once a month. Because of that, decisions to buy and sell can only be made once a month. The stocks the club invests in should be ones that have an earnings history, companies that are followed by Value Line. The companies in which your club invests should be familiar to club members, or at least the products the company makes should be. Companies that need instantaneous decisions to sell shouldn't be part of the club's portfolio.

The monthly format is a hindrance because of the limitation to purchase risky stocks. Investment clubs can't purchase stocks that are so volatile, or speculative, because decisions to sell must be made by committee. This is also helpful. If you really want the "high fliers," invest in them on your own.

Several investment clubs with which we're familiar, knowing the volatility of the stock market, have attempted to have a telephone tree to make decisions between the monthly meetings. It was found to rarely work, and if it did, only because one or two of the members were persistent enough to make certain that enough members had a vote. As discussed before, everyday life gets in the way of investment decisions and makes it difficult to get club members to decide about a stock between meetings.

Emergency meetings can be a useful means of getting between-meeting decisions about stock sales. These should only be for emergency situations, however, or members will get tired of the extra commitment required for the club.

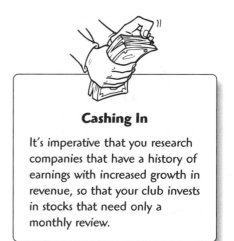

Cashing In

It's imperative that you research companies that have a history of earnings with increased growth in revenue, so that your club invests in stocks that need only a monthly review.

Understand the Company's Product or Service

It's interesting when investors talk about broadband companies, chip manufacturers, computer storage, and networking. Maybe you know what all that means, but probably most of your fellow club members do not. The first item of business when discussing stocks is for the members of the club to understand the products or services produced by the companies you're considering investing in. Are they good for investment?

Although increased profits may be found in more risky stocks, the investment club portfolio should be invested in stocks that have reasonable price-to-earnings ratios. Try to stick mostly with companies that manufacture products your club understands—that they can feel, touch, even smell.

Where Do You Start?

Okay, you must pick a few companies to research, but where do you turn to find them? The S&P 500 Index is comprised of the 500 largest companies in the U.S. The composite is "weighted" with a portion of the total stocks being technology stocks, oil stocks, financial services stocks, and so on.

Taking Stock

Beta (B) is a mathematical measurement of the risk on a portfolio or a given stock compared with rates of return on the market as whole. A beta of less than one is less volatile than the general market. A beta above one is more volatile than the market.

Before you begin to look into companies to research, the first decision your club will have to make is in which direction it wants to go with its investments. Should you look toward large companies like Coca-Cola, Exxon Mobil, and General Electric—or toward growth stocks like Amgen, Oracle, or Computer Associates?

There's an investment tool used by analysts called *beta (B)*. This mathematical measurement tells the investor how volatile a stock is compared to the market. A stock with a beta of one means the stock goes up and down with the market. A beta of less than one means the stock is less volatile than the market. Then, of course, a stock with a beta greater than one means that stock is more volatile.

So, unless you are in an investment club that is designed to invest in growth stocks, your club's first investments should be in companies that are known to members, and that have a reasonable beta and a good growth record. Your club, as it grows and gathers experience, can move toward other investments down the road.

Don't Forget to Diversify

Besides picking good stocks, it is of the utmost importance for an investor to diversify. Diversification is as important a concept as stock analysis and is imperative for any investor. Intel was up 70 percent in 1999, but the stock has been known to drop almost as quickly.

Ask somebody who has stock in Hershey Foods. The value of Hersheystock dropped almost 50 percent in less than m18 months. If you had your entire portfolio in Hershey Foods stock, you'd have seen the value of your portfolio drop by 50 percent—yikes! Investors love their portfolios when the stocks they own go up in value, but wish they belonged to somebody else after a big drop in the market. Diversification helps somewhat control this volatility.

Hershey Foods dropped in price for several reasons. The first reason is that the stock price dropped along with many of the large cap stocks, like Coke, McDonald's, GE, and so on in late 1998. The large cap stock had skyrocketed and the sector seemed to drop in value or at least stagnate as investors went after the "new economy" (Internet) stocks.

Then, in 1999, Hershey announced they were having distribution problems due to computer problems. A glitch with a computer conversion created a debacle. In today's high-priced stock market, any news can create a significant price adjustment.

Diversification is difficult when your club is new. You start with one stock, then you purchase another, and then a third. Although it's tempting for clubs to keep investing in the first stock, particularly when the first stock is a winner, it's important to keep increasing the number of stocks for diversification.

Everyone knows that investing money is never risk-free. The idea is for you to find the investments that offer the best chance for a good return, with the least amount of risk.

The risk of your stock going up and down in value because the entire stock market goes up and down is called systematic risk. Chances are, if the stock market drops by 10 percent, your stock will drop in value. The same is true if the market increases in value. It may not be the same percentage up or down, but the risk associated with a stock following the market is something to be considered when you buy stock.

Unsystematic risk is an individual investment's risk that can be eliminated through diversification. What that means is that you can plan your investments to protect against one incident, for example an oil embargo, bankruptcy of a firm, and so on, but you can't protect a portfolio of stocks against a drop in the entire market. Protecting against one company's problems is called protecting against unsystematic risk, while diversifying a portfolio against a plummet in the market (like the one that occurred on October 17, 1987) is called diversifying against systematic risk.

Systematic risk can be controlled by investing in more than just stocks. Owning a variety of different types of investments is called diversification. Investing in real estate (your home), bonds, and certificates of deposit help against systematic risk. Also, investing in a variety of stock types, for example utility stocks, value stocks, growth stocks, cyclical stocks, and so on, help diversify against systematic risk.

Know the Risks

We talked earlier about the categories of stocks. But, what risks are involved when purchasing a stock and how do these risks affect your club's portfolio and the choices you make?

That question takes some know-how to answer. First of all, there are many kinds of investment risks. Some of the different types are ...

➤ **Business risk.** Risk from the way in which the business that issued the security is managed. Can a new CEO turn a floundering company around?

➤ **Financial risk.** Risk associated with the finances of the company. Does the company have too much debt—are they expanding too quickly?

➤ **Purchasing power risk.** The effect that inflation might have on the value of your holding. This is a risk found when investing in fixed investments. Will the income produced by your investment be reinvested in a return as good as the initial investment? This risk is usually associated with bonds and similar investments.

➤ **Interest rate risk.** The changes in interest rates may affect your investment. This risk is found in the stock of companies and in bonds that are affected by increasing interest rates. Examples are bank stocks, utility companies, and insurance companies.

➤ **Market risk.** The tendency for stock to move with the market. This is measured by the beta factor.

➤ **Default risk.** The chance that the company you've invested in will be unable to service the debt.

➤ **Foreign currency risk.** The risk that a change in the relationship between the value of the U.S. dollar and the value of the currency of the country in which your investment is held will affect your holding. This is an important consideration for any foreign investment.

There is an equity investment known as an *ADR* (*American Depository Receipt*). An example of an ADR is the drug company, Glaxo Welcome. The funds are held in U.S. dollars, so the currency risk is less applicable than if you are buying stock directly in a foreign company.

Reading about all those possibilities for risk can be scary, but it's important for you to understand as much about the risks as possible. Now, exactly how great are these risks, and where are they the most likely to occur?

Taking Stock

ADRs (American Depository Receipts) are trust receipts for shares of a foreign company purchased and held by a foreign branch of the bank. The ADRS are legal claims against the equity interest that the bank holds. ADRs are an excellent alternative to direct investing in foreign companies.

The stock market is subject to some pretty significant fluctuations, and many possibilities for risk. If you can put your money in and ride it out for the long haul, you'll probably do okay. But if you have a limited period in which to leave your money in stocks, you risk having to take it out at a time when the market is down. If that happens, you'll lose money. Investments in real estate carry similar risks. The real estate market can be very rewarding—or it can drop dramatically.

On the other hand, if you invest in something really safe, you're almost sure to get a lower return. It's just one of those things. If it's feasible for you to have your money invested for a long time, then stocks are probably a better investment than low-risk, low-yield bonds. Take a look at the statistics below. They'll show the chances of the returns on stocks beating the returns on bonds at different lengths of time after the initial investment.

Diversification can't stop market risk. If the entire stock market drops, chances are your stocks will drop. However, diversification helps alleviate some of the other risks stated above: business risk, interest rate risk, and industry risk.

Limit Your Exposure

Another form of diversification is limiting your exposure to one company's stock. Most investment experts don't invest in any one stock for more than 10 percent of a portfolio. Some money managers even go as low as 7 percent as a maximum in any one stock, but that's usually when an investor has a large number of investments.

Heading for a Crash

Owning 20 shares of stock in companies that are in the same sector of the market is not diversifying a portfolio. An investor must diversify a portfolio by purchasing a variety of stocks in different types of companies.

For example, your club purchased a stock, let's say Motorola, in 1998, at $60 a share. It totaled 5 percent of the club's portfolio. Motorola has skyrocketed in price. It is now $145 per share, or 14 percent of the portfolio. Although it's difficult to sell because you like the company and feel the stock has more growth potential, it's important to limit the portfolio's downside potential by selling enough shares to bring the total to less than 10 percent.

We know it's difficult to keep stock at less than 10 percent when you are just beginning to invest, but this should be your club's goal as you grow.

But another diversification situation that we see often is when an investor has too much invested in one sector. It doesn't help to have all your stocks invested in computer chip companies, or all telecommunication companies or all Internet companies. Having 20 stocks of the same type of investment is not diversification.

Targeting Growth Industries and the Companies in Them

Twenty-nine percent of the composite of S&P 500 Index is technology stocks. Growth companies are where the action is. Buying the next Microsoft or Cisco takes research, but the rewards can be phenomenal.

Financial information provided on television and the radio gives information about new growth areas of the economy. One analyst recently stated that the Internet and telecommunications technology are the second industrial revolution.

A financial magazine that an investment club provided to their membership displayed a bar graph showing the United States increase in Internet access over the last 10 years. The growth was quite interesting. Year by year, the number of new accesses increased. An even more impressive comparison was the worldwide Internet access increase worldwide. The increase was geometric.

This new technology won't go away. Cell phones are used by about 25 percent of the U.S. population. The number is 70 percent in Sweden. I've just changed cell phones for the third time in seven years, updating technology for a lower price.

How to Find Them

Be alert to the new products that your children and their friends are buying and pay close attention to what you buy. Understand and ask questions about the technology within the product, so you know how to discuss the product with your club.

A family member received a DVD player for Christmas. Several family members spent time patiently explaining the technology to me and how it will change televisions in the future. Then, I researched the companies that provide this technology and made my next equity purchase.

Your club should decide on a sector in which it wants to invest, and then start researching to find the best companies within that sector. If you decide you want to invest in the retail sector, for instance, you've got to pinpoint retail companies in which you're interested. What will it be? Gap? Home Depot? Starbucks?

Once you've identified some companies, it's important to check out their competition. Maybe the companies you've identified aren't the best ones within the sector. You can learn about the competition by asking Investor Relations or by reading Value Line's analysis. You should also be able to find financial information about the competitors of your target companies on the Internet, particularly for technology companies. Ask your area appliance, stereo, or video technology dealers about the different products on the market. Which DVD player works the best? Who has the best price? Who provides the technology for the companies that manufacture the DVD players?

If you are researching cell phone companies, the questions to ask may be similar. What cell phones do customers purchase most frequently? What are their complaints? Which ones come in for service the most? This will give you an idea of what people are buying, and what consumers like and dislike.

Talk, ask, learn. Read online about news of the latest inventions. If your neighbor raves about the experimental cardiac drug (which costs $3,000) that enables

Cashing In

There are many online sites with information about various companies. Obviously, you could go directly to the company's site. We like America Online's Personal Finance section. It has an investment research area that provides different types of reports about many companies. You can check out a company's balance sheet, SEC filings, past dividend records, 52-week highs and lows, and so forth. The AOL site also lets you know about stock splits and which stocks are most active on a given day. It's a great place to start.

his wife's 98 percent blocked artery to open up overnight to only 70 percent blockage, find out which pharmaceutical company produces the drug. Read the information on their Web site. Although information might be available on the company's Web site or in the financial news, look also on the World Wide Web for other sources of information about the drug, device, or product you're interested in finding.

Warner Lambert is one company that has performed outstandingly for one area investment club. The stock was discovered when a member's husband's doctor prescribed Lipicor for his cholesterol years ago. The club membership got online and found that Lipicor was manufactured by Warner Lambert. From there, the club performed a financial analysis, decided to buy, and has had a very good return.

Growth Industries for 2000 and Beyond

You hear a lot about growth industries when you start exploring the stock market and the companies in which you may invest. Nearly everybody will tell you that growth industries are where you want to be.

But what exactly are growth industries, and how do you find them?

Growth industries are simply industries that are expected to expand significantly. Some are real obvious, like the electronics and computer industries. Some are less obvious, like the captive deer industry.

Yep. You read it properly. The captive deer industry. Just in case you haven't heard about it, it's the industry of raising deer that are eventually slaughtered and sold to fancy restaurants.

Take This to the Bank

Once an industry is identified as a growth industry, financial communities get behind them and invest in them heavily. This just about ensures that they'll continue to be growth industries in the coming years.

You can learn about growth industries from reading market research reports, trade journals, business newspapers and magazines, and from many Internet sites. You also can get an idea of growth industries from looking in the Yellow Pages, or taking a walk around your town or through the local mall.

If five new coffee shops have opened downtown or in the mall during the past year, it might correctly occur to you that coffee is a growth industry.

After you check out the shops, head over to a department store like Macy's, and have a look in the housewares section. You'll notice a vastly expanded line of cappuccino makers, espresso machines, fancy European coffee makers, bean grinders, and so forth. After you've seen all that, take a walk over the gourmet food section of the store and check out all the different coffee blends and accessories available. Everything from your favorite Kenyan blend to those chocolate-dipped stirring sticks and spoons.

Americans are definitely having a love affair with coffee.

If you want to be a bit more scientific about identifying growth industries (although personal observation is a great way to go), the U.S. Bureau of Labor and Statistics has predicted the industries slated for the most growth between 1996 and 2006.

The listing of the growth industries, along with the percentages that they're expected to grow within those years, is shown in the following paragraphs.

The Ten Fastest-Growing Industries Between 1996 and 2006 According to the U.S. Bureau of Labor and Statistics.

Computer and data processing services	109
Home healthcare services	90
Automotive services, except repair	80
Water supply and sanitary services	66
Management and public relations	60
Residential care	59
Freight transport arrangement	56
Personnel supply services	53
Individual social services	50
Offices of physicians	46

Notice that all of these predicted growth industries are in the service-producing sector. The industries expected to lose the most jobs during the same time period, on the other hand, include farming, private households, clothing stores, and the federal government.

Growth companies are good investments, and you should make sure to include some of them in your portfolio.

Before you get carried away, however, and throw all your money into Starbucks or Microsoft stock, remember that, while they're often great investments, growth industries aren't the only ones you should consider. A company doesn't have to be in a growth industry in order to be a solid investment (remember the blue chips).

Checking Out the Stocks You Targeted

Say your club has decided to invest the next several months' dues into one of a group of stocks they've been *targeting*.

It's the feeling of your investment club that drug companies would be good investments. One member mentioned that his parents' monthly pharmaceutical bills are in excess of $500, and other members have similar stories to share. Your club wants to invest in a drug company. One or several members get together and do an analysis of several drug companies. The analysis is comprised of price-to-earnings ratios, price-to-book value of the stock, sales and revenue increases, and cost of goods. All of this information will be discussed in Chapter 17, "Buying Stock—the Cornerstone of an Investment Club." The analysis presents three possibilities, all of them biggies: Eli Lily, Merck, and Pfizer.

Another area your club may find interesting is the financial service industry—specifically banks. With the repealing of the Glass-Steagell Act prohibiting banks from selling stocks, banks can now offer brokerage services, broker insurance, and provide all aspects of financial services. This should make banks very attractive for mergers. Knowing that bank stocks have been in a downward spiral for a while, they seem like a bargain. But which one is best? That is the question.

You can get important information about a company and its stock by calling the company's investors' relations office and requesting an annual report. Also ask for the quarterly report that has come out since the annual report was published. The next step is to get online and look for any news you can find about the company you're investigating. You may see information about stock splits, or read that the earnings of

Cashing In

The process of **targeting** is discovering a sector of stock you think might be a good investment, then researching that type of stock until you find the companies best for your investment club.

Taking Stock

Charting, as the name implies, is an analysis system that uses charts to show the ups and downs of everything from the price per share of individual stocks to the overall Dow Jones Industrial Average. Charting can be very helpful when trying to decide in which companies to invest.

a particular company didn't, or aren't expected to, reach expectation. This is information that affects a company's reputation and the value of its stock. And, it can help your club decide whether or not to invest. While online (or using Value Line's hard copy information from the library), look at performance of the stock over the 1-, 3-, and 10-year periods (if available).

Most of the financial online services can give you a graph or chart of the performance of the stock over a period of years. Although using charting analysis is not how an investment club works, it is still good to know (see) if the stock has recently skyrocketed or dropped or if there is a steady increase in value.

Charting is a technical analysis activity of plotting the behavior of everything from the DJIA to share price movements of individual stocks by means of charts.

An example of charting the high, low, and close.

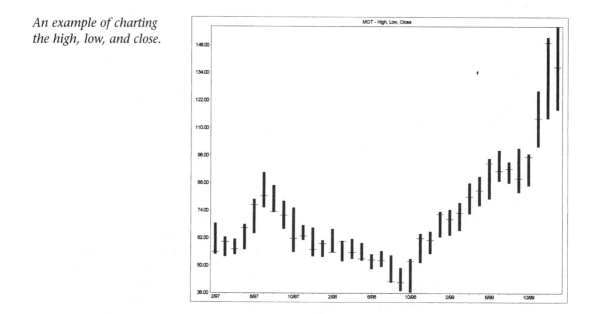

Using Annual Reports to Evaluate Companies

The annual report provides the financial statement for the company. This statement is comprised of four parts:

➤ **Balance sheet.** The part of the financial statement that shows the financial condition of a company on a particular date. It lists the assets of the company that equal the company's liabilities and stockholder's equity.

➤ **Income statement.** The portion of the financial statement that presents the revenues and expenses of a business for an accounting period.

➤ **Statement of change in stockholder's equity.** The financial statement that summarizes a firm's financing and investing activities for an accounting period and explains the change in financial position for one period to the next.

212

➤ **Flow of funds statement.** The financial statement that shows cash flow from operations. This has become increasingly important in recent years as an analytical tool to determine the financial health of a business enterprise.

By themselves, corporate financial statements are a very important source of information to the investor; when used with financial ratios and fundamental analysis, they become even more powerful.

What ratios are we talking about? The most significant contribution of financial ratios is that they enable an investor to assess the firm's past and present financial condition and operating results.

Now, before you close this book and decide this is too much for you to do, please know that this information is important, but not all these ratios are needed for every stock analysis. We'll review many ratios, and then tell you the major ones you need for financial analysis. From there, your club can decide which to use.

Understanding Liquidity

The liquidity, or cash flow, of a company shows the ability of the firm to meet its day-to-day operating expenses and satisfy its short-term obligations as they come due. It's a measure of how well the company can pay its bills.

Liquidity, along with the most common ratio, current ratio, goes hand-in-hand to indicate to potential investors how well the company will be able to meet its financial obligations. Current ratio, calculated with information found on the balance sheet, is calculated as follows:

Current Ratio = Current Assets ÷ Current Liabilities

A current ratio of one shows the company's assets are equal to the liabilities; a ratio of two shows that the assets are double the liabilities, and so on. Review this ratio as a comparison over the last five years. Is the ratio the same, increasing, or decreasing? Decreasing current ratio would be a warning sign for the investor.

Net working capital, also calculated with information found on the balance sheet, is an absolute measure of a company's liquidity, and is calculated as follows:

Net Working Capital = Current Assets – Current Liabilities

This figure is a more precise measure of liquidity because it measures actual funds held by the firm to pay expenses, not buildings, equipment, and assets that aren't easily available to pay bills. It's a measure of what the company can quickly turn into cash, if needed.

Another ratio often used to analyze a firm is the measure of activity ratio. This ratio, using the income statement and the balance sheet, compares the way the company is utilizing its assets by comparing company sales to various assets categories.

213

Accounts receivable turnover, inventory turnover, and total asset turnover are measures not commonly used by investors. Just know that the higher the turnover for any of these categories, the better for an investor. These ratios are calculated with figures from the income statement and the balance sheet. It's not hard, it's just a matter of knowing which figures are needed, and where to plug them in.

Understanding Leverage

Leverage measures different types of financing for firms, and indicates the amount of debt being used to support the resources and operations of the company. The amount of the indebtedness a company has, and the ability of the firm to service its debt should be concerns of an investor. Low-debt companies survive in bad times, while highly levered companies are less likely to survive a downturn in the market. Debt equity ratio is measured as follows:

Debt Equity Ratio = Long Term Debt ÷ Stockholders' Equity

The higher a firm is leveraged, the higher its risk of going bankrupt. Different firms have different ratios, but know the higher the ratio, the riskier the investment.

Understanding Profitability

Profitability is a relative measure of success. But how is it measured?

Net Profit Margin = Net Profit After Taxes ÷ Total Revenues

A firm's Gross Profit Margin measures profit generated after consideration of cost of products sold.

Gross Profit Margin = Gross Profit ÷ Net Sales

Gross profits as a percentage of sales is an important financial measurement for a potential investor to review. Because this ratio moves with costs, it reveals the type of control management has over the cost structure of the firm. A very important area to review is how management is controlling costs. If revenues are increasing, that's wonderful; however, if costs are out-stripping revenues, that's a detriment to the company.

Another measure of profitability is Return on Total Assets (ROTA), which looks at the amount of resources used by the firm to support operations. It reveals management effectiveness in generating profits from the assets it has available, and is perhaps the single most important measure of return. This is an important ratio when reviewing banks, but not regular companies. ROTA is calculated as follows:

ROTA = Net Profit After Taxes ÷ Total Assets

Return on Investment (ROI) or Return on Equity (ROE) measures the return to stockholders by relating profit to shareholders' equity.

ROI = Net Profit After Tax ÷ Stockholders' Equity

This ratio should be around 13, 14, or 15 percent.

Understanding Performance

Market or common ratios convert information about the company to a per-share basis, and are used to assess the performance of the company for stock evaluation purposes.

One common ratio is the P/E (price-to-earnings ratio), which determines how the market is pricing the company's common stock. It is calculated as follows:

P/E = Market Price of Common Stock ÷ Earnings per Share

Thirty-six times last year's earnings is the current P/E ratio for the S&P 500 Index; 28 times last year's earning is the current ratio for the entire market.

Another common ratio is the earnings per share (EPS), which measures the company's growth; it is calculated as follows:

EPS = (Net Profit After Taxes – Preferred Dividends) ÷ Number of Shares Outstanding

Finally, net book value is the difference between the original cost of property, the plant and equipment, and any accumulated depreciation to date. It tells you what you would receive if the firm were liquidated. Currently, the stock of Philip Morris is selling for less than its book value.

Book Value Per Share = Stockholders' Equity ÷ Number of Common Shares Outstanding

Although extremely useful as analytical tools, financial ratios also have serious limitations. They serve as screening devices to point to areas of potential strength or weakness and to indicate matters that need further investigation. But financial ratios do not provide answers in and of themselves, and they are not predictive. Financial ratios should be used along with heavy inputs of common sense.

Other Methods to Check Things Out

Word of mouth from employees, neighbors, local newspapers, and so on are great ways to learn of companies in which you may be interested in investing. These are not good reasons to go plunk your money down, but a good way to trigger research.

Although this isn't foolproof, many of the investment clubs in our area invest in companies they know about. One club member, watching Tyco's stock value drop in half, mentioned how his neighbor was working all the time. They couldn't keep up with orders.

Another club comprised of hospital personnel was able to research companies offering new drugs and state-of-the-art medical equipment. They knew which HMO companies were a threat to their hospital, and so on.

The Least You Need to Know

➤ When looking for companies in which to invest, target those with which you're familiar, have reasonable risk, and good growth records.

➤ It's tempting to put all your money into one company or one area when you're first starting to invest, but remember that diversification is one of the 10 commandments of buying stock.

➤ Look for growth industries such as computer and healthcare services, but don't overlook other good industries that are out there as well.

➤ Once you've targeted the companies you're interested in, check them out on the Internet, in trade journals, market reports, and so forth.

➤ Learning to read and understand annual reports can give you access to valuable information about the companies you're interested in.

➤ Understanding ratios also can help you better assess the health of a particular company.

Chapter 17

Buying Stock— the Cornerstone of an Investment Club

In This Chapter

➤ Recognizing what's good stock and what's bad stock

➤ Understanding how to use fundamental analysis and other methods to help you choose stock

➤ Putting your computer to work when choosing stock

➤ Socially responsible investing

➤ Knowing the mechanics of investing

➤ Keeping the whole club involved with buying stock

You may have looked at the title of this chapter and breathed a big sigh of relief. Finally, you think, we're getting to the fun stuff. Learning about investing is why you became a member of an investment club. Getting to know what stocks to buy is probably one of the biggest—if not the biggest—reasons that you decided to start a club in the first place.

There are more than 3,000 stocks listed on the New York Stock Exchange. There are thousands more on the American Stock Exchange and the NASDAQ. Where does your club begin?

People will give you all kinds of advice about buying stock. Your cousin is more than happy to tell you all about how he made a killing last year on a hot technology stock. He's sure that you ought to rush right out and buy some of it, too.

And then there's that tip that your boss gave you at your office holiday party. He said he'd heard that a certain company was coming out with a new product that was going to send its stock through the roof. Anybody who bought now, he said, would stand to gain big.

Even your mother is telling you about the dividend she just received on some stock she owns. Maybe, she says, you ought to consider buying some of the same.

Yep. You'll get all kinds of advice, if you ask for it. Looking for hot tips and advice from well-meaning relatives, however, is not the way to choose stocks.

The way to choose stocks—you knew this was coming, didn't you—is to carefully study and evaluate a lot of different companies and their stock. You consider how your interests compare with the interests of the company, the cost of the stock, the health of the company, and many other factors.

When it's all said and done, you'll have enough information to make informed and knowledgeable choices.

Knowing What To Buy—and What Not To Buy

A dynamic that seems to be unique to investment clubs is the tendency for clubs to hang on to their investments long-term. The average length of time an investment club holds a stock is seven and a half years. That's a big difference from the day-trader mentality.

Part of the reason that clubs hang on to their stocks has to do with the process they go through to get them in the first place. There's a lot of homework involved with buying stock, and members usually are pretty committed to what they decide to buy.

Another reason for the long hold has to do with the rules clubs establish for selling stocks. It's not always easy to sell a stock when 50—and maybe 75—percent of your members have to agree to it.

Take This to the Bank

The National Association of Investors Corp. encourages its members to look for companies that have "a reasonable prospect of being worth substantially more in five years." Notice that it doesn't say tomorrow, or next week, but in five years. This guideline encourages clubs to buy stock and hold it while it has a chance to increase in value over time.

Knowing that whatever stocks your club decides to buy will probably be held for a long time, you certainly should choose ones from good, solid companies. Consider companies that have been in business for many years, and companies that look like they'll be in business for many more years.

That doesn't mean you can't consider Microsoft or America Online as an investment possibility for your club. AOL wasn't even in business 20 years ago, and now it is one of the largest companies in the world.

You should, however, use caution when buying stock, and rely on facts, not rumors.

We have a friend—let's just call him Tom—who bought Microsoft stock at just the right time. He bought $10,000 worth of the stock after the market dropped in August 1998. Within a month, the stock price skyrocketed, earning him $4,000 in one month.

Tom was on a roll, so he bought some Intel stock, too. Yep. The value of Intel stock increased, and Tom made some more money. He was more than a little pleased with his stock market aptitude.

Tom's investing began to get riskier and riskier. At a dinner party one night, he was talking to a friend he hadn't seen for a while. Naturally, the conversation turned to the stock market, because Tom could hardly think about anything else. The friend told Tom about this great stock.

The next morning, Tom invested $15,000 in a company that was supposed to split, or announce stupendous earnings, or whatever. By lunchtime, the value of Tom's stock had dipped in half. The moral of this story is that a hot tip from somebody you talk to at a party is an extremely poor reason to buy stock. The only way to know what you're getting is to research the company and look at the stock's historical performance.

Heading for a Crash

Investments are purchased after careful consideration, based on facts and reliable information. Buying a stock on a tip from a friend isn't investing—it's speculating. Speculating is really just a fancy name for gambling.

Not All Stock Is Created Equal

Knowing that all stock is not created equal is a very important concept for the beginning investor to understand. If you don't get that right up front, it could affect the success you'll have in meeting your investment objectives.

Stocks fall into various categories. Remember in Chapter 14, "Understanding the Stock Market Before You Jump In," when we listed some of the different kinds of stock, like blue chip and growth stock? Let's look at that list again and review some of what we talked about in Chapter 14. Knowing what kinds are out there can be a big help when you start thinking about what you should buy. You can refer to Chapter 14 for more information about the stocks that were described there, such as ...

➤ Blue chip stocks

➤ Growth stocks

➤ Emerging stocks

➤ Mid-cap stocks

➤ Large-cap stocks

➤ Income stocks

➤ Cyclical stocks

➤ Defensive stocks

➤ Interest-sensitive stocks

➤ Value stocks

All of this information about different kinds of stocks can be confusing, to be sure. Basically, if your club plans to be aggressive, small- and mid-cap stocks may be the direction you'll want to go.

If you want to learn the fundamentals of investing without having to worry that the stocks you may buy will crash into the abyss, then large-cap or blue chip stock is where you should look.

The Basics of Buying Stocks

We heard a great explanation a few years back about how an investment manager chooses stocks. We use the story all the time to explain the investment process.

This manager says that he decides it's time to buy stock from a certain type of company when stock in that sector has been taking a beating. That's the time that he looks to buy—when prices are low.

Let's say that he's interested in buying a chemical company's stock. He researches chemical companies, then lists all the companies that have sufficient capitalization to meet his criteria.

Then he takes the next step, narrowing down the field of companies from which he might buy stock a little more. He compares buying stock to sifting through sand, or panning for gold.

Try to think of it this way. You start out with a bucketful of all the stocks within the sector in which you've decided to invest. They're all in there, waiting for you to decide which you want.

You start sifting through the stocks, sorting out the ones that are too expensive, the ones from companies that don't interest you, and so forth.

After you've sifted all the stocks in the bucket four or five or six times, you're left with only a few companies left. A bit more sifting, and you've got the stock you want to buy.

Understanding Fundamental Analysis

Fundamental analysis is the study of the financial affairs of a business. It enables an investor to better understand the nature and operating characteristics of companies that issue stock. Fundamental analysis rests on the belief that the value of a stock is influenced by the performance of the company that issued the stock.

Although this might be argued in today's overvalued stock market, fundamental analysis is the basic premise for financial experts. Fundamental analysis also is very important when you're thinking about getting rid of a stock. We'll go into the topic in some detail in Chapter 21, "Know When to Walk Away."

Cashing In

Understanding Financial Statements: Through the Maze of a Corporate Annual Report, by Lyn M. Fraser, can be a great help to those confused by the complexity of an annual report.

An important tool in fundamental analysis is a company's annual report. Knowing how to read one will take you far in learning about a company—where it's been, and where it's heading.

A company's annual report provides a wealth of useful information regarding the financial position of the firm, the success of its operations, the policies and strategies of management, and insight into its future performance.

It will tell about expansions that occurred during the year, changes in key personnel, plans for acquisitions, mergers, and so forth, and all kinds of other interesting tidbits.

The objective of the financial statement is to provide the reader with information that answers questions about the company.

The information in an annual report should tell a potential investor the following things:

➤ Whether or not the company's stock generates attractive returns

➤ Whether the company would be able to repay interest and principal on borrowed funds if existing investment holdings are liquidated

➤ Composition and trends of sales

➤ Profit margins and company earnings composition

➤ Liquidity of corporate resources

➤ The competitive position of the company

Industry Analysis

Annual reports and fundamental analysis are important tools when it comes to evaluating companies and their stock.

Another method of evaluating stock is to use an industry analysis. These analyses are found in several places. Analysis is found by brokerage firms, Value Line reports, newsletters, and magazines. People who do a great deal of equity investments are always reading, looking for new companies in which to invest. They read for changes in the companies that they currently own, which might have continued potential or which don't seem to be growing in today's economy. Industry analysis considers factors such as ...

➤ The nature of the industry. How does the industry that you are considering investing your club's funds compare to others? What is the future of the product line? How will this industry hold up in the new millennium? Railroads were once outdated industries; are they an area of growth in 2000 and beyond for freight and/or high-speed transit? If you are interested in the computer industry, what is the future of the industry, and who are the leaders?

➤ The extent to which the industry is regulated. Gas producers have recently been deregulated. The government has previously controlled the amount a company could sell its product for and could hold down profits. However, many companies no longer were guaranteed a certain profit margin when the government deregulated their industry, and many companies didn't make it through deregulation. Remember the major truck carrier companies? Deregulation brought many to bankruptcy while many new, young companies entered the market place. Same thing happened with the airline industry, telecommunications, and so on. Will regulation hurt the company you are thinking of investing in or help it? An investor should know.

➤ The role of "labor" in the industry. Labor is a major factor in the auto industry. Labor problems struck Caterpillar several years ago, and the ensuing tussle was very difficult for investors. The stock price plummeted, and stayed there for many, many months.

➤ The importance of technological development within the industry. Technology has been and will continue to be the wave of the future. Is the industry you are choosing able to move into the new century? What is needed for the company to move ahead?

➤ The economic factors that are important to the industry. Control by OPEC for the oil producing companies in America, the effect of interest rates on the banking or insurance industry, and so forth are economic factors that affect innumerable industries. Understanding how the economy affects an industry is why students studying finance in college are required to take at least one course in economics.

➤ Other important financial and operating considerations, such as the presence or lack of an adequate supply of labor, material, capital, and capital needs within the industry.

An industry analysis can tell you a lot about what will be happening, both to the industry as a whole and the companies that reside within that industry.

You'll also gain valuable stock analysis information from publications such as *Value Line's Investment Survey, The Wall Street Journal,* and other financial publications.

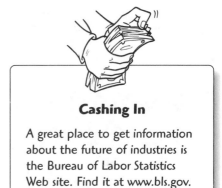

Cashing In

A great place to get information about the future of industries is the Bureau of Labor Statistics Web site. Find it at www.bls.gov.

Personal observation isn't a very scientific tool for evaluating stock, but it can be useful. If possible, check out the companies from which you're considering buying stock.

Wal-Mart and Home Depot are both popular companies for investors right now, and there certainly is no shortage of them around to visit. Check some out and see what you think. Some things to look for include:

➤ Is the store clean?

➤ Are the shelves well stocked?

➤ Do the salespeople seem to know what they're doing? Are they helpful?

➤ Is the store crowded?

➤ Do you get through the check-out line in a reasonable amount of time?

➤ Is there management around to help with any problems that might occur?

➤ Do employees seem happy?

Cashing In

Be alert to the trend in this country that bigger is better. It used to be that the Rickel Home Center stores were big stores for do-it-yourselfers, and a good company in which to invest. Then, along came Home Depot, and Rickel stores everywhere started shutting down.

Don't underestimate your ability to get a feeling for a company in which you're thinking about investing. If you observe that the four Wal-Mart stores in your general area are always crowded, with the parking lots completely full, you can get a pretty good idea that Wal-Mart is doing just fine.

There's one last important tool for evaluating stocks that we haven't yet mentioned. It's not based on numbers, or ratios, or reports, or even your observations or the opinions of your mother-in-law or the guy down the hall in your office. It's your gut.

No, a gut reaction is no way to choose stocks—you're right about that. When all the homework is done, however, all the numbers crunched, all the reports read, and you're still not sure about what the best stock for your club to buy is, then check your gut.

Using Your Computer to Help You Choose Stock

Your personal computer can be a great resource when it comes to choosing stock. In addition to the Web sites for the companies you have chosen to research, there are a host of financial Web sites that offer all kinds of information about financial companies and their stock.

Some of the sites you may be interested in looking at are …

➤ **Stocks.com.** A financial resource site providing information, charts, and the latest quotes on stocks.

➤ **Marketplayer.com.** Stock screening available.

➤ **NetStockUpdate.com.** Stock research, technical charting, SEC filings, analyst reports, institutional ownership.

➤ **Morningstar.com.** In-depth analysis and ratings of companies.

➤ **ValueLine.com.** In-depth analysis and ratings of companies.

➤ **AForecastingStockSplit.com.** A Web site specializing in forecasting stock splits.

➤ **MerrillLynch.com.** Provides access to reports of more than 1,500 companies.

➤ **Investertech.com.** Online technology; industry charts available.

➤ **Labpuppy.com.** Odd name, but the site offers investment research, stock quotes, message boards, chat rooms, investor education, market commentary, and lots of investment-related links.

➤ **MarketCentral.net.** Features free investment newsletters, stock quotes, news, mutual fund information, online stock brokers, world markets, IPO report, and investment guides.

➤ **MarketGuide.com.** Gives timely and accurate company reports, quotes, news, estimates, price charts, stock screening tools, industry, and sector and company rankings.

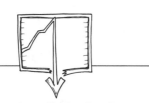

Heading for a Crash

These are just a few of the thousands of online sites that contain information, advice, and tips about buying stocks. Much of the information is very good, and comes from reliable sources. Be aware, however, that there's a lot of bogus information on the Internet, and it's sometimes difficult to discern that from the good stuff. Use good judgement and stay away from offbeat sites that you've never heard of. Not all information and advice are helpful.

You also can buy software to help you choose stocks. The NAIC has a software program that will help your club begin the process of investing. It is highly recommended, particularly when you are setting up your club.

Other packages to look into are …

➤ MetaStock at metastock.com.

➤ SuperCharts at supercharts.com.

➤ TC2000 at tc2000.com.

➤ Vanguard stock choice at vanguard.com.

➤ T. Rowe Price at troweprice.com.

Being Socially Responsible When Buying Stock

In the 1970s we refused to eat Nestles candy bars or buy other Nestles products. We didn't like that the company was selling infant formula in third-world countries, where mothers loved the status that came from using formula, but babies suffered badly when the formula was mixed with dirty water, or drastically diluted to make it last longer.

In the 1980s we avoided the cosmetics and shampoos of certain companies that were said to use animals for testing. In the 1990s we looked for dolphin-safe tuna and didn't buy grapes from Chile because of sanitation and workers' issues.

There are many ways to express and practice social responsibility, and many opinions on what exactly social responsibility is.

Socially responsible investing is a much-talked-about issue, but one that perhaps isn't very well understood. There are a lot of misconceptions about socially responsible investing and investors.

Socially responsible investors are not all vegetarians who wear Birkenstock sandals year round. They don't all live in Denver or Portland, and they don't all have long hair and beards.

The Beardstown Ladies are socially responsible investors—refusing to buy companies that contribute to "personal misery" by producing products related to liquor, tobacco, or gambling.

The guy who sits next to you at work might be a socially responsible investor. Your mother may be.

Being socially responsible as far as investments go became popular in the 1970s, when investors questioned making money at the expense of the environment or people. Socially responsible investors objected to companies that bought and sold products to South Africa. Investors objected to apartheid, and felt that hurting South Africa in the pocketbook might rectify the situation. And it did!

Since then, the meaning of being a socially responsible investor has expanded to mean any and all of the following:

➤ Investing in companies that are ethical, environmental, and socially responsible

➤ Not investing in companies that are anti-family, anti-environmental, or that produce or deal with pornography

➤ Investing in companies that fund renewable energy

➤ Investing in humane and environmentally conscious companies

Some socially responsible investors look for companies that have equal employment opportunities or good working conditions. Some look at consumer protection issues. There are many criteria for being social responsible, and many opinions about which companies are, and which aren't.

The issue of socially responsible investing can affect your club. Let's say that your club has set parameters for the stocks it's interested in buying, and one of the companies that sounds good is Raytheon. The earnings per share are 2.15, the stock yields 4 percent, the P/E is 9. The price has dropped from $76.56 per share to $19.625 per share.

The presentation for this stock has been given, and club members are about to take a vote. Suddenly, one member speaks up, objecting to purchasing the company because Raytheon is a defense contractor. It makes the Scud missile.

The Scud missile became a household word during the Iraqi invasion of Kuwait. The Scud missile was used to protect Israel from the Iraqi missile attacks. Many people object to missiles, which kill living things and cause great destruction of property. Because of that, many people would prefer not to support companies that manufacture missiles.

It's easy to know that Phillip Morris is a tobacco company, and that Lockheed Martin is a defense contractor, but many investors don't know that Coca-Cola owns Taylor Wines and Great Western Vineyards, or that General Electric is a defense contractor, or that Raytheon makes Scud missiles. If your club is interested in socially responsible investing, it will have to establish its standards, and be willing to do its homework.

Your club could hire a money manager who specializes in socially responsible investments, but that would pretty much defeat the purpose of an investment club. You can invest in socially responsible stocks by doing the work yourself and choosing from this list, rather than the entire gamut of stocks.

If your club is interested in investing in a socially responsible manner, ask your broker to point you toward funds that only deal with socially responsible companies, or get on the Internet and find them yourself.

Don't assume that every socially responsible mutual fund is the same. If you take a look at some of those funds listed on various Web sites (just type in "socially responsible investing" when you use a search engine to get the Web sites), you'll see that there are big differences.

226

Some invest only in companies that promote family values, while others focus on companies with good environmental records, and others primarily look for companies who are attuned to human rights issues.

One mutual fund, the Labrador Mutual Fund, lists the following criteria that it demands of a company in order to be considered socially responsible. It must be concerned with, and have good records in ...

Cashing In

For a list of socially responsible mutual funds, go to www.sociallyresponsible.com/mutual_funds.htm. You can find out the companies in which each fund is invested by clicking on the individual fund name.

➤ Consumer protection and product safety.

➤ Environmental concerns and use of natural resources.

➤ Equal opportunity employment.

➤ Occupational health and safety.

If you look at the companies in which the Labrador invests, you might be surprised at which ones it considers to be socially responsible.

Some of them include: Abbot Laboratories; Cisco; General Electric; Hewlett-Packard; Intel Corp.; Lucent Technologies; Merck and Co., Inc.; Microsoft; Proctor and Gamble Co.; Sun Microsystems, Inc.; Wells Fargo and Co.; and Xerox Corp.

Because the Labrador doesn't include defense issues in its social responsibility criteria, it doesn't preclude General Electric from being one of the companies in its fund.

A list of some other socially responsible mutual funds and their Web sites are ...

➤ **The American Trust Allegiance Fund.** Find it at www.amertrust.com/allegianceFund.

➤ **Ariel Mutual Funds.** It's located at www.arialmutualfunds.com.

➤ **Bridge Way Fund, Inc.** On the Web at www.bridgewayfunds.com.

➤ **Calvert Group Mutual Funds.** Located at www.calvertgroup.com.

➤ **Catholic Values Investment Trust.** Find it at www.catholicinvestment.com.

➤ **Dreyfus Investor.** It's located at www.dreyfus.com.

➤ **Evergreen Funds.** On the Web at www.evergreen-funds.com.

➤ **Labrador Mutual Fund.** Located at www.labradorfund.com.

➤ **The Noah Fund.** It's located at www.noahfund.com.

➤ **Meyers Pride Value Fund.** Find it at www.pridefund.com.

➤ **Timothy Plan.** Located at www.timothyplan.com.

Socially responsible investing is an interesting topic for your club to discuss and consider, whether or not you decide to do it. Many people feel they can balance social responsibility with making money on their investments.

It's Everyone's Business

Chapter 20, "It's Trading Time," explains the specifics of trading stock, but it's important for club members to know that once they vote to buy or sell a stock, the broker, or a club member, probably will leave the meeting to do just that.

If your club doesn't have a full-service broker, the trade will be transacted either by calling a discount broker, or trading online. If your club does use a full-service broker, he or she will make the trade.

Although the club has designated the person who actually makes the trade, buying stock is everyone's business. It's necessary for one person to be responsible for actually making the transactions, but everyone should review the records to verify that the trade occurred as it was approved.

Verifying trades is important for several reasons. One is to verify that the brokerage firm is making the trades as directed. Mistakes do happen, and although the treasurer or club member who is responsible for the record keeping should be checking each trade, people get busy and things sometimes fall through the cracks.

Cashing In

Club members should be sensitive to the workloads that other people are carrying, and the club should shift the work around if it becomes clear that one or two people are doing more than their share. There's nothing more discouraging than for somebody to think she's doing twice as much work as anyone else, and that no one else is noticing.

Everyone should take responsibility for checking the books to make sure your club's transactions have occurred and been properly recorded.

Perhaps the most important reason, however, for everyone to get involved with buying and selling stock is that everyone should have a chance to benefit from the learning process that comes with making transactions.

That, after all, is the primary purpose of belonging to an investment club.

Once stock has been purchased, the member who presented it to the club will follow the stock. Or the stock might be assigned to a new member who isn't watching as many stocks as other members.

Following a stock on a month-by-month basis is very important for the club's portfolio review. Some clubs have their members rotate leadership of the monthly meeting. At that time, that member makes a review of all the stocks. This forces each member to know about each stock, although it does make more work for the leaders during their particular months.

The Least You Need to Know

➤ It's extremely important that you fully understand the stocks that your club proposes to buy before voting on them.

➤ Fundamental analysis is an excellent method of evaluating stock, but there are other methods you can use, as well.

➤ In our age of technological advances, your computer is, and will remain, an increasingly valuable tool for researching and tracking stocks.

➤ Knowing how much to pay for a stock is sometimes difficult, and sometimes requires a judgement call, depending on how important your club thinks it is to own the stock.

➤ There are many opportunities for your club to buy stock of companies that are considered socially responsible.

➤ All club members should be involved in deciding what stock to buy, and in making sure the necessary transactions were made and properly recorded.

Part 5

Keeping Track of Your Investments

Buying stock is a major part of the process, but keeping track of what you own and how it's doing is equally important.

Knowing how to track and monitor your investments will help you make good decisions about buying, holding, and selling stock. Investment clubs are known for holding on to the stock they buy, but there are certain situations when it may be to your advantage to trade.

All the members of your club need to be involved with the decisions of whether to hold or trade. In order to do that, everyone needs to understand the processes and logic behind buying and selling.

Making sure that all members participate in the club's buying and selling decisions keeps everyone interested and accountable. We'll give you some tips in this part about how to keep the members' enthusiasm high.

Chapter 18

Watching out for What You've Got

An investment portfolio is like a child—it bears close and frequent watching.

This doesn't mean that you've got to spend hours every day at your computer, frantically looking for the most updated stock sites.

Nor does it mean that you've got to be on the phone with your broker every couple of hours, or get to be intimately acquainted with *The Wall Street Journal*.

You should, however, make sure that you have a good, up-to-date knowledge of what's happening in the stock market and the general economy (both national and international).

That might sound like a tough assignment, but it's really not very difficult.

Do you listen to the news at night? Or maybe while you're driving to work in the morning? Pay careful attention to the financial reports and the general news, as well. Remember that many factors—from the weather to the world political scene—can affect the stock market and the economy.

Do you read a newspaper every day? Maybe you get *Time* or *Newsweek* each week. Newspapers and magazines contain financial news—just take the time to read it.

Also, talk to others about financial topics. Many people are interested in the stock market. Nearly everyone is interested in the economy—after all, it affects us all. Consider all opinions and insights, they'll help keep you aware of what's going on.

In this chapter, we'll learn about the importance of watching out for your investments and how you can best do so. You might be surprised at how easy it is.

Investments Don't Always Take Care of Themselves, You Know

Anyone who owns a house, a car, a boat (especially a boat), or any sort of property knows the importance of maintenance.

We paint, we change the oil, we check the engines, we rake the leaves … Fun? Not too much. Necessary? You bet.

It's the same thing with your investments. A certain level of maintenance is required to make sure they stay healthy and desirable. We live in a world that changes quickly. What's true today won't necessarily be true tomorrow. Let's look at an example of a company that underwent big changes that affected its stock.

Cashing In

Don't immediately assume that your stock will increase or decrease in value when a change occurs within the company, but keep a close watch on what's going on. Try to learn to anticipate how changes will affect the company.

New Holland is a large corporation based in Lancaster County, Pennsylvania. In the past 20 years, the corporation went from being called New Holland to Ford New Holland to Fiat New Holland to Case New Holland. Stockowners in the original New Holland Corporation, which produced tractors and other farming equipment, certainly had their work cut out for them, keeping up with all those changes.

The problem is that you might have bought stock in New Holland because you thought it was a strong, local company. Located in a large farming area, there was a built-in market for its product, and Lancaster County is blessed with a dependable and plentiful work force.

You may have bought New Holland stock for those reasons, only to have the company sold to Ford, which is hardly a local corporation. That isn't to say that Ford New Holland wasn't a good company, but it wasn't the company whose stock you purchased.

Next, Ford sold off the New Holland division to Fiat, and in a moment, New Holland became a foreign corporation. Again, the acquisition by Fiat might have strengthened the company. Or, it might not have. As an investor in the company, it's your job to keep tabs on what's happening to your company and how it affects the value of its stock.

When Case, another farm equipment producer, merged with New Holland, it created a great deal of new debt. That's definitely a reason to evaluate the company. All of these changes happened independently of other factors that could affect a company like New Holland.

If farmers aren't making money, they're not likely to be buying expensive farm machinery. Factors that affect farmers—weather, the prices their crops will bring, and so forth—also will affect a company like New Holland. As New Holland is affected, so is the stock that you're holding.

New Holland is a good example of why it's necessary to work to maintain your portfolio. In these days of mergers, acquisitions, and takeovers, it's certainly not unique.

Maintenance might not be your favorite part of owning a house or car, but you can't argue that it's a necessary process. Fortunately, when you're a member of an investment club, the maintenance work can be spread out. If everyone does a little bit, your club portfolio should remain in good shape.

Cashing In

Sit down some day and consider all the companies that are in your portfolio. Have you been keeping up with what's going on with them? Is it possible that you've missed something major? It's a good idea sometimes to get an overview of your portfolio by considering all the companies whose stock you own.

Keeping Track of Your Investments

So, just how do you go about keeping track of your portfolio? Some days it's hard enough to keep track of your kids, let alone worry about your portfolio.

Where does the process begin?

Let's say that your club recently purchased 300 shares of Lincoln National (LNC), a Midwestern insurance company. Lincoln National is the fifth largest publicly traded life insurer in the U.S. The stock is yielding 3.2 percent and has a price-to-earnings ratio of 13.12.

It's also important to know that Lincoln National charged off (took business losses on the company's tax returns) $53,000,000 in the fourth quarter of 1999—quite a chunk of change.

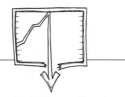

Heading for a Crash

While it's wise to track the stocks in your portfolio, don't fall into the trap of becoming fixated on them. Some investors spend hours every day watching the market, tracking every move their investments make. Trust us, there are much better uses for your time. All your watching isn't going to change the course of the market. This becomes a real problem for some people, so just be aware of it.

Your club will need to look at whether that move will affect its holding. If it does, you'll need to decide whether you should hold the investment. You'll need to keep a close watch on what the company's stock does. You can do that in several ways.

Reading the Stock Reports

There is more written every day about investing and investments. Keeping up with it all can be a complicated and time-consuming process.

Let's face it. We all have plenty to do in the course of a day. It's a constant source of amazement how, with all the time-saving devices we come up with in our society, we continue to get busier and busier.

Probably the last thing you want to do is spend a lot of time keeping track of your stocks. That's why it's important to know where to get the information you need and know how to use it once you find it.

Learning to read stock reports, sometimes called stock tables, is arguably the simplest way to keep tabs on what you own. They look terribly daunting at first, to be sure. Once you get the hang of it, however, it's not at all difficult, and you'll no doubt find it extremely interesting reading.

Take This to the Bank

Check out the business pages of your Sunday newspaper for a review of what's happened during the week on Wall Street. *The Sunday Reading Eagle* (Reading, Pennsylvania), for example, includes a weekly wrap-up of stocks of local interest, Dow Jones 30 Industrial stocks, market indicators, and the activity of each of the three major exchanges. It also includes a market roundup, a column about investing, and a market outlook.

Stock reports are published daily in business papers and most good-sized newspapers. The report that you'll read summarizes the trading from the day before. For example, Monday's paper lists Friday's transactions.

Each of the three exchanges (the New York Stock Exchange, American Stock Exchange, and the NASDAQ) has its own stock table. Stocks are listed in alphabetical order, with abbreviated company names.

Some examples of the abbreviations are ...

➤ America Online is AmOnlne

➤ General Motors is GnMotr

➤ General Electric is GenElec

➤ Home Depot is HomeDp

➤ Philip Morris is PhilMor

To the left of each abbreviation, you'll see the high and low prices that the stock has reached during the last year.

It'll look something like this:

$48\frac{1}{2}$ $33\frac{1}{2}$ Boeing

The prices are quoted in points, and each point is worth $1. Each eighth of a point is worth $12\frac{1}{2}$¢.

Take This to the Bank

Many of the stock abbreviations are obvious. Some, however, like Wal-Mart, can be a little tricky to figure out. Wal-Mart is listed in the reports as WMT.

Just to the right of the stock abbreviation, you'll find the dividend rate (the amount of the current dividend payment) and percentage yield (the ratio of the dividend to the closing price).

Next, proceeding from left to right across the page, will be the stock's price-to-earnings ratio (remember, that's the price of a share of stock, divided by the company's earnings per share).

Then comes the high price that the stock reached on the previous day. Next is the low price that the stock reached on the previous day. The next column—the one marked "last"—lists the stock's closing price for the previous day. And the last column—marked "chg"—gives the difference in the closing price from the previous day, as compared to the day before that.

If you're looking at Thursday's paper, for instance, the "chg" column would tell you the difference between the stock's closing prices on Tuesday and Wednesday.

If there's a plus sign next to the number, that means the stock has increased in price. A minus sign means the value has dropped.

This sounds complicated on the surface, but once you know what you're looking at, it's not at all difficult. You don't need to be a financial expert to read stock reports, you just need a bit of knowledge and some interest.

Other Methods of Keeping Up

Reading the stock reports is a great way to keep up with what's happening, but there are other sources that you'll also find useful. You'll also want to consider:

➤ Statements sent from your broker

➤ Literature from the company in which you own stock

➤ *Value Line's Investment Survey*

➤ Business and financial newspapers and magazines

Keep an eye on the monthly brokerage statements you get regarding your investments. They'll reiterate any transactions that occurred, and tell you the values of everything you own and how your holdings have changed.

Always be sure to read any information you get from companies concerning your investments. A representative of your club should make sure that this information is made available to all members and everyone should take the time to look at it.

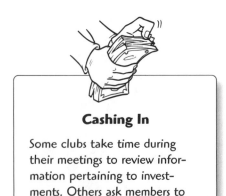

Cashing In

Some clubs take time during their meetings to review information pertaining to investments. Others ask members to do so individually, so it doesn't take up club time.

It can be cumbersome reading, and it might not be necessary to read every word of every paper you get, but you should at least get an understanding of the topic and see if the information is important to your investment.

There will be quarterly reports and an annual report. Some companies even send all of their press releases to shareholders.

When you get the reports, compare the data with the past quarter or year. Is the company growing? What do the company's chairperson and president have to say? What's the tone of the information? Upbeat and optimistic? Cautious? Apologetic?

Remember, though, that information you get about the company in which you hold stock, comes from that company. You'll get the news that the company chooses to release.

Another source of stock information is the *Value Line's Investment Survey.* You can buy the hard copy service, which means you'll get a weekly report on the stocks the service follows. It has loads of information and is a great publication, but it's expensive. If you want to check out Value Line, look in the reference section of your public library.

There are a number of business and financial publications from which you can learn a lot about the stocks you own and what's happening that could affect those stocks.

The Wall Street Journal is a great business publication. It's filled with information and is interesting to read.

Forbes and *Fortune* magazines, *Business Week,* and other business and financial publications can help you keep up with what's happening with your investments. Some magazines have indexes that list the companies they cover in the current issue. Some articles are brief, while others are more in depth.

Barron's is a comprehensive weekly newspaper that has in-depth articles about stocks and trends in the market. It lists the price of stocks on all exchanges, and each week includes informative interviews and features.

While all of these are good methods of keeping up with your investments, they seem a little outdated compared to the newest financial tool—the Internet.

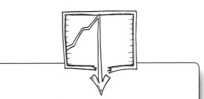

Heading for a Crash

It may be tempting to ignore the correspondence you get concerning your investments, but don't. Many people have been burned because they didn't keep up with what was going on and didn't have the information they needed to make informed, intelligent decisions. If you don't read it, you risk missing something you should know.

Cashing In

Find *The Wall Street Journal's* Web site at www.wsj.com. You can subscribe online, either to the printed newspaper or its electronic version. There are also lots of articles that you can access from the Web site.

Using the Internet to Track Your Stocks

There's no longer any need to sit around, anxiously awaiting delivery of your daily newspaper so that you can see how your stocks are doing. You can jump online and see what's happening any time you want.

Heading for a Crash

While the Internet is a great tool for investors, it contains a potential danger. Some investors, able to check on their stocks whenever they want to, become obsessive about keeping up with what's happening. If you find that you're unable to resist the temptation of constantly checking your stocks, you'll need to limit the time you spend online.

The Internet provides up-to-the-minute prices, major stock announcements, dividend amounts, and so on.

Most companies have their own Web pages, containing investor relations information, current press releases, and so forth. Fantastic! Maybe you're driving along and you hear something on the radio about a company in which you own stock. When you get to where you're going, you can log on to the company's Web site, where you'll probably find a press release on the matter you heard mentioned.

Many Internet service providers have financial pages to keep track of stock prices. The prices are updated throughout the day.

America Online contains a personal finance site that's extremely useful. There's a service that keeps track of your portfolio, updating stock prices and gains and losses. It totals your entire portfolio, listing your gains or losses. You can follow your club's portfolio all day—if you want to.

The AOL site also has the ability to get quotes for all stocks, all day long. Along with the recent price, it will tell you the stock's highest trade for the day, the day's low-trade price, the yield, price-to-earnings ratio, earnings per share, 52-week high and 52-week low price for the stock.

On AOL's Market News Center site, you can see how the markets are performing at any time. The site lists the most active stocks on all three stock exchanges, stock splits, initial public offerings coming onto the market, and 52-week highs and lows for stocks on all three exchanges.

There's certainly not enough space in this book to list all the useful Internet sites. Take some time to look around and bookmark the sites you find most interesting and helpful.

Knowing About Market Timing

Market timing is a method of investing, but it's also important when you're looking after the investments you have.

Timing is important in what happens to stock. If you're diligent in keeping track of your investments, you'll read and hear important information that could affect the value of your stocks.

Let's say that you're looking through *The Wall Street Journal*, and you see an article about one of the companies in which your club is invested. Naturally, you read the story carefully.

While doing so, you find out about a big shakeup in the company's European division. You know this is important, because a good percentage of the company's earnings come from its foreign operations. You do your homework, check out Value Line and some other publications, and learn even more about the trouble your company is having.

You share the information with other club members, who are also concerned. You keep a close watch on this company for another week, and reports continue that the company is in trouble. At that time, you decide you're going to sell your stock.

What you've done in this instance, based on information you gathered and processed, is time the market.

Cashing In

There are lots of market-timing methods. The problem is that most of them don't work—at least not consistently. Most people who try to time the market are wrong much of the time.

You sold your stock because you thought the time was right to do so. Based on solid information—which is the only way to do it—you predicted that your stock would lose value due to problems within the company.

That scenario is a simplified explanation of market timing, but it's important when you're looking out for what you've got. We go into more detail about knowing when to sell stock in Chapter 21, "Know When to Walk Away."

There are other forms of market timing, as well. You can time the market for an individual stock, or for a sector of the market (for example, oil stocks or financial service stocks), or for the entire market.

Market timing can be a matter of common sense, such as studying information concerning your investments and using it to decide when you should buy or sell. Some people, however, make a game of buying and selling depending on what the market's doing, which can be risky.

While your investment club may find it necessary to get involved with market timing every now and then, it's not something that you should be doing frequently.

Your club is—or probably should be—investing for the long term. Market timing forces the sale of your investments in order to create realized capital gains.

Keeping an Eye on Cycles

Investing is a process of choosing stocks that you think are going to go up in price. You want to purchase the stocks that your club feels are a good value, in companies that have the potential and opportunity to expand.

Take This to the Bank

A great financial program is National Public Radio's (NPR) *Marketplace*. It offers all kinds of information on financial and business issues in a clear, understandable manner. Check out your local NPR station to find out when *Marketplace* is aired in your area.

Sometimes, though, no matter how well you choose, trends in the market work against you. There are dozens of these trends, called *cycles*, that can influence how the market performs. Investors should know how these cycles work, and how they affect their investments. Stocks tend to move up when the economy is strong and retreat when the economy weakens.

We'll tell you about two important cycles: business cycles and inflation cycles—all of which affect the financial market.

A business cycle is an indication of the change in total economic activity over time. It is a measure of economic, political, and social activity. Two widely followed measures of the business cycle are gross national product (GNP) and industrial production.

The GNP represents the market value of all goods and services produced by a country over the period of a year.

Industrial production is a measure of the activity and output in the industrial or productive segment of the economy. Normally, the GNP and/or the index of industrial production move up and down with the business cycle.

Taking Stock

Inflation is the upward movement of prices for goods and services.

Inflation cycles, which are tied closely with interest rates, have a great influence on whether the stock market increases or declines.

When there's high *inflation*—that's when prices go up—the demand for goods and services decreases. Low inflation boosts demand.

The inflation rate determines how much things will cost.

To keep informed about what's happening with inflation—other than noting if you're paying more at the grocery store or the gas station—is to monitor the producer price index and the consumer price index.

➤ **Producer price index.** If this index goes up, it means that producers are raising prices on the products they sell. Sometimes these increases are passed along to consumers—but, depending on things like competition and the state of the general economy—they may not be.

➤ **Consumer price index.** This index is based on the products and services that most people buy. If the consumer price index goes up, just about everything we buy will cost more. Those who track this index start to get worried when it's increased 5 percent or more. If it increases 10 percent or more, it starts to cause big trouble for the stock market.

Nearly every industry is affected by inflation cycles, but some are affected more than others. We always need to eat, for example, but we'll put off buying new cars when inflation is high and prices are up.

Some industries that tend to hold their own in times of high inflation include supermarket chains, drugstores, clothing manufacturers, and alcoholic beverages.

Some industries that are more affected by inflation are airlines, hotels, chemical/pharmaceutical, and home construction.

Indicators for Financial Health

There is a lot of information to help determine financial health and how the general economy is performing.

Some of the things we look to as indicators include personal income, retail sales, consumer prices, producer prices, employment numbers, and housing starts.

Leading indicators are the movement of statistics that tend to predict or "lead" changes in the nation's economy.

The indicators are numerous. They include: layoffs of workers, new orders placed by manufacturers, changes in the money supply, and the prices of raw materials. If the index moves in the same direction for several months, it's a sign that total output will move in the same direction.

Investors use leading indicators to decide if the economy is contracting. If the stock market is going to be flat or will go down because of how the economy is doing, it may not be the time to invest in the stock market.

The United States currently is experiencing the longest economic expansion in the history of this country, and the stock market has expanded along with the economy.

Taking Stock

Leading indicators are factors such as housing starts and new orders placed by manufacturers that can tell us the direction in which the economy is heading.

Explanations of the some leading indicators are ...

➤ **Personal income.** This is the before-tax income, received in the form of wages and salaries, interest and dividends, rents, and other payments such as Social Security, unemployment, and pensions. This report helps explain trends in consumer buying habits. When personal income rises, it often means that people will increase their buying.

➤ **Retail sales.** These are total sales at the retail level, including everything from cars to groceries. This figure gives a rough clue to consumer attitudes and can indicate future conditions. A long slowdown in sales can lead to cuts in production. If retail sales are dropping, your club shouldn't rush out and buy Gap, Limited, Sears, and so on.

➤ **Consumer prices.** Consumer prices indicators are changes in prices for a fixed market basket of about 360 goods and services. The changes are used as a measure of inflation.

➤ **Producer prices.** These indicate price changes of goods at various stages of production—from crude materials such as raw cotton, to finished goods like clothing and furniture. An upward surge may mean higher consumer prices later. Watch for changes in the prices of finished goods. These don't fluctuate as widely as crude materials, which makes them a more accurate measure of inflationary pressure.

➤ **Unemployment.** Measuring the percentage of the work force that's currently involuntarily without jobs, this is a broad indicator of economic health. Another monthly figure available is the number of payroll jobs. This may be a better indicator for spotting changes in business. A decreasing number of jobs is a sign that firms are cutting production.

➤ **Housing starts.** A pickup in the pace of housing starts follows an easing of credit conditions—the availability and the cost of money—and is an indicator of improvement in economic health. Housing starts include the number of new building permits issued across the country, which is an even earlier indicator of the pace of future construction.

As you can see, there are many factors to consider when keeping track of your investments, and many ways in which you can get information that might affect them.

The Least You Need to Know

➤ Choosing investments is the first step of the process, buying them is the second, and keeping watch over them is the third step.

➤ It's extremely important to use stock reports, company information, financial publications, and other sources to keep up with your investments.

➤ Internet sites can give you up-to-the-minute information on the stocks you own and the factors that could affect them.

➤ Market timing is important and can be applied practically, but it can be a dangerous practice.

➤ Understanding cycles that affect the market can help you keep track of what's happening with your investments.

➤ Factors that tell us the direction in which the economy is heading are called indicators. They can be helpful in predicting what the stock market will do.

Chapter 19

To Have and to Hold

In This Chapter

➤ The wisdom of keeping what you've got

➤ These things called dividends

➤ Reinvesting dividends makes a difference

➤ Different ways to reinvest dividends

➤ What to watch for when reinvesting

Deciding what to buy with your monthly dues is exciting—one of the fun parts of belonging to an investment club. Deciding what to do with the stocks that you've already purchased, however, can be a different story. If the stocks the club owns are doing well and have considerable capital gain, it could be that a few club members are rearing to take the profits. After all, it's pretty tempting to know that you could sell that stock today and walk away with a profit on it.

Other members, however, are thinking more long-term and want to leave the club's investments where they are. One of the most difficult decisions that investment clubs face is if—and when—to sell stock. It can be extremely frustrating to watch your investments lose value, or to remain flat for a period of time.

Still, all the research shows that if you have stock that's basically sound and you leave it alone for the long haul, it will increase in value. That's not to say that there never is a time when it's appropriate to sell stock. In fact, we spend a whole chapter discussing that in Chapter 21, "Know When to Walk Away."

Generally, however, the advantages of holding onto your stock outweigh those of frequent trading and selling. In this chapter, we're going to tell you all the reasons to hang onto the stocks you have.

Advantages of Keeping Stocks Long Term

You often hear people talk about keeping their investments for the long term. What exactly is the *long term?* Is it 30 days, 12 months, 5 years, or 20 years? The concept of long term varies from circumstance to circumstance, and can be interpreted differently by different people.

Long-term hospital care, for instance, might mean several months. But several months don't cut it for a long-term relationship. Anyway, you get the idea.

Taking Stock

In the context of stocks, short-term is the one that you buy, and then sell within a year. **Long-term** is the one that you keep for more than a year before selling.

Long-term also means different things to different people in the investment area. For income tax purposes, as discussed in Chapter 12, "A Taxing Topic," long term means that the holding period of a stock is greater than one year. If you buy a stock and keep it for a year, you've had it long term, at least in the context of paying income tax on it.

As a refresher, once you've held a stock for 12 months, any capital gain incurred due to the sale of stock is taxed at either 10 or 20 percent, depending on your tax bracket.

If you hold your stock only short term, that is, for less than a year, the capital gain you'd realize when you sell it is taxed at your regular income tax bracket. That means you'd pay either 15, 24, 31, 36, or 39.6 percent in income tax—depending on your tax bracket.

So, unless you've quadrupled your investment in a stock that, for whatever reasons, most club members want to get rid of, it's strongly recommended that you hang on to the shares for at least a year.

This past summer, an investment club we're familiar with had a spin-off company go public from one of its current holdings. The stock came on the market August 10, selling for $15 a share and the club bought. The stock immediately shot up in price, and by the club's September meeting had risen to almost $100 per share.

The club decided to sell its shares of the stock—Internet Capital Group—for $100 a share. After all, it had made $85 a share. Club members decided they were going to take their gains and run. Try to imagine how club members felt as they watched the stock continue to rise, and rise, and rise. It topped out at $212 a share, coming back down to $132 at the time this book was written. All of this occurred within five months.

So, was the club's decision to sell its stock wrong? Or did the club do the right thing? Should it have held the shares for the long term? Who can say for sure? Investments are a subjective business, because nobody can know for sure what they'll do.

Certainly, if the members of the club discussed above had known the stock would continue to rise to $212 per share, they wouldn't have sold it for $100. Some members, however, thought that $100 was as high as the Internet Capital Group stock could go, and that the stock was going to start devaluing.

While it seems that $85 per share was a great profit, remember that a good percentage of that had to be paid in capital gains taxes. The club still made money by selling its Internet Capital Group stock, but it did pay higher taxes than if it would have held on to it. Who knows, however, what the stock will be worth when August rolls around again?

Cashing In

A major theme throughout this book is that investment decisions must be based on facts. Members should learn about company fundamentals and the parameters that drive their decisions to buy and sell stock. Income tax considerations, although notable, are secondary. If you feel a stock is too risky to hold long term—sell it. Pay your taxes and take whatever's left over.

Another reason that investors hold stock long term is to wait and take gains on shares sold after the end of the year. They wait to sell their stock until January, knowing that will delay the payment of income taxes due on the gain until April 15 of the following year.

Take This to the Bank

If you sold a stock for a profit in January 2000, the income tax you owe on the capital gains from that sale isn't due until April 15, 2001.

Many investors will wait for the stock to become a long-term investment (longer than one year) before they sell. They're often glad to wait in order to delay the inevitable tax payment. Just remember, though, that you can run, but you can't hide when Uncle Sam's concerned. He'll get you—and your tax money—sooner or later.

Up to now, we've focused primarily on tax considerations as the criteria of whether to hold stocks for the long term. And while long term means one year for tax purposes, we think that a year really isn't long term, at all.

249

Our definition of keeping stock long term is to hold on to the shares for years. If you invest in a good company, such as Microsoft, General Electric, or AT&T, and hang onto them, you'll realize an increase in the value of your investment. Don't we all wish we'd bought $10,000 of Microsoft stock way back in the early years of the company? If we had, it would be worth more than $1 million today.

A big advantage of investing long term is that the total funds are invested. Your money earns more and more as it increases in value. If you sell stock at a profit and have to pay tax on the gain, the money you pay in taxes is gone and can't be reinvested.

Another problem with selling stock instead of hanging onto it is that the club receives proceeds from the sale of a good company. The club takes the gains from a good company and has to figure out something to do with the proceeds. You'll need to find another good company in which to invest. It's not a smart move to take your money out of a good company and put it into a not-so-good company. It's usually better to consider a good company as a safe bet and stick with it.

The last advantage of holding stock long term that we'll discuss in this section is that by hanging on to your stock, you avoid paying out money for trading costs. We'll discuss this a lot more in the next chapter, but remember that when you buy stock, there's a commission involved. Selling stock also involves paying a commission. When you purchase a stock and hold it, you're only paying commission on one side of the equation.

Desperately Seeking Dividends

Sometimes individuals, investment clubs, or companies will invest in particular stocks because they pay *dividends*.

Taking Stock

Dividends are payouts, or distributions of a company's profits to shareholders in a fixed amount for each share held. Dividends can vary on common stock, but are usually fixed for preferred stock.

The Hershey Trust Company, for example, is a company set up to administer and oversee the trust established by Milton Hershey, founder of the Hershey Foods Co. The purpose of Hershey's trust is to support the school for underprivileged children that Mr. Hershey founded in Hershey, Pennsylvania.

The school, of course, needs income to remain in operation. To that end, the Hershey Trust Company has a policy that it won't invest in any company that doesn't pay dividends.

The dividends, or payments to Hershey Trust, a stockholder, were used as income for the school. Hershey Trust wanted to receive dividends as it waited for the stock it had purchased to increase in value. A stock that pays dividends will provide income to stockholders, even in the event of a down market.

Not everyone, however, targets only stocks that pay dividends as investments. Very few of the Internet and technology stocks that have led the dramatic rise in the market recently pay a dividend.

What Are Dividends?

Simply, dividends are a share of a company's profits that are distributed by the company to a class of its shareholders.

The dividend is paid in a fixed amount for each share of stock held. Dividends are usually fixed, or set in preferred stocks, but dividends from common stock vary as the company's performance shifts. Common and preferred stocks are two different classes of stock.

Dividends normally are paid quarterly, and have to be approved by the board of directors of the company that's paying them before they're distributed.

As discussed in Chapters 16, "Targeting Companies from Which to Buy Stock," and 17, "Buying Stock—the Cornerstone of an Investment Club," there are various types of stocks. Emerging and growth stocks rarely pay dividends. Well-established companies that have sound profits pay dividends. *Value Line's Investment Survey* contains a report that lists companies that have paid continuous dividends for the past 20 years.

Dividends are nice and many investors like them—a lot. They shouldn't, however, be the only reason you purchase stocks.

If you're retired and looking for a hedge against inflation while still owning stock, dividends might make sense for you. This reason for choosing dividends, however, is almost assuredly not the investment objective of your club.

Dividends should be a consideration. When you look at a stock report, it will give you the dividend yield. It will tell you that the company pays 1 percent, or 2 percent, or whatever. Philip Morris currently is paying a whopping 7.9 percent dividend. The dividend factor should be taken into consideration when you purchase a stock.

How Do Dividends Affect a Company's Stock?

Dividends, as you might expect, affect a company's stock price. Companies with lower profits are often forced to lower their dividends. This move is not taken lightly by the company's board of directors, because they know that the price of the company's stock will probably drop after the announcement to cut the dividend is heard on Wall Street.

Steady dividends, as discussed above, assuredly create a feeling of confidence in a company. If the company has the growth to pay out a dividend continuously over a

Cashing In

For more information on dividends and the companies that pay them, check out these books: *The Dividend Growth Investment Strategy: How to Keep Your Retirement Income Doubling Every Five Years,* by Roxann J.D. Klugman or *The Dividend Rich Investor: Building Wealth with High Quality, Dividend-Paying Stocks,* by Joseph Tigue and Joseph Lisanti. Both are available online from Amazon.com or BarnesandNoble.com.

period of years, or is even able to increase the dividends, this can be taken as a sign of a healthy company. This type of company might be the one in which your club should consider investing.

Too high a dividend, however, can be a problem. A higher than market dividend yield is often a warning sign for the investor to dig deeper into the company's fundamentals to learn why the dividend is so much higher than other stocks in the industry.

Philip Morris's dividend is high compared to the average stock. That's because the stock has dropped significantly since cigarette litigation has turned against the company.

Your club shouldn't invest in a high-dividend-paying company without reviewing the pros and cons of all the firm's statistics. These include the price-to-earnings ratio, the debt-to-equity ratio, and whether its revenue is on the rise or has fallen, and so forth.

Historically, there are companies that pay a higher dividend than the S&P 500 average. Examples of these are utility stocks, oil stocks, and even some insurance companies. These stocks are known for their steady increases in value. Keep in mind, however, that it's difficult for a company to pay high dividends and still have funds for corporate reinvestment in research and development.

Reinvesting Dividends

While some investors may use dividends for income, others reinvest them. There are several ways to reinvest dividends. One way is to reinvest within a dividend reinvestment plan. We'll get to that in the next section, "Dividend Reinvestment Plans."

The other way for an investment club to reinvest dividends is for the treasurer to accumulate the dividends that are received each month. They can be added to members' monthly dues, giving more money to invest.

This is a good thing for clubs, because as your club grows in size, the dividends you receive also should grow. Of course, this wouldn't hold true if you invest only in emerging or growth stocks that don't pay dividends. If you get dividends, however, you should have a little bit more each month to invest.

If you use this system of reinvestment, you need to think about how you're reinvesting the dividends. It's usually good to reinvest some back into the original stock.

A problem experienced by many newer investment clubs is that its first holding can be nearly 100 percent of its portfolio. It's recommended that most investors shouldn't hold more than 7 to 10 percent of their portfolios in any one holding. If you only have one or two holdings, however, how is that possible?

This is, indeed, a difficulty for any new investor. You can't be diversified if you own only one stock. As we discussed in Chapter 15, "Considering Mutual Funds as Investments for Your Club," mutual funds can provide diversification, but buying mutual funds doesn't teach you much about investing in individual stock.

One way to get around the no-diversification problem when you're first starting out is to defer buying stock for a few months, while your club

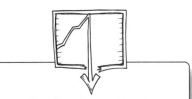

Heading for a Crash

One of the biggest problems with any new investment club often is a lack of diversification. Working toward diversification must be a common goal of the club. If it's not, and the club doesn't diversify, you could be facing big problems down the road.

accumulates some cash. That would give you more time to research and decide what to purchase, and allow you to get more than one or two companies when you do buy.

Accumulating all the dividends your club receives and adding them to your new monthly dues also will help you to gradually be able to buy more stock and work toward diversifying your portfolio. And as Martha Stewart would say, that's a good thing.

Another form of dividend reinvestment can occur within your brokerage account. Let's say that your club has decided that every quarter, when it receives its Ford Motor Company dividends, it will reinvest those dividends right back into more Ford Motor Company stock.

If you instruct your broker of that plan, he'll make sure that your dividend payments are immediately reinvested in more Ford stock.

The brokerage house method of reinvesting is a great way for an investment club to add to its initial holding in a company. If your club was only able to buy 30 shares of Ford stock as an initial investment, however, but wants to increase its holding to at least 100 shares, reinvesting dividends puts you on the road to accumulating more shares.

Maybe your dividends will only buy another couple of shares. Still, you're heading toward your goal of 100 shares. But remember, just because you haven't received the dividend directly as cash, you still have to pay income tax on the amount of the dividend reinvestment. You really did receive the funds, you just immediately put them to work, again, in another investment.

Dividend Reinvestment Plans

Adding dividends to your monthly dues, or having your brokerage house reinvest them, are methods of reinvesting dividends. They're not, however, real reinvestment plans.

In this section, we'll talk about dividend reinvestment plans, known as DRPs (sometimes pronounced *drips*). Basically, a DRP is an automatic system of reinvesting the dividends you receive from a company back into that company.

How DRPs Work

Once you've set up a dividend reinvestment plan (DRP), it works as follows. Every time a dividend is paid on a stock you own, the money is put back into your account and used to purchase as many shares (both whole shares and fractional) as possible.

Dividend reinvestment can occur in two ways. The first occurs within your brokerage account, as we discussed earlier in this chapter. That's how your club can gradually increase its amount of Ford Motor Company stock, while still using its monthly dues to buy other kinds of stock with which to diversify its portfolio.

Your broker will handle the dividend reinvestment for you, but you'll need to keep records of the additional shares of stock your club accumulates.

If your brokerage house does not offer a dividend reinvestment plan, or for some reason you don't want to do the reinvestment through the brokerage house, the second way to reinvest is to go directly to the company's DRP. Many companies, especially large ones, such as ExxonMobil, Ford, and Bristol Myers, offer their own DRPs.

The second method of dividend reinvestment is going directly with the company. You can go to ExxonMobil's Web site, and click on the dividend reinvestment spot. Many companies advise you of their DRP plans when you first purchase their stock. If you sign up for the plan, then each quarter when the dividends are paid, the company will reinvest the funds immediately in additional shares of stock. Sound easy? It is!

Why DRPs Work

DRPs work because they enable small shareholders, such as your club, to keep buying additional shares of a company without incurring a brokerage commission every time you buy. You'd only pay a commission on the initial buy.

DRPs work because they free your club from the reinvestment decision. You can worry about other things, knowing that your dividend will be automatically reinvested back into the company they came from every quarter.

It can be a slow process, but DRPs work. We've known investors, who over time have increased the shares of a company three times by using a dividend reinvestment plan.

Some clubs have even sold their original holdings and are only holding the DRP shares for future gain.

Some investors are fanatic about timing their trades—only trading when they think conditions are absolutely right. When you reinvest dividends through a DRP, you don't have the luxury of market timing. You have to depend on dollar cost averaging. This means that you buy the stock at the going price, trusting that you'll get a good average, over time. Studies have shown that an investor's stock performs better if shares are held for the long term, rather than trying to time the market.

Caution Signs for Dividend Reinvestment Plans

DRPs are great for all the reasons mentioned in the last couple of sections. Be very careful, however, of the costs involved with these plans. Some questions to ask include:

➤ Is there a fee charged to purchase the shares?

➤ If so, what is the fee?

➤ What percentage of the price of the stock is that fee?

➤ Is there a minimum fee for the shares purchased?

Another concern with DRPs has to do with record keeping. It's very important that your club treasurer pays close attention to any dividend reinvesting your club does and makes sure that all is in order with the statements you'll receive.

Finding the Companies That Pay Dividends

As we mentioned earlier, most stock reports will tell you whether the company in question pays a dividend. Remind your club members to look for that information when they're researching companies in order to recommend or not recommend stock.

We use the America Online finance center to get quick information about stocks. When you get a stock quote from the AOL's finance center, it tells you the dividend yield. To have a dividend yield, the company must pay a dividend.

We already mentioned that you can find out about dividends in Value Line, which usually is available at your public library,or online at www.valueline.com.

While dividends can be fun and exciting, they're not, in themselves, the best reason to purchase a particular stock. If you get stock in a good company that's likely to increase in value, then the dividends are just the icing on the cake. You should, however, have more reasons for buying stock than the dividend it pays.

The Least You Need to Know

➤ Trading stocks might seem appealing, but hanging onto them is usually a smarter option.

➤ Dividends are a portion of a company's profit that's distributed to shareholders.

➤ Reinvesting dividends can make a big difference in your club's earning power.

➤ You can reinvest dividends on your own or through a dividend reinvestment plan.

➤ There are some things to watch for when reinvesting dividends.

It's Trading Time

The stock market, as you've no doubt figured out by now, is a funny thing. It has fascinated people for years. It sometimes can be your best friend, and other times seem like your worst enemy.

Because the stock market is so mysterious and difficult to figure out, it can be very intimidating. Sometimes it's hard to know what to do, or how to get started and keep your investments moving ahead.

We're all pretty optimistic about the stock market at this point in time, but there's always the question of what it's going to do and how our investments might be affected.

On January 15, 2000, 98 stocks on the New York Stock Exchange hit 52-week highs in the market. That's great, if you owned one or more of those stocks. On that same day, however, 41 stocks on the Exchange (including Hershey Foods and I ask you, how can you go wrong with chocolate bars?) hit a new 52-week low.

On the same day, 247 stocks hit 52-week highs on the NASDAQ, but 42 stocks hit new lows. The point of all this is to emphasize how important it is to know about the companies in which you're buying stock. If you're going to trade in the stock market, it pays to know as much about those companies as possible.

What Does It Mean to Trade a Stock?

When you trade stock, you execute a buy or sell order, either with a broker or online. Once your club has voted to execute a trade, your broker, or a club member, will call and order the purchase.

Cashing In

If you want an in-depth look at the stock market, try reading *How the Stock Market Works,* by John M. Dalton. Available through Amazon.com or BarnesandNoble.com, the book gives an interesting overview of the market and how it operates.

Cashing In

Companies issue a specific number of shares of stock. Once those shares are all issued, a buyer can only purchase shares if a current shareholder is willing to sell his.

After the order is made, the brokerage house sends a message to the New York Stock Exchange (NYSE) for execution of the trade. If the stock is not listed on the NYSE, the brokerage house would contact the appropriate exchange.

If the stock is listed on NASDAQ, a computer message is sent, directing the trade. As discussed in Chapter 14, "Understanding the Stock Market Before You Jump In," NASDAQ is a computerized system of stock trades. Trades aren't made in person—all transactions are handled by computer.

Trading stock is a lot different from most of the other transactions you make. If you go to Wal-Mart to buy tires, for instance, you simply walk over to the automotive department and tell the salesperson what it is you want. He takes four tires off the shelf, you pay the stated price for them, and out you go. If you decide not to buy the tires, they'll sit on the shelf until somebody who wants them comes around. If there's suddenly a big demand for tires because of a worse-than-normal pothole season, or some other reason, Wal-Mart can order more from the tire manufacturer.

Purchasing stock is very different from buying tires. For every share of stock that's purchased, a share of stock must be sold in order for a trade to be executed. There's only a certain amount of stock out there. Each company only has so much stock issued, so there are only so many shares available to sell.

If there isn't much interest in selling a particular stock, the price keeps rising until shareholders decide it's too good to pass up and they agree to sell their shares. There still, however, are a limited number of shares to be had.

The stock market keeps track of what's available to buy and sell through a system of bids and asked prices.

Once the trade is executed, your club has three business days in which to get the money to your broker for settlement. This can be accomplished in two ways. One way is for your club treasurer to send a check immediately to the brokerage house in order to meet the three-day requirement. Or funds might be sent ahead of time to the brokerage house, and held there in a money market fund until they're needed for a trade.

It's usually required to have funds in the account before your club's first trade, unless the broker knows your club well.

The Pros and Cons of Trading

Some of the reasons you've chosen to be part of an investment club is to get to the point where you understand the process of investing. Therefore, you're able to base your decisions to buy and sell stock on solid information about companies, rather than on feelings or instinct.

Your club's decisions to purchase or sell stock should be based on knowledge, not gut feelings or tips you picked up at last week's happy hour or soccer game.

Trading stock is serious business for numerous reasons. For starters, trading costs money. Even with online trading, there is a cost involved with going in and out of a stock. If your club is using a full-service broker, the cost to make a trade is signifi-cantly higher than with a discount broker.

Your club will have to pay a *transaction cost,* called a brokerage fee, to purchase shares of stock. It'll have to pay another cost to sell the stock. No mat-ter what the charge is, it factors into the total re-turn for the holding. The costs of trading stock should be taken into consideration.

A good thing about trading is that it ties in your club's gains on a security. Let's say, for instance, that you bought Hewlett-Packard stock at $52 per share, and let's say that the current price of your stock is $134 per share. If you sell that stock, the gain you realize can never be taken from your club. If you hold the stock, the gain is only on paper, and could disappear if the value of the stock falls.

Taking Stock

Transaction costs (commissions and fees) add to the costs of purchasing shares of a stock, and in reverse, lower the total amount you'll get when you sell a stock. These costs lower the total return that your club makes on the stock.

Take This to the Bank

Talk about a roller coaster! Hewlett-Packard stock started at $60 per share in the beginning of 1999. Within a year, it rose to $118 per share, dropped back to $70 a share, and rebounded back to $134 per share.

Some stocks do drop and stay down permanently, or for a very long time. We know of a club that held a stock that was as low as $40 per share. They held onto the stock and watched with great frustration as it went down and down, until the company eventually declared bankruptcy.

In the final analysis, sometimes it's beneficial to trade stock, and sometimes the best thing you can do is sit tight and see what happens.

How Do You Trade Stock?

We all know that stock is traded constantly—it's what keeps the market interesting and stockbrokers in business. But exactly how does stock get traded?

How can your investment club, located in the heartland of America, connect with the stock exchanges in New York City to get the stock you want at the prices you want to pay?

We gave you a basic explanation of the mechanics of trading stock in the "What Does It Mean to Trade a Stock?" section of this chapter. In following sections, we'll talk about some specific trading techniques and explain what they can do for you.

Market Orders

The standard way to trade stock is through a market order. When you make a *market order,* you call your broker and tell him that you want to buy a stock. The broker orders the stock for you and you pay the market price. If your club wants to buy 10 shares of General Electric (GE), for instance, you could end up paying $150 a share, or $149.50 a share, or $150.25 a share. You'll pay the price of the share at the time the order is made.

The volatility of some of today's high-priced Internet and technology stocks is so great that you can never be certain throughout the day about the price of the stock. You could think that you're buying stock at a particular price, when it could actually be much higher or lower.

So, while a market order is the easiest method of trading stock, it's not always what your club may want to do.

Taking Stock

When you place a **market order,** you get the stock you specify for the price it's selling at when the order is placed.

Good-Til-Cancelled Orders

If your club has reviewed the fundamentals of a company and agreed to buy the stock, but doesn't want to pay more than a specific price, it can submit a *good-til-cancelled order*.

By doing so, you're directing that your broker only purchase the stock at the price you specify. This eliminates the possibility of you paying too much for the stock.

Let's say, for example, that your club has decided that Sovereign Bank stock is a good buy at $6.50 per share. Rather than put in a market order and maybe end up paying $7 or $7.50 a share, you can put in a good-til-cancelled order.

A good-til-cancelled order is held on the books, either for the day, for 60 days, or indefinitely, depending on your brokerage house. Your broker will ask when you put in the good-til-cancelled order if

Taking Stock

A **good-til-cancelled order** directs your broker to purchase stock for your club, but only at a specified price. It allows him to hold the order for a certain period of time to see whether the price will match that specified by the club.

it applies for the day, or for an indefinite time period. For a variety of reasons, many brokerage houses will permit the standing order for only 30 or 60 days.

If you really want a particular stock at a particular price, you can re-up your good-til-cancelled order. Just call your broker when the 30- or 60-day time period expires and renew the order.

Stop-Loss Order

Let's say that your stock has tripled in value. You're thrilled, but you're not yet ready to sell. Still, you'd love to be able to protect your profits on the investment. To do that, your club can submit a *stop-loss order*.

A stop-loss order protects your gain in the event that the value of your stock plummets.

This is an interesting type of trade. If you paid $40 a share for a particular stock, for instance, and it's currently worth $80 a share, you've got a paper profit on the share. As you know, however, what goes up in the stock market sometimes comes down. If you're concerned that the value of your stock could take a drastic downward turn, you could put in a stop-loss order at, say, $60 a share.

If the stock starts falling and hits $60, your broker should automatically trade it. That way, you've still made $20 per share on your investment.

The danger with a stop-loss order, of course, is that the stock could drop for a while, then rebound and go higher than ever. If your stop-loss order has kicked in and your stock is sold, you miss the rebound.

This happened to a club that owned American Express stock. The value of the stock dropped from $108 per share to $98 and the club's stop-loss order kicked in at $100 per share. The stock rebounded back, and currently is worth $159 per share. Club members still realized a gain on their investment, but they're not happy when they look at the current value.

As you can see, trading occurs in different ways. While market trades are the most common and simplest, good-til-cancelled orders and stop-loss orders can be useful and beneficial to your club.

Getting Input from All Club Members Before a Trade

Part of every club meeting should be spent reviewing the current stock holdings of your investment club. Each member has a particular stock to follow, and is required to apprise other members of any company news or pertinent information that could affect the value of the stock.

Because your club primarily purchases stock as investors and not traders, most of your stock will be held. Normally, unless the stock has reached its target price or the earnings are suffering due to unforeseen problems at the firm, no action will be necessary.

Quarterly report figures and other pertinent information should be presented so that members know how the stock is performing. Although most club members might not care that the revenue for a particular company is $10,000,000 for the quarter, everyone needs to know the direction of the revenue trend.

Higher revenue within a company is good, while lower revenue needs to be examined. Maybe there's something going on within the company that will affect its stock value. These are the kinds of issues your club should be examining.

All club members should be involved in any discussion about whether a stock should be traded. The temptation, sometimes, is to listen to the member who's responsible for the presentation, and take his or her recommendation at face value.

The only way that all members can be involved in the club, and learn from it, is to get involved in discussions. A vote on whether to hold or trade a stock should only occur after everyone is fully aware of all the implications of each option and understands them. If there is extensive discussion about whether to trade a stock, and some members aren't comfortable with voting on the matter at the present time, it's okay to hold off voting until the next meeting. If there are members who are in a hurry to vote, you may have to vote on whether or not to vote, and defer to the wishes of the majority.

Cashing In

Each member should have at least one stock to follow throughout the month. The member should look for any news articles about the stock and come prepared at each meeting with a recommendation to buy more, sell, or hold the stock.

If your operating agreement calls for a majority vote in order to sell a stock, you only need more than half of your membership to agree. Some clubs require 60 percent approval to trade stocks, while others even require 75 percent.

If members vote not to trade a stock, discussion on that particular stock can be opened again at the next meeting.

We know of several investment clubs that, rather than having one member responsible for tracking the stock of one company, have one or two members review the entire list of holdings each month. Those members recommend any changes they might think are necessary and what to do with the club's monthly dues.

Heading for a Crash

If your club requires 75 percent of the membership to approve a stock trade, you might find that you're bogged down and unable to get the votes needed to do so. The higher the percentage required to approve a trade, the more difficult it is to secure agreement to trade.

This method forces each member to review all the holdings at least once a year. It's more work during the month that it's your turn to review the holdings, but it makes all members aware of all the companies in which the club's invested.

It's imperative that the club members have a good general knowledge of the club's holdings so that they understand and feel comfortable with the monthly recommendations and are able to make knowledgeable decisions when they vote.

Recognizing When the Time Is Right to Trade

When your club purchases a stock, it should set a target price. The target price establishes where you want your investment to be within a specific time period.

It should be reported to the club when you reach a target price. A discussion should follow about whether the target price should be upped, the stock should be sold, or the club should hold onto the stock and see what happens.

After all the information is presented and discussed, club members can vote on whether to keep or trade the stock.

We will spend all of Chapter 21, "Know When to Walk Away," discussing how to know when the time if right to sell a stock, so we won't get into it much now.

A few of the signals that it might be time to consider selling are ...

➤ You notice a sudden large increase in a company's debt.

➤ There's a drop in the company's revenue.

➤ The price of the company's stock has a sudden and unexplained increase.

➤ The company undergoes a drastic change in management.

➤ The fundamentals of the company have changed.

➤ The company's product is becoming outmoded or outdated and there's nothing to replace it.

Cashing In

Many investment advisers recommend selling if a holding is greater than 7 percent of your account. Others say it's okay to keep a stock until it's greater than 10 percent.

Another possible signal to sell is if a particular stock has grown so much that the holding is greater than a percentage of your total portfolio.

Members may find it difficult to sell a stock that has been a part of their portfolio for a long time, or if it has performed particularly well.

Motorola stock has recently tripled in price. If your club bought its shares at $60 each, and now the stock is worth $151 a share, what should you do? Should you hang on to the stock, or trade it?

If they think that the stock price has the potential to continue to move even higher, club members might be very reluctant to sell off this great stock. But if the value of the total Motorola holding has increased to more than 7 or 10 percent of your club's portfolio, it probably should be scaled back. If not, it can become a liability.

One piece of bad press or an unforeseen problem can create a large drop in one stock and end up hurting your club's entire account. As an example, the value of Tyco International stock dropped almost 50 percent in one day when an allegation was made about the company's accounting method. If Tyco represented 10 percent of your portfolio, you'd have really taken a hit when the value of the stock dropped. See the following table for more examples.

	Value	Cost	Potential Gain
Computer Associates (CA)	$10,750	$5,252	$5,498
Cisco (CSCO)	$60,850	$12,000	$48,850
Hershey Foods (HSY)	$9,350	$4,263	$5,087
General Motors H (GMH)	$11,850	$3,549	$8,301
Packard (HWP)	$27,050	$10,550	$16,500
TYCO	$22,432	$11,252	$11,180

This is why diversification in your portfolio is imperative. If a holding increases in value until it reaches more than 10 percent of your total account, some of that holding should be sold. You don't need to sell all of the stock, but you should scale back. It should be specified in your club's operating agreement that no single investment should represent more than a certain percentage of the total portfolio.

When a holding doubles in value, many investors will sell their initial investment, figuring that whatever happens from that point on is "gravy." This isn't a reason to hold a stock until the end of time, but it's a way to protect the club's initial investment, while keeping the stock for its future investment.

Most investment advisers base their decisions to buy or sell a stock either on the company's fundamentals, or because the stock has risen beyond the recommended 7 to 10 percent value of the portfolio.

Club members also should review their company's fundamentals monthly, make informed decisions, act on those decisions, and protect their profits.

Taking Stock

Although diversification is the accepted rule of thumb, and is considered the smart thing to do by most financial people, not everyone agrees. Phil Weiss, a CPA, argues in an article that appeared on the Motley Fool Web site (www.fool.com) that diversification is overrated, and it actually is better to limit the number of companies in which you invest and get to know the companies well.

The Least You Need to Know

➤ Trading stock is executing—either with a broker or online—an order to buy or sell.

➤ There are advantages and disadvantages associated with trading stock.

➤ There are different methods of trading stock that can be beneficial to your club in certain situations.

➤ It's important to fully understand what happens when stock is traded.

➤ Every member of your club should be involved with the discussion of whether or not to trade.

➤ There are situations in which trading is not only appropriate, but recommended.

Chapter 21

Know When to Walk Away

In This Chapter

➤ Resisting the temptation to sell unnecessarily

➤ When your stock turns out to be no good

➤ Recognizing when the price of your stock has peaked

➤ Bad reasons to sell your stock

➤ Getting emotionally connected to your stock

To everything there is a season. A time to overindulge; a time to spend some additional hours at the gym; a time to throw on sweats and your running shoes; a time to dress for business; a time to take a good, long vacation; and a time to put in some extra hours at the office.

There also is a time to sell stocks, and a time to hang on to them. There's a well-known and much-circulated story among the financial crowd involving the famous, and extremely wealthy, investor Warren Buffet. Somebody, the story goes, asked Buffet one day what was the average length of time that Buffet held onto stock. Buffet's reply, according to the story, was "forever."

Not everyone, however, thinks that all stocks should be held forever. There are some very convincing reasons to sell stock in certain situations.

In this chapter, we'll discuss how you can recognize when it's time to sell. Deciding whether to sell or hold can be tricky, and there are many factors to consider. So, let's get started.

Don't Be in a Big Hurry to Bail Out

Watching the stock market is sort of like eating dinner with a six-year-old boy.

Scrutinizing either one too carefully can make you a nervous wreck and ruin your appetite. On the other hand, if you leave both alone, they'll probably do just fine.

Keeping an eye on how your stocks are doing and evaluating them from time to time is a great idea. Checking on them every hour, however, is likely to serve no other purpose than to cause you great anxiety.

It has been documented that less experienced investors are more likely than veterans to sell off stock when the price drops below what they paid for it, or if the market starts to look a little shaky.

While that's a natural reaction, it's generally not the smartest thing to do. In some ways, investors are like poker players. They sometimes have to sit tight, act cool, and hang onto their cards.

Cashing In

When you're tempted to sell stock that has faltered, remember the process you went through before buying that stock. You didn't rush into buying it. You researched, analyzed, and did your homework. You should do the same thing before selling it, even if you're tempted to get rid of it fast.

If the stock you own isn't performing as well as you think it should be, you've got to find out why. Is it just a temporary dip in the market? Or are there real problems within the company that are unlikely to be resolved any time soon?

There are many instances in which smart investors have patiently and trustingly hung onto stock in good companies while, for one reason or another, it lost much of its value. If the company is fundamentally sound, the stock is likely to rebound nicely and reward those who had the faith to keep it.

In fact, many experienced investors rush to buy stocks when their value takes a dive. A broker can show you investment funds made up of big, respected companies that for one reason or another are experiencing slumps.

We saw one investment fund recently that offered companies including Toys 'R Us, Sears, Hershey Foods, AT&T, and K-Mart. These are fundamentally sound businesses, which for one reason or another have recently gotten clobbered and the value of their stock dropped dramatically. Some investors welcome the opportunity to buy at that point, figuring that the companies—and their stock values—will rebound.

It's important to remember that investing is different than trading. Online investing has given rise to a whole new world of day trading, that's now available to anyone with a computer, Internet service, and the considerable time and interest necessary to participate.

While day trading sounds glamorous—we recently read about a former CPA who moved to an island off of Florida, where he's made millions of dollars as he merrily makes dozens of trades each day—it's by no means a model for investment clubs.

Day trading might be exciting and profitable (although we all know that isn't always the case; in fact, studies have shown that the majority of day traders don't turn profits), but it's a very different thing from investing.

So, if you're tempted to get rid of a stock, think carefully about your reasons for wanting to do so. We're certainly not saying that selling is never warranted. In the very next section, in fact, we'll give you some very valid reasons for selling stock. All we're saying is that you shouldn't be in a big hurry to bail out, especially if you're fairly new to investing and haven't had much experience in selling.

Heading for a Crash

Don't let the collective opinion of your investment club be too influenced by the desires of one member. Watch out for the domino effect that can occur if one member panics over a decrease in stock value and tries to get other members to agree to sell. Panic is contagious, and your club could end up making a bad decision fueled by the anxiety of just one member.

There's a time to sell and a time to hang onto stocks. Before you do either, though, consider all the pros and cons, and make a well thought-out, responsible decision.

Reasons to Get Rid of an Investment

Having explained the importance of not selling stock impulsively, or for the wrong reasons, we'll now discuss circumstances and situations in which you probably should get rid of investments.

Unlike Warren Buffet, we don't buy into the "never" theory of selling stock.

One reason for that might be because we don't have as much money as Warren Buffet. Chances are pretty slim that Warren's going to have to sell off some stock in order to have enough money to pay for an in-ground swimming pool in his back yard.

Chances are much better, however, that you'll want to sell some stock in order to put in a pool, or finance another major expense. After all, what's the point of investing and earning money if you're never going to use it?

Sure, it's nice to think about leaving a legacy for your kids. It's great to know that your spouse will be well provided for if you die first. And it's great to think about having tons of money to spend after you retire. While those all are considerations, there's also the point to be made of living now.

You've no doubt heard some of those stories about people with millions of dollars worth of investments or other types of assets who live in desperately poor conditions, refusing to spend any of their money. You've also no doubt heard stories about people who hoard their money in order to have a great retirement, only to die before they reach retirement age.

What's the point?

If your investments have been successful, and you want or need the money for a good reason, then go ahead and sell what you need to sell to get it. This doesn't mean you should rush out and sell every investment you have, just don't ignore what you have, if you need it for a good reason.

Needing money is a good reason to sell stock, but not the only one. Let's have a look at some other situations in which you might consider getting rid of an investment.

Your Stock Turns Out to Be a Big Loser

Sometimes, no matter how carefully you research a company and analyze its stock, or how much time your club spends discussing, debating, and finally deciding to buy the stock, it turns out to be a loser.

If that's the case, you're better off getting rid of it.

Before you do, however, you need to make sure that it really is a bad stock, not just a stock that's not doing well at the moment. There are sources to help you make that determination. There are all kinds of reports and newsletters to help you keep track of how your stocks are doing and why. Some of the biggies include:

Cashing In

Remember that in an investment club, everyone shares responsibility for stock selection. If the stock turns out to be a winner, everyone takes credit. If it turns out to be a real loser, everyone shares the blame. Don't be reluctant to get rid of a bad stock because you're afraid you'll hurt the feelings of the person who recommended it. The club voted to buy it, so it's not the fault of any one member.

➤ **Moody's.** Moody's Investor Service is well respected when it comes to rating stocks and bonds. Most of its publications can be found in the library. Moody's can be reached toll-free at 1-800-342-5647, or accessed on the Internet at www.moodys.com.

➤ **Value Line.** The *Value Line's Investment Survey* includes not only facts and figures, but analyzes and gives you all sorts of information about different companies. Also usually available in the library, the Value Line Investment Survey is a comprehensive, extremely useful publication. Value Line can be found on the Web at www.valueline.com, or reached at 1-800-833-0046.

➤ **Standard & Poor's.** Yep. The same company that produces the S&P 500 Index offers *The S&P Reports OnDemand*, which is another popular resource for investors. It provides information on more than 4,000 companies, with more than 10,000 price and index charts. Standard & Poor's can be reached at 1-800-292-0808, or located on the Web at www.standardpoor.com.

➤ **Bloomberg.** One of the best informational services provided to investment advisers and brokers over the years is now available to everyone via the Internet. Up-to-the-minute information about most securities is available online, along with good amounts of research information. Find it at www.bloomberg.com.

There are many more research houses that publish stock reports and analyses, but these four are some of the best known and respected.

Another financial source that you might find useful is *The Wall Street Journal*. *The Journal* contains all kinds of helpful and interesting information, and it's not difficult to read and understand.

Publications such as these will help you understand what's going on within the company and how it's affecting the value of the stock. It could be that something temporary is happening, and the stock will rebound as soon as the situation is resolved.

Take This to the Bank

Remember that if you sell stock for less than what you paid for it, you can claim a capital loss on your income tax statement, which decreases the amount of taxable income you have. That can sometimes be a factor in deciding whether or not to sell.

If the president of a large company dies or retires, for instance, the value of the stock certainly will be affected. But if there's a smooth transition to new leadership and the company continues to run as it had before, the value of the stocks most likely will quickly recover.

A good example of this occurred in 1999, when General Electric CEO Jack Welsh announced that he would retire in the summer of 2001. GE stock took a hit, but quickly rebounded when investors came to their senses and figured out that GE has a well-trained and competent management team ready to step into place.

If, on the other hand, 90 percent of a company's top management has resigned within the past month due to extremely serious circumstances within the company, then the stock is likely to be permanently affected.

Stock for Rite Aid Pharmacy had hit a new high of $51 per share in the spring of 1999, when it was discovered that the firm was transacting inappropriate business. Stock fell to $4 per share, and has since rebounded slightly to about $10 per share. If you owned any Rite Aid stock during this time, you would have been faced with the decision of whether to accept your loss and bail out, or wait and hope that the new management can turn the company around.

If the stock isn't performing well and you're not sure whether it's a bad stock or just a temporary setback, don't rush to sell it. Wait it out for a couple of months and keep an eye on what happens. If the stock is still sliding, then you'll have to re-evaluate.

You Think Your Stock Is as High as It's Going to Go

When you buy a stock, it's a good idea to set some expectations for it. This is called setting a target price, and it's a decision you should make when you decide to buy a stock. Many investors consider a reasonable expectation to be that their stock will double in value in five years.

Unfortunately, you can't predict the value of your stocks in five years like you can predict what a bond will be worth at a certain date, or what the money you put in a certificate of deposit will be worth when the term of the CD is up.

If you're lucky, you'll double your money in less than five years. It could, however, take longer. When it does reach the goal that you've set for it, however, you should take a close look at the stock and its company.

While you're doing your homework, you might find out that analysts are predicting the stock you own won't appreciate in value any more than it has. This would be based on information about what's happening within the company.

Taking Stock

Fundamental analysis is a system that evaluates a company's overall condition based on various criteria that measure the company's health. Many investment clubs use fundamental analysis when deciding whether or not to buy a company's stock.

A system commonly used to evaluate companies is called *fundamental analysis*. Many investment clubs rely on it when deciding whether to buy or sell a company's stock.

Fundamental analysis looks at a variety of factors concerning companies. Some of those factors include:

➤ **The company's industry rating.** You can find a company's ranking in publications such as *Value Line's Investment Survey*. If the company you're investigating isn't in the top third of its industry, warning bells should sound.

➤ **The amount of debt the company has.** A company with a huge amount of debt probably isn't a smart choice in which to invest. A company's total debt should be no more than one third of its total assets. You can get this information from S&P Reports, Value Line, or the company's annual report.

➤ **The price of the company's stock.** The price of the stock will, naturally, affect how much your club can buy. Young clubs often look for stocks that are fairly inexpensive so that they can buy a round, or even, lot. A *round lot* is a group of 100 *shares,* the opposite being an *odd lot.* If you buy a round lot of a stock that costs $35 a share, for instance, you'd have to pay $3,500. If you're thinking about selling your stock, consider how many shares you have, and whether or not you want to sell all of them, or hold some.

➤ **The company's sales and earnings.** Take a look at the sales and earnings of the company over the past five years or so. Has it been consistently profitable, or have there been a lot of ups and downs? Also, note the company's projection for future growth. That information is available in Value Line or one of the other investment reports. If the company is not projected for growth, it could be that your stock value has peaked.

➤ **The amount of risk associated with the stock.** No stock is risk-proof, but some are more risky than others. Investment reports list risk factors, which you should consider in your fundamental analysis. If you see that the risk factor of the stock you're holding has increased, you might want to think about selling it.

➤ **The company's product line.** Is the product line diversified, or does the company depend on one product for its success? A company that makes and sells only miniskirts, for instance, will be okay as long as women are wearing miniskirts. When fashion tastes change, as they're bound to, and hemlines fall, the company will be out of luck. Make sure the company in which you've invested manufactures and sells enough products so that if one fails, the company isn't entirely dependent on it.

➤ **The company's management.** Management can make or break a company. Do your homework and find out what experts have to say about the management

Taking Stock

Shares of stock are usually sold in **round lots,** which are groups of 100. Groups of less than 100 are called **odd lots.**

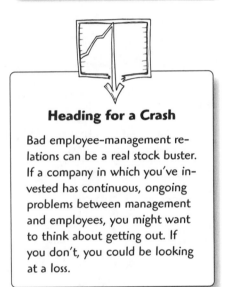

Heading for a Crash

Bad employee-management relations can be a real stock buster. If a company in which you've invested has continuous, ongoing problems between management and employees, you might want to think about getting out. If you don't, you could be looking at a loss.

of the company in which you've invested. Be particularly cautious if there have been a lot of recent changes in management, or if you've heard of employee problems, the threat of strikes, and so forth. A publication such as *The Wall Street Journal* would contain that kind of information.

These are some of the factors to consider when you're trying to decide whether or not your stock has reached its top value. They all affect whether or not it's a good idea to sell your stock.

When deciding whether or not to sell, you'll take into account many of the same factors that you considered when trying to decide whether or not to buy the stock in the first place. You have to do the same homework, but for a different reason.

If, after careful review, you decide that your stock is probably as high as it's going to get and you can sell it at a good price, go ahead and get rid of it.

Bad Reasons to Sell Your Stock

While there are some good reasons to sell stock, there also are some bad ones.

We already discussed the dangers of nervous selling. Almost every experienced buyer will tell you that unless there are extenuating circumstances, such as those mentioned in the last section, the best thing to do is to hang onto your stock and wait for a rebound.

Cashing In

Trading stock is different from investing in stock. Trading stock is when you buy and sell stock actively, with the intention of turning a profit. Investing is when you buy stock with the intention of keeping it for a significant period of time.

Sometimes that's hard to do. If you have a lot of money invested, it's hard not to panic when the market takes a nose dive, as it does from time to time. It's natural to think you're losing your shirt (or whatever) and want to cut your losses the best you can.

However, experience shows again and again that stocks of good companies, when left alone for the long haul, tend to increase in value.

So, if a particular stock that you have, or the market in general, starts to dip, try to stay calm and hang on. Assuming that the company in which you're invested is fundamentally sound, you can trust that better times are coming.

There are some other bad reasons to sell stock, as well. Some investors get bored if they don't see a lot of action, and they sell so they can buy something that might be more exciting. Again, that goes more toward trading than investing, and it's investing that your club was formed to do.

The National Association of Investors Corporation (NAIC) warns against reacting to paper losses and profits. A paper loss is when the price of your stock drops and, if you sold it, the loss that you'd take. A paper profit, on the other hand, is the amount that you'd gain if you sold your stock at an increased price.

These calculations are just that—calculations. Profit and loss don't become real until the stock has been sold. Thinking about making or losing money, or looking at it on paper, isn't a good reason to sell your stock.

Don't sell your stock because of a temporary condition that adversely affects the company. We mentioned this briefly earlier in the chapter, and it's an important tip to keep in mind. Things can go wrong within a company, just as they can in a family, or church, or school. There could be a fire, a natural disaster, or a case of bad management that couldn't be anticipated.

As long as the company is fundamentally sound, it's best to leave your stock alone and wait for the trouble to pass. Factories get rebuilt when the insurance money becomes available. Unethical or bad managers can be fired and replaced with top-notch people.

There probably are at least as many reasons not to sell stock as there are to sell it. Granted, however, there are cases in which selling is the best thing you can do.

When that situation arises, it's important to be able to recognize it and to act decisively. Your club has got to be able to work together to do what's best for your portfolio and the future of the group.

Perils of Getting Emotionally Involved with a Stock

Every now and then, we hear about a situation in which members of an investment club, or perhaps the entire club, become emotionally involved with a stock that it purchased.

This is a bad situation, and one that is potentially dangerous to the health of the club.

Emotional involvement with a company and its stock occurs sometimes if the club has invested in a local company, or a company at which some club members are employed.

It may happen if club members really believe in the company's product. Sometimes a person develops some sort of attachment to a high-profile company executive, and wants to invest in the company for that reason.

As you can imagine, none of these are smart reasons to hold onto stock. If all indicators show that the stock you're holding is bad, or that it has peaked and will go no higher, you should sell it, regardless of any attachment you might feel to the company.

Some people buy stock because they really love the product. If you're one of just a handful of people across the country who love Dolly's Double Chocolate Delights, however, you're looking at a losing proposition. If Dolly's stocks are dogs, get rid of them, no matter how much you like her chocolate delights.

275

When you're done selling your stock, you might want to think about stockpiling some of those treats. They probably won't be found in your grocery store for much longer.

Buying and selling stock should be done in a thoughtful manner, based on facts and indicators—not emotion.

To Trade or Not To Trade

There no doubt will be times during the life of your investment club when members will disagree on various subjects. Whether or not to trade stock is a likely source of those disagreements.

Hopefully, the problem of whether or not to trade stock will be resolved with a vote. After all, that's the spirit of an investment club, or any type of club, for that matter. You win some, you lose some. Not everyone always gets their way in a club situation—that's just not how clubs work. You've got to go with majority rule, or whatever is specified in your operating agreements.

If there are club members, however, who are in disagreement with the majority of the club about whether or not to trade a stock, and they're insistent about their point of view, the subject can be re-opened for discussion at more than one meeting.

Make sure that all members get their say, but, on the other hand, don't waste too much time debating the merits of a stock on account of a few members.

The Least You Need to Know

➤ Hanging on to a stock that's dipped in value, or when the market is in a downturn, can be nerve-wracking and difficult, but it's often the best course of action.

➤ Although it's usually good to sit on your stock until the value comes back up, there are some instances in which the best thing you can do is sell it.

➤ There are some invaluable tools available that can help you determine whether you should hang onto your stocks or sell them.

➤ There probably are more bad reasons than good reasons to sell stock.

➤ Getting emotionally involved with a company and its stock is not a smart way to operate. Buying and selling stocks should be objective and based on fact.

➤ Consider the viewpoints of all members, but don't spend too much time debating the merits of one stock on account of a few people who disagree with the majority view.

Chapter 22

Keeping Club Members Invested

In This Chapter

➤ Getting everybody to pitch in

➤ Encouraging club members to work as a team

➤ Avoiding being overly disappointed at losses

➤ It's okay for members to disagree

➤ Keeping everybody involved

We think that by now it should be clear to everybody that, while belonging to an investment club has plenty of rewards, it also entails a certain amount of work.

Work such as researching companies, tracking investments, and reporting back to other club members.

We talked a lot about these jobs in earlier chapters, and hopefully, you understand the mechanics of how they should be done. In this chapter, we want to focus more on the spirit of your investment club and how members are pulling together to make the club operate at its full potential.

It's discouraging, but true, that one or two people really can bring down an organization, and investment clubs aren't immune to that danger.

We just can't emphasize strongly enough how important it is that everyone in your club pitches in and does his or her part. Just as with any group that's working toward a common goal, your investment club should be operating with a spirit of teamwork and cooperation.

In this chapter, we'll ask you to think about the health of your investment club. Are members working together to make the club effective and profitable? Is every member doing his or her share of club work? Let's have a look.

Everyone Should Be Responsible for Tracking Investments

The work that's required to keep an investment club running doesn't belong just to the club president, or the treasurer, or the men and women of the group. It belongs to everyone.

As you've probably learned by now, tracking investments is one of the primary jobs for club members. We've talked a lot about how to track stocks in earlier chapters. You can refer back for a refresher if you need to.

The point of this discussion is not to go over the mechanics of tracking investments, but to stress how important it is that everyone does it.

Some investment clubs assign one member to track one or more particular stocks. It is the responsibility of that member, and no one else, to keep up to date on everything that could affect that stock. Other members, presumably, are busy keeping track of their assigned stocks.

Some clubs report that this system works very well, but we see a danger in it.

Take This to the Bank

An old-fashioned phrase is "many hands make light work." It means that everyone pulling together can accomplish a lot, without any one member having to do too much. Makes sense to us!

We all have days when we don't accomplish as much as we'd like to. Sometimes it feels like that's true of most days, not just occasionally.

Maybe you don't feel very well for a couple of days and it's all you can do to drag yourself into work, sit at your desk, then come back home to lie on the couch when the day ends. Your investment club stock is the last thing on your mind.

Or, perhaps you're extremely busy with a personal project that consumes all your free time. Maybe, for instance, you're helping your daughter plan her wedding. By the time you get back in the evening from helping her try on gowns and pore over hundreds of different invitation samples, you're completely exhausted. It occurs to you that you should do some reading, or get on the Internet to see what's going on with your stocks, but you'd much rather just sit and leaf through the newest copy of *Brides* magazine to get an idea of what the best-dressed mothers will be wearing this spring.

You get the idea. Although we make commitments to our investment clubs that we'll be conscientious and do our homework, stuff happens, and sometimes the homework just doesn't get done.

Ideally, there'd be another member of your club you could call and ask for help if you needed it. Somebody who would keep track of your stocks, as well as his own, until you felt better, or until the wedding was over. Some people, however, find it difficult to ask for help. In some cases, members who are busy with their own club work might feel imposed upon if another member asks for help.

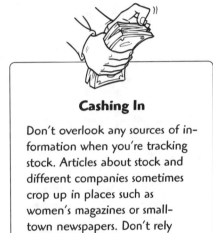

Cashing In

Don't overlook any sources of information when you're tracking stock. Articles about stock and different companies sometimes crop up in places such as women's magazines or small-town newspapers. Don't rely solely on business publications.

We think it works best when members are asked to concentrate on particular stocks, with the understanding that all other members will act as backups.

What that means is that everybody in the club is responsible for tracking every stock, but each member has one, or several stocks for which he or she is responsible for *closely* tracking.

You report to the club on the stocks you track closely, with other members providing additional information when applicable. This works well for several reasons:

➤ **Not everyone has access to the same materials.** Some of the members of your club might get *The Wall Street Journal*. Others use *Value Line's Investment Survey*, while somebody else relies on a financial magazine. Some members regularly use the Internet to keep track of what's happening with your club's stocks, while others check out the stock report in the daily newspaper. Different information regarding stocks and companies will appear in different sources. To make sure you didn't miss anything, you'd have to keep up to date with every available source. Wow! Talk about time consuming. Having everyone on the lookout for information regarding all the club's stocks assures you'll get a wider range.

➤ **You give each other backup.** When a club member gets sick or is busy planning a wedding, she'll have the security of knowing that her appointed stock is not going unmonitored. Other members will be gathering information that can be discussed at the monthly meeting. While club members shouldn't use this security to avoid doing their homework, it's nice to know that somebody's backing you up when you need it.

➤ **It keeps everyone interested in every stock.** Sometimes, when each member is assigned one or two stocks to track, he gets possessive or overly concerned with "his" stocks, and becomes uninterested in the rest of the club's investments. When everyone is responsible for keeping an eye on all of the stocks, it tends to keep members more interested and aware of the big picture.

➤ **It sets the tone for teamwork.** Having everyone work together on tracking stocks tends to create a feeling of common ownership and a sense of camaraderie and teamwork. Assigning one person to a particular stock may sometimes create a feeling of isolation.

It's really important that the members of your investment club feel connected to one another and are willing to help out and share jobs. As you'll read in the next section, teamwork is essential to your club.

The Name of the Game Is Teamwork

Teamwork was mentioned briefly at the end of the previous section, but it's such an important quality of an investment club that it's worth further discussion.

When somebody joins a group, she wants to feel that she belongs. She wants to feel comfortable and that she's accepted and liked.

This is true with almost any situation. Think about the times when you started a new job. Remember how uncomfortable those first couple of weeks were, until you started feeling that you were part of the gang—a member of the team? How about when you first went away to college and you didn't know anyone, or when you moved into a new neighborhood, or joined a professional group?

People generally are social creatures who want to be accepted as part of a group. We also like to feel that we're useful, and most of us are willing to pitch in to achieve a goal we believe in.

Take This to the Bank

The eastern part of the United States experienced a severe drought during the summer of 1999, and it was interesting to see the public's reaction. Most people stopped watering lawns and washing their cars long before those restrictions became law. They did so voluntarily, because they wanted to pitch in and help avert a crisis. They were working as part of a team to accomplish a goal.

Consider the examples of rationing and other public efforts that occurred during World War II. It was a time when everyone pitched in to make sure the country had what it needed for its war effort. Everyone recognized that it was necessary to sacrifice for the good of the country.

Homemakers were told to "use it up, wear it out, make it do, or do without," and they responded admirably. They tore apart old clothing and made it over into new clothes. They used blankets to make coats and jackets, and accepted with little complaint their rations of butter, sugar, and meat.

Women even gave up their beloved nylon stockings, which had been introduced to an extremely receptive public only a short time before the United States got involved in the war. Gas was rationed. Women took over men's jobs in the factories, where they wore overalls and cut their hair.

Cashing In

Smart business leaders recognize the importance of camaraderie and teamwork. Think of your investment club as a business, and you as its leader, as you attempt to motivate the members of your club and get them to work together as a team.

It was a massive effort, in which people willingly participated. They were invested as part of a team, and were willing to do whatever needed to be done to achieve the goals of the team.

Of course, the goals of your investment club aren't on the same level as those of United States citizens during World War II, but we think you'll get the idea.

People work together better when they feel that they're working toward the same goals as part of a unified team.

Think about the best jobs you've had. Chances are they weren't the ones that paid the most, gave you the most vacation, or supplied the fanciest offices. They probably were the ones in which you had a sense of camaraderie and belonging. They were the ones in which you worked as part of a united and committed team.

You'll understand this concept if you've ever been a part of an athletic team, or involved in a theater production, or worked with others for a cause that was very important to you. If you've never experienced true camaraderie and teamwork, being a member of an investment club will give you good opportunity to find out what it's all about.

Beware the Bully Syndrome

Every now and then, you meet up with an honest-to-goodness, bona fide bully. This starts out when you're a kid when there's the constant danger of encountering a bully. Although the bully threat seems to lessen as you move into adulthood, it's still there.

Bullies are people who enjoy intimidating others. They may do so in order to get their own way, or just to give somebody else a hard time.

Psychologists have field days analyzing bullies. All we're going to say is that you never know where or when a bully might show up. It could be in your kid's school, or a new guy at work, or a member of your investment club.

If you notice any intimidation occurring within your club, be sure to address it immediately. Bullying sometimes occurs at a subtle level, so it might not be easy to recognize. It's not unheard of, however, for a member of an investment club to bully another member. This could happen in order for the bully to convince the other guy to back off of a stock choice that the bully doesn't like. Or, maybe the bully proposed a stock for purchase and it was shot down by the other members. The bully might engage in a bit of intimidation to get members to reconsider.

It doesn't happen often, and it's not something to worry about. You should be aware of the intimidation possibility, however, and have an idea of what you'd do about it, should it occur within your club.

We mostly think of children as both being bullies and being bullied, but it occurs within adults, as well.

If you, or someone in your club is being bullied by another member who insists on having his own way, or for some reason doesn't like another member, there are some things to keep in mind.

Bullying can be verbal, physical, emotional, or a combination of those things. It can be a one-on-one thing or can involve several people "ganging up" on another. All bullying involves …

➤ An imbalance of power.

➤ Blaming the victim for what's happened.

➤ A lack of compassion.

Psychologists and counselors say that people who bully others often have been bullied or abused themselves, are experiencing something in their lives that they're unable to deal with, or feel a need to have control over others. Meanwhile, this won't help to improve the situation within your investment club, should bullying occur there.

If it does, here's what you should remember:

➤ Do something about the situation as soon as it's recognized. If the person being bullied is unable or unwilling to assert himself, have a club officer or leader do it for him. Confront the person who's bullying and ask him to explain his actions.

➤ Be specific. Tell the bully that he was observed on three occasions demanding that Jake agree to the trade the bully favors, and on one occasion he was seen following Jake to his car.

➤ Make it very clear that this type of behavior will not be tolerated in your investment club, and if there is one more complaint or incident, the bully will be thrown out of the club. Don't, however, yell at, or demean, the bully. If he's already dealing with some sort of control issue, you don't want to upset him to the point where he might do something stupid, or even dangerous.

➤ Whatever you do, don't ignore a bullying situation. There's just no place for it within your club.

Making Sure You're Not Too Polite

On the flip side of the bully syndrome is the "too polite" situation. It can be equally detrimental to your investment club.

Jake may hesitate to tell Nancy that he thinks her stock recommendation for this month is less than desirable. Lindsey might be reluctant to criticize Robert's choice of investments, or to point out that Dennis hasn't been keeping up with the stocks he's assigned to track.

Jake and Lindsey don't want to offend anybody, or hurt anyone's feelings. They don't feel that it's their place to say something that could be insulting, or cause any resentment. They're far too polite to do anything like that.

People who feel comfortable with one another and respect each other understand that criticism is okay when it's offered in the proper spirit. We all can learn from each other, and it's a darned shame not to say something that could be helpful because you're afraid you'll offend the person you're speaking to.

Be aware of the tone of voice you use and the words you choose when you offer criticism or suggestions. You can be polite and friendly, while telling someone what you really think.

If you have a club member, or members, who is afraid to express his or her opinions and viewpoint, try the following strategies to draw them out:

➤ Encourage them to share their views. Tell them that their opinions count, and assure them that other club members are anxious to hear what they have to say.

➤ Initiate a brief discussion among the entire club relating to communication and why it's important for all members to participate. This sends the signal that everyone is not only invited to join in, but expected to offer opinions and information.

Heading for a Crash

Members who are new to a club often are hesitant to express their opinions or criticize other members. If you think this is the case in your club, encourage the new member to speak up. If you don't, you could be missing out on valuable input.

➤ If a member is really having a hard time expressing viewpoints and opinions, consider teaming her with another member for a month or two. Working with someone may help her develop the confidence she needs.

Remembering That You Won't Always Be a Winner

Members of investment clubs sometimes get cranky and irritable when the club's stocks don't perform as well as they'd like them to.

This happens frequently after a club has just completed a great run, during which the value of its stocks has appreciated considerably.

Cashing In

Remember that holding onto the good stocks you own is less risky than constantly buying and selling while trying to turn a profit. Historically, the stock market has always rebounded, even after its worst moments. A long-term approach to the market is the safest way to go.

It seems that, when that happens, club members start thinking that the appreciation is their due, that they deserve to have the value of their stocks go up. Then, when the value levels off or dips a bit, they feel cheated and angry.

You know as well as we do that the stock market is never a sure thing. Sure, it's arguably the very best place there is to invest money after a certain point. And sure, there are plenty of opportunities associated with it.

There also, as you know, are risks. You don't always win—sometimes you lose. While it's okay to celebrate a big win, club members should be able to accept losses as part of the package. No investor wins all the time, and it should be understood that losing isn't the end of the world.

If your club experiences a big loss, take it in stride, and use the loss as a learning experience. What went wrong? Is there a way to ensure that the same situation won't occur again? Analyze what occurred, learn from it, and chalk it up to experience. Encourage club members to not be overly disappointed or bitter when a stock they've chosen doesn't work out. Remember that it's all part of the game.

Agreeing to Disagree

Disagreements happen. Many people are afraid of disagreements and will go to great lengths to avoid them. That, however, is not always the most useful or healthy tact.

Within any organization—family, church, club, school, or workplace—you'll find a great variety, and sometimes a great clash of ideas. The trick is to realize that varying opinion is good. It's healthy and it shouldn't be avoided.

If we all held the same opinions about everything, what would we ever find to talk about? We'd have no reason to challenge what we, or anyone else, thinks or believes. We would severely limit our capacity to grow and develop new ways of thinking and understanding.

If we recognize, however, that positive confrontation is normal and healthy, and it's okay for us to agree to disagree, we'll be on the road to learning and expanding our ideas and understanding.

Positive confrontation is encouraged in business, and it should be encouraged within your investment club. It allows people who disagree to exchange ideas and thoughts, with the understanding that the exchange will be respectful and without hostility.

Taking Stock

A **positive confrontation** is a frank, open exchange of ideas that allows people to discuss and debate without being critical of one other.

Let's say that Julie, a long-time member of your investment club, insists that buying stock in Martha Stewart's company will be the very best move the club has ever made. Stephen, on the other hand, is adamant that doing so would be the club's downfall. The argument has dragged on for months now, and other club members are tired of hearing Julie and Stephen bicker. They're disturbed by the accusations Julie and Stephen are casting back and forth, and confused about the stock.

Julie and Stephen are badly in need of some positive confrontation. They should sit down and agree to discuss the matter calmly and rationally. As a leader of your investment club, you should encourage them to do this, and even provide some mediation, if necessary. Lay down the ground rules of positive confrontation, and insist that things remain civil.

Once Julie and Stephen are able to calmly discuss their reasons for loving and hating Martha Stewart's company, they'll probably come to a better understanding of each other's opinions, and possibly to some kind of middle ground concerning the purchase of the stocks.

It's perfectly normal to disagree, but it should be done in the proper spirit, with respect and courtesy.

Not Taking It Personally

A dangerous kind of person to have in your club is one who takes everything too personally. You've no doubt met this kind of person, who's easily offended and tends to misinterpret comments and conversation.

Members of investment clubs have to be willing to have their ideas questioned, and sometimes to accept criticism. It's simply the nature of the beast. Buying and selling stock are very subjective processes. There's no perfect or unshakable formula for doing so, and the uncertainty of the processes often leads to debate and discussion.

Cashing In

If you have a person in your investment club who has apparent problems that are affecting the health of the club, try to build a feeling of trust between you and the troubled member. Once he trusts you, he'll be more likely to talk to you about what's going on. Just be sure, however, that you never betray a confidence to other club members.

If there's a member of your club who can't stand to be questioned and gets upset when she is, take steps to remedy the problem early on. You can't have the rest of your club walking on eggshells because they're afraid of upsetting an overly sensitive member.

If you find that this situation occurs in your club, keep the following suggestions in mind:

➤ Pull the overly sensitive person aside and talk to him about the problem. Perhaps he doesn't realize that he's a source of discomfort to other members. Explain that his attitude is hindering the progress of the club.

➤ Keep him involved in decision-making and point out that others who make decisions also get criticized—and their ideas sometimes shot down. Help him understand that he's not being bullied or picked on, but that a degree of criticism is normal within a group setting.

➤ Try teaming him with another member for a couple of months to research and present stocks. Criticism that is directed not solely at him, but at his team, might be easier for him to accept. And, once he gets used to the idea that criticism is part of the deal, he might be better able to deal with it.

Keeping Everyone Involved with the Club

One of the best things you can do to keep every member of your investment club involved and interested is to let each person know how important he or she is to the health and well-being of the group.

Try to get each member to recognize the value of her role, whether she's a new member or an officer. Be sure that everyone understands exactly what your club is trying to accomplish, and how the work of each member contributes to those goals.

Make sure that everyone has the opportunity to share their ideas, and that those ideas are at least acknowledged, even if they're not implemented.

Keeping everyone up to date on how their efforts contribute to the greater good of the club accomplishes several things:

➤ It makes all club members feel important and invested in the group.

➤ It gives members a better understanding of the overall purpose of the club.

➤ It motivates club members and encourages them to keep each other motivated.

Involve your members in any way you can think of. In addition to listening to their stock reports and recommendations, get them to do other things for the club, as well.

Ask somebody who seems a little standoffish to help the club secretary contact all members about a special meeting, or to help set up for the meeting, or to give an extra report. Do what's necessary to get members involved and keep them motivated and invested in their club.

The Least You Need to Know

➤ Tracking investments is one of the most important jobs in a club and everyone should be responsible for doing so.

➤ Having every member keep an eye on all the club's stocks provides backup and extra eyes for the person who has primary responsibility for tracking a particular stock.

➤ A sense of teamwork and camaraderie is essential for a healthy investment club.

➤ Club members need to understand that the club won't always be a winner.

➤ It's okay to disagree, as long as it's done respectfully and positively.

➤ There are lots of ways to keep club members interested and invested, and it's extremely important to do so.

Part 6

The Evolution and Life Span of Your Investment Club

Setting goals and keeping track of how your club is progressing toward them will help keep your club operating effectively. Without goals, it's easy to lose sight of where you're heading.

In this part, you'll learn how to monitor your club's goals and expectations, and how to deal with the changes that will occur within your club.

One thing we can be sure of is that nothing stays the same, and this will apply to your club. Anticipating the changes, and knowing how to use them to your advantage will keep your club strong.

Also in this part, we'll look at what should be done if your club decides to disband. Clubs break up for many reasons. As much as you want your club to succeed and stay together for a long time, breakups are sometimes inevitable.

If it happens to your club, you need to remember that your time and work have not been wasted. You will have acquired a lot of knowledge and experience that you can use for personal investing, or for starting another club.

Chapter 23

How're You All Doing by Now?

In This Chapter

➤ Taking a look at the overall picture

➤ Evaluating the goals of your investment club

➤ Keeping expectations attainable, understandable, and measurable

➤ Making sure your goals and expectations fit into the purpose of your club

➤ Keeping an eye out for big-time disasters

➤ Outside help is sometimes necessary

Every now and then, it's a good idea to step back and take a good, hard look at how things are going. This is true not only for investment clubs, but also for many other areas of our lives.

If you work for a company, chances are that you get periodic evaluations to let you know how things are going. These help you take a step away from your own perceptions about your job to get an idea of a bigger picture. Maybe you're in a supervisory position and you're the one letting others know through their evaluations how things are going.

Every now and then, the President of the United States gets on television and delivers a State of the Union address to the American public. This address is intended to give Americans an overview of how the country's doing, and where it seems to be heading.

Students get report cards to inform them of their progress, or sometimes lack of progress.

We get physical examinations and tests to give us an overview of how our bodies are performing.

Business owners keep track of their daily operations by using balance sheets, cash flow statements, and short-term profit and loss statements. They look at production statistics, orders, and shipments. They step back and look at a bigger picture, however, when they write a 3-, 5-, or 10-year plan.

Maybe you and your significant other talk about where you want to be and what you'd like to be doing in 5 or 10 years. If so, you're stepping away from the day-to-day goings-on and looking at the bigger picture.

It's healthy to do this every now and then. Let's face it. Daily life is pretty demanding, and most of our lives are segmented into different areas that we must balance and manage. Work and home, school and work, kids and work, kids and school, and work and home. Throw in a social life, a spiritual life, your kids' social life, and a hobby or two, and you've got a real balancing act in progress.

A friend who has started and run several companies says he loves to hire working mothers as managers in his companies. Why? Women make excellent managers, he says, because they're so used to managing. Traditionally, women have managed homes, meals, transportation, scheduling, and finances. Many women also work outside of their homes, which means they're adept at managing time, as well.

The point is that our society moves extremely fast, and most of us scramble to keep up with it. Sometimes we find ourselves going through the motions of completing a task, or belonging to a club, or spending time with our families, just so we can get it done and get on to the next thing. Sometimes, we start to lose perspective on our various activities and responsibilities. And that's when we need to step back and take a fresh and objective look.

In this chapter, we'll tell you how you can evaluate the health of your investment club. You've been through a lot up to this point—setting up the club and finding members, writing an operating agreement, learning how to select good stocks and keep track of them once you have them, and many other aspects of club life.

It's time to step back and take a look at how your club's doing—at the bigger picture concerning your investment club.

Evaluating the Health of Your Investment Club

In this section, we'd like for you to take some time to really think about the questions we'll be asking. Think of it as a quiz. You may even want to write down your answers and discuss them with other club members to see if your perceptions concerning the club are similar.

Take This to the Bank

Perhaps the best example of how perceptions vary within a single unit is a family living in the same house. A 9-year-old boy certainly has different perceptions of home life than his 15-year-old sister, who has extremely different perceptions than her 40-year-old father. You probably could talk to those three people separately and never know that they live in the same house!

It's surprising sometimes, how four, or five, or any number of people who belong to the same group can have such different perceptions of what goes on within their group. Let's try to get an overview of how your club is doing.

Q: Are members working together toward a common goal?

A: The goal, of course, is making successful investment choices. What to look for is people helping and advising one another about stock selection, and respectful and considerate discussion concerning stocks. Also, members should share a feeling of happiness when a particular stock does well, and a feeling of disappointment when one does not. If you're noticing smugness or satisfaction on the part of a member or members when a stock that another member recommended takes a nose dive, you've got a problem within your club.

Q: Is every member doing his or her share of the work?

A: If you notice a couple of members (keep an eye on your officers, they sometimes tend to get overburdened) who seem to be doing more than their share, find out why. Some people naturally do more than they need to, but they could be picking up the slack for other members who aren't doing their share. If that happens and is allowed to continue, you risk having dedicated, willing members get burned out because they're trying to do too much.

Q: Are your club meetings well attended?

A: If most members attend most meetings regularly, give yourself some points. That means your members are interested and dedicated. If your attendance roster is noticeably empty, you'd better get on the phone and find out why members aren't showing up at the meetings.

Q: Are your investments doing reasonably well?

A: Of course, not every investment you choose is going to turn out to be a big winner, but you should anticipate that most of your picks will do reasonably well. Consistently bad returns can cause consistent disappointment among club members. Many will leave the club if the situation doesn't change.

Q: Do members basically agree on the investments your club makes?

A: You want to, of course, encourage discussion and debate among club members over which stocks you buy, sell, and trade. If every meeting turns into a shouting match, however, you may have too broad of a range of investment philosophies among your members. You can't, and shouldn't, expect everyone to agree on everything. If disagreements among your club members seem to be extreme or constant, however, you need to do something to improve the situation.

Q: Are all members following the club's rules, as outlined in your operating agreement?

A: An investment club is no different from any other structured organization. It's important that everyone play by the rules so that the club can operate effectively. One or two people who are allowed to set their own guidelines can create resentment and bitterness among the rest of your club's members. It's a good idea to review the operating agreement occasionally during club meetings.

Q: Are all members participating in discussions and club business?

A: Sometimes clubs develop cliques leaving some members feeling left out. If you notice anybody in your club who seems to get left out and not included in discussion or activities, make it a point to get them more involved.

Q: Is your club learning more about investing each month?

A: Education should be one of the top, if not the top, priorities for your club. Does your club schedule speakers to share information and education on a regular basis? Are club members looking for educational opportunities outside of the meetings? Hopefully, there's a feeling of enthusiasm among members regarding educational presentations. If education in your club is lacking, try to move it up on your priority list. Your club will benefit greatly from education and will suffer if it's not provided.

Q: Have you found competent outside help that's available when necessary?

A: Your club might not need outside help very often (other than your broker), but you should have a lawyer, accountant, and perhaps a tax adviser available in the event that you do. If you don't have these professionals available, start looking for them now. It doesn't hurt to know whom you'll call if you need to. If your club never needs a lawyer or accountant, that's fine. But if you do, you should have someone available with whom you can work effectively.

Q: Are your officers acting as leaders and setting the tone for the club?

A: Your president, vice president, secretary, and treasurer (or whatever you call their equivalents) should be recognized as leaders and should be instrumental in establishing the mood or tone for your club. They should lead by example, making sure they keep up with their club work, and encourage members to be respectful of one another. Officers shouldn't be permitted to form cliques or to take privileges that other members don't have.

These questions are intended to help you step back and take a look at how your club is moving along. If you're happy with all your answers, your club probably is on target and progressing nicely.

If you're not happy with some of your answers, it might be a good idea to meet as a club and discuss the situation. Talk about the problems you've pinpointed, and about how you may be able to improve the club.

We intentionally omitted two questions from the list above, because we wanted to talk about them separately. Let's have a look.

Is Everybody Happy?

If most of your answers to the questions above were positive, then it's pretty safe to assume that the members of your club are getting along and everyone is happy.

If you're dealing with factions or cliques, however, or there are a couple of people who are bringing down the atmosphere of the whole club, then it's time to do something about it. Refer to Chapter 9, "Ensuring That the Club Runs Smoothly," for tips on dealing with disagreements. Just don't be hesitant to take action when it's necessary.

Are You Having Fun Yet?

With all the work involved in getting a club up and running, it's easy sometimes to lose sight of an extremely important goal—having fun.

If your club meetings and activities are no fun, it's time to step back and figure out the reason, and then think about how you're going to fix it. Members soon will tire of meetings that are boring or tedious, and eventually they'll stop attending.

Hopefully, club members will let you know if they're not having fun. It could be that officers are taking the proceedings too seriously, not leaving any room for levity. We're not saying that every meeting should be one laugh after another, but it doesn't hurt to lighten up and let everyone enjoy themselves.

If you're not sure what club members are thinking about the fun factor, ask them. If you're uncomfortable, or think they might be, with asking them to respond directly, hand each person a short survey on his or her way out the door after a meeting. Include an envelope in which members can return the surveys before the next meeting, and make it clear that they don't need to identify themselves if they don't want to.

That should give you a clear indication of how members think things are going within the club. Survey questions could include the following, and others that might pertain to your club:

➤ Do you find the club meetings to be generally enjoyable?

➤ Do you think the meetings are too long, too short, or about right?

➤ Can you offer any suggestions about how the meetings could be made more interesting?

➤ Are you happy with the balance of business and social interaction during club meetings? If not, please explain.

➤ Do you look forward to attending meetings? If not, please explain.

➤ Would you describe the relationship between club members as being generally (choose at least one): (a) friendly (b) comfortable (c) respectful (d) tense?

Looking at Your Members' Expectations

Everyone has a different level of expectations. Some people expect that everything they do will turn out just fine, while others are apprehensive and fearful, and don't expect much at all from their lives.

Some people expect a lot out of everyone they meet. They expect their kids to be outstanding in everything they do (talk about pressure!), their employees or co-workers to go above and beyond the call of duty, and their elected officials to overcome all sorts of obstacles in order to accomplish goals.

Take This to the Bank

Psychologists say our expectations concerning life are shaped by our core beliefs. Those are the beliefs we form in the very early years of life, in response to what we see, are told, and experience.

Others accept people just the way they are, without expecting any more than they see the person can do.

All this has to do with how we look at the world, and the beliefs we've acquired during our lives. In your investment club, you probably have a mix of people, all of whom might have different expectations about what the club will do for them.

Some of your club members might expect that they're going to get rich as a result of belonging, while others are afraid they'll lose everything they invest. Some members might expect that every investment the club makes will double in less than a year, and they'll be retiring when they're 52.

It's a good idea to have a look at the expectations of your club members, and try to get a handle about who's thinking what. There may be expectations that your club members share, or there might be a lot of individual expectations, without any shared ones. Evaluating expectations can be difficult, but it's important.

Once you've evaluated expectations, you can set goals for your club. Goals should be attainable, understandable, and measurable.

That means that the expectations of your club should be neither too high, nor too low, and that the goals should make sense for the overall mission of your club.

Your club's goals also should be measurable. Not keeping track of your goals is sort of like playing a football game without a scoreboard. It reduces the game to a bunch of guys crashing into each other, without the benefit of knowing the score, elapsed time, penalties, and so forth.

Setting reasonable goals for your club also encourages you to keep track of where you are in relationship to those goals. If you have the expectation, or goal, that your investments will double in five years, you can track the progress, or lack of progress, of those investments along the way. Tracking goals is as important as realizing them, because it keeps everyone aware of where the club is and how it's doing.

Are They Too High?

If somebody's expectations are unrealistically high, chances are that they'll end up disappointed and disillusioned. Sure, it's great to have dreams and lofty aspirations, but to be unrealistic is setting yourself up for a big letdown.

If Charlie is sure that his investment is going to double by the end of the year, despite evidence that it's actually decreasing in value, Charlie is going to be one disappointed guy.

In Chapter 21, we told you that many investors consider a reasonable expectation to be that their stock will double in value in five years—not 15 years, not a year and a half. A reasonable expectation is five years. This is called setting a *target price*. If you invest $1,000 in 2000, it's reasonable to set a target price of $2,000 for the year 2005. You're stating an expectation that your investment will double between 2000 and 2005.

Taking Stock

A **target price** is what you anticipate your investment will be worth at a future time. If you expect your $1,000 investment to double in five years, for example, your target price is $2,000.

Cashing In

The primary quality of a good goal is that it's realistic. That doesn't mean that we'll meet all our goals, but that we can have reasonable expectations that a goal is attainable.

Sometimes, an entire club will get unrealistic expectations about their investments. This can happen if an early investment the club makes turns out to be a phenomenal one, and club members mistakenly hold it up as the standard.

If that happens in your club, you'll need to bring your members back down to earth by showing them more realistic reports and statistics.

High expectations can work in your club's favor. If members expect great things, they're more likely to strive to reach them than if their expectations were very low. It's best, however, to try to strike a balance and keep expectations at a reasonable and realistic level.

Once unrealistic goals have been established and club members see that their investment choices have fallen short of their expectations, it will be hard to get them excited about choosing other investments.

Are They Too Low?

On the flip side of expecting too much is, of course, expecting too little. If you're thrilled to find out that your investment increased in value by 2 percent over the past year, you'd better think about raising your expectations.

While you can't expect that every stock your club chooses will be a big winner, it's reasonable to expect that you'll be at least moderately successful.

Goals or expectations that are set too low can be real morale busters for your investment club. If you anticipate only minimal earnings on your investment, you might as well stick your members' contributions into a money market account and save everybody the trouble of researching and tracking stocks.

Again, try to set goals that are reasonable and realistic. If you find that you've set goals that are either too high or too low—change them.

People sometimes get in the mindset that once a goal is set, or an expectation established, it's fixed—never to be changed. The fact is that people change and adjust their goals and expectations all the time.

And it's also important to realize that goals are final, and that there's usually a series of steps leading to achieving the final goals.

The Miami Dolphins, for instance, might start out the season with the goal of winning the Super Bowl—a lofty goal, indeed. To reach that goal, the team has to accomplish a series of steps along the way. You can work backward from the goal to see what the steps are.

In order to win the Super Bowl, the Dolphins first have to get there. To do so, they have to be one of two teams to survive the National Football League playoffs. To get into the playoffs, they have to qualify by either winning their division, or by having a regular season record good enough to get in as a wild card team.

In order to do that, the team has to work very hard in training. There sometimes are many steps necessary to complete when attempting to accomplish a goal, or to meet an expectation.

Cashing In

Some investment clubs start out with very low goals, thinking they'll raise them as members gain experience and confidence. It's better to start with higher, reasonable goals and work toward them. You might meet low goals more quickly, but in doing so curtail the success you may have had if the goals had been higher.

Remembering What Your Club Is All About

As you set goals and think about your expectations, it's important to remember why you formed the club in the first place.

Make sure that the goals you set are in tune with the larger purpose of your investment club. Way back in the beginning, we said that a club should serve to educate its members, to be an enjoyable experience, and hopefully, to make some money.

Try to keep those reasons in front of you, and not get too bogged down with where you're going and how you're going to get there. Goals and expectations are very important, but don't forget to learn from the process, and try to have a good time as you do so.

Preventing Disasters from Derailing Your Club

Nobody expects that something terrible will happen within his club or organization, but sometimes it does.

It's not pleasant to think about, but there have been a few instances in which a club member has found a way to bolt with the club's portfolio, leaving the rest of the group disillusioned and distressed, as well as broke.

299

Cashing In

If there's any worry among your club members about the integrity of its account, you can look into getting insurance bonding. Bonding would protect the club's assets in the event of a disaster.

This is the sort of disaster from which a club would never recover, and it tarnishes the reputation and integrity of all investment clubs.

Keeping a close watch on your club's brokerage statements is the best way to prevent financial impropriety from occurring within your club. Don't ever leave financial record keeping strictly in the hands of one person. Make sure the books are open for everyone to see at any time, and review your accounts carefully at every meeting.

This type of situation isn't something that you need to spend a lot of time worrying about—the great majority of investment clubs never experience any problems of this sort. Just be aware, however, of the possibility of such a thing occurring, and if anything within your club seems wrong, don't hesitate to check it out.

You can do this without being heavy-handed or judgmental. Everyone has the right to examine the club's books whenever they want to. Simply exercise your right.

Knowing When You Need Some Help

We've said this several times in earlier chapters, but if you feel that your club needs some help, don't hesitate to go find it.

Trying to handle a complicated legal or financial matter on your own can severely undermine your investment club and could result in lasting trouble.

Hopefully, you've established rapport with a good lawyer and accountant on whom you can call if necessary. There also are tax experts who can help you with special situations. Make sure that everyone in your club understands that seeking outside help is perfectly acceptable, and sometimes the smartest thing you can do.

If your club is experiencing serious problems because of personality clashes or other people problems, and you've tried unsuccessfully every way you can to solve the problems internally, you may also need to get some outside help.

Maybe one of the members of your club knows a counselor who would be willing to help you sort out your club's problems for a reasonable fee.

There are psychologists and counselors who are trained to work with group and workplace situations, so help is available, if you really think you need it. If your area has a large counseling center, you might try there first. It's likely to have counselors who specialize in various situations, including group counseling.

If one person is causing a lot of trouble within your club, it's certainly within your rights—and in the best interests of the club—to ask him to leave. If you anticipate the person may be very upset when you do this, make sure you have at least one other person with you when you deliver the news.

Situations that are this serious rarely occur within investment clubs. These days, however, you can't be too careful. If you feel that you need help dealing with a club member or members, don't hesitate to ask for it.

The Least You Need to Know

➤ It's important to periodically assess the health and progress of your investment club.

➤ The goals and expectations of your club should be reasonable and attainable.

➤ Setting goals that are too high can result in disappointment and cause members to lose interest in the club.

➤ Remember that goals most often are reached through a series of steps, not all at once.

➤ Your goals and expectations should mesh with the overall purpose of your club.

➤ Be on the lookout for possible disasters that could threaten your club's existence.

➤ Don't hesitate to consult help when you think it's necessary.

Chapter 24

The Ebbs and Flows of an Investment Club

In This Chapter

➤ Change is the very nature of an investment club

➤ Dealing with changes in membership

➤ Understanding how group dynamics change

➤ Replacing your club's officers

➤ Knowing when to look for help

Ebbs and flows—subtle changes—occur in nearly all aspects of life. You look at your son one day, for example, and you wonder how it happened that he got so darned tall. Or exactly when was it that your father started to look so old?

When did the paint start peeling off the side of your house? Or at what point did your car get so beat-up looking? At what moment did the piano get out of tune? Or the grass got so tall, again?

Rivers are great examples of ebbs and flows. So are continents and oceans. They shift and change, most often so gradually that it would go unnoticed if there weren't folks who specifically look for and track those kinds of things.

The stock market is another great example of change. Sometimes it's subtle, and other times it hits you right in the face. But you can count on the fact that it won't stay the same.

Change is for certain, that's for sure. Nothing stays the same, especially nothing in which people are the primary players.

Your investment club is no exception to the "everything will change" rule. In this chapter, we'll explore some of the kinds of changes that will, or could, occur and how you can successfully handle those changes.

Remember That Nothing Stays the Same

Sometimes we'd like to capture a moment, or a situation, and make it last forever. Anyone with children has probably wished at one moment or another that she could stop time and keep her children at exactly the age and temperament that they are right then.

Or things are going so well at work that you'd like to hit the freeze frame and never have anything change for the rest of your career.

Fortunately or unfortunately, depending on your point of view, we can't stop time from advancing, or prevent changes from occurring. It's just the way it is, and your investment club is no exception. It will ebb and flow and change. Some of the changes will be subtle, causing you to wonder just how and when they occurred.

Others will be sudden changes, such as members leaving and new ones coming in, or new officers replacing the existing ones.

The very nature of an investment club forces it to undergo constant change. Because one of the primary goals of your club is to grow and succeed, change is an absolutely necessary component. Without change, you could have no growth.

Think about it for a minute. If your club never changed, it would be exactly the same as it was the day it was formed. You'd have the same members, the same number of members and the same attitudes, hopes, and beliefs. You'd also have the same amount of money (not much), the same knowledge of investing (perhaps quite limited), and the same portfolio.

Constancy might be a plus for some groups, but not for your investment club. A year or two into your club's endeavor, you've no doubt acquired many times the amount of knowledge that you started with. You've built up your portfolio, and hopefully made some money. As Martha Stewart would say, change, in this case at least, is a good thing.

We think it's fair to say that change is not only necessary and unavoidable, but it's desirable for an investment club.

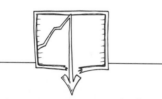

Heading for a Crash

If you're in an investment club and you're one of those people who simply can't deal with change, you've got some tough times ahead. Investment clubs have to change, or they can't fulfill the purpose for which they were formed. If you simply can't stand change, you probably won't enjoy being in an investment club.

Okay. Now it has been clearly established that change will occur within your club, and that change is necessary and positive. Because it will happen, you've got to learn how to deal with change. You've got to get ready to grow and evolve, just as the club will.

If you're in a leadership position, you've got to be ready and willing to lead other members through changes, and to encourage the *changes* that will benefit the group.

There probably will be some changes to and within your club that you'd wish you could avoid. We're not saying that all change is good—just that it's necessary and unavoidable.

> **Taking Stock**
>
> **Change** means to be altered or made different, to undergo variation, or to be transformed. We know that change occurs constantly, with many variations. The only certainty about change is that it will happen.

An important thing to remember is that it's extremely beneficial to watch for and anticipate change. The more attuned you are to the changes that may occur, the less likely the chance that you'll be caught offguard and left wondering how to deal with them.

You need to watch your club as diligently as you watch the stock market. In time, you'll get to recognize the club's ups and downs, and its ebbs and flows, as well as you're able to recognize those of the market. Let's look at some of the changes you might anticipate and how those changes could affect your club.

Changes in Membership

There are some investment clubs that run for many years with the same group of members that were in it at the start. These groups, however, are few and far between. Just as change is the nature of investment clubs themselves, it's also the nature of their members.

Jack's job changes and he and his family move to Cincinnati, where he has better career opportunities. Janet has another baby and finds that she just doesn't have time to do the necessary club work and attend the meetings. Sharon gets engaged and the investment club doesn't seem very important to her right now. Richard finds out he has a fast-spreading form of cancer and starts aggressive chemotherapy that leaves him weak, sick, and unable to do much of anything at all.

As members leave your club, for whatever reason, you'll want to think about getting new ones to replace them. You can choose not to replace members if you want to, especially if you think the club is too big. Too many members can sometimes make club operations difficult, and the club can become inefficient. If the remaining members feel the club was too large, it's fine to reduce its size as people leave.

If the club is working well with 20 people, however, you'll probably want to add new members as old members leave. If you have a small club, you might want to add new members to increase its size without waiting for existing members to leave.

Let's have a look at the implications and practical aspects of bringing new members into your investment club.

Adding New Members

For the sake of good record keeping, potential new members should submit an application to be reviewed by all existing members and filed in the club's records.

Anyone interested in joining the club also should be required to attend at least one meeting as a guest. This gives both the prospective member and existing members the opportunity to make sure that the person will fit into the club and be comfortable there.

We've mentioned several times earlier in the book the potential perils of mixing high risk and conservative investors. Or, the new member may be uncomfortable with the type of stocks your club has purchased. Or, she might not feel that she's a good mix with some of the people already in the club.

If she does feel comfortable and expresses a desire to join, members should vote on whether or not to admit the new member at the next meeting. Be sure to ask the prospective new member to leave the room while the vote takes place.

Generally, most people are pretty accepting of proposed members who are recommended by other people within the club. There may be times, however, when your club votes not to accept a particular person for membership, and those wishes must be honored.

If the other club members vote not to admit the person on whom they're voting, that's their prerogative. Your operating agreement states that a certain percentage of the club membership must approve a new member before he's admitted.

Cashing In

Your operating agreement should state a maximum number of members that will be permitted in your club. You can't exceed that number without modifying your agreement, but you may have fewer members.

Taking Stock

Your club may require the unanimous or majority consent of its partners to admit new members. **Unanimous consent** means that all members must vote in favor of admitting the new member. **Majority consent** means that more than half of all members must be in favor. Some clubs require a 75 percent majority vote.

Some clubs require *unanimous consent* to admit new member, which means that every person must vote in the affirmative. Other clubs require *majority consent,* which means that more than half of the members must vote in favor of admitting the new person.

Once the new member has been voted into the club, you'll have to take care of some business.

Some clubs require new members to pay a starting, or initiation, fee. If your club is a member of the National Association of Investors Corp. (NAIC), the money would be used to cover the cost of membership for the new club member and for any other expenses associated with adding a member to your club.

A new member, obviously, will not have as much money in the club initially as members who have been contributing for several years. Many clubs give new members the option of putting in as much money as they want to when first joining the club—up to the amount that has been contributed by charter members.

Let's say, for instance, that Rhonda joins a club that has been together for three years. Members of that club who were in from the start have contributed $20 a month for three years, or $720 each. Upon joining the club, Rhonda has the option of paying, in addition to her starting fee, if there is one, up to $720. Whatever amount she contributes above the starting fee will be credited to her capital account.

Cashing In

Be sure that prospective members understand exactly what will be required of them if they join your investment club. Tell them about any starting fees, the amount of money they'll need to invest each month, and so forth. Make sure that they read and understand your operating agreement and have an understanding of how the club is run.

Some clubs require that new members pay for a share of the club. For instance, if there are 15 members in a club, and each member owns one share of a portfolio that's worth $45,000, then one share is worth $3,000 ($45,000 divided by 15 members). Each applicant would have to contribute $3,000 to become a member of this club. When a new member joins and pays for a share, the value of the club's portfolio increases. In this case, the value of the portfolio would increase to $48,000, equally divided between 16 members.

When new members come into your club, make sure they're warmly welcomed and introduced to all the other members. It sounds like something that goes without saying, but we've heard about clubs where new members were pretty much ignored and ended up feeling very discouraged and out of the loop.

When Members Leave the Group

When members leave your investment club, you'll have to give them back their share of your club's portfolio.

To do this, you'll need to determine the amount of their share, then decide how the group will finance the payback.

There are several options to consider:

➤ **Other members can "buy out" the exiting partner.** This means that some or all of the remaining members would contribute an amount of money equal to what the person leaving has invested.

Samantha is moving to Seattle and has to leave the club. She has a one fifteenth share of the club, valued at $1,600. The value of each share of the club is based on the dues that members have paid, and the appreciation, or growth of their dues.

Linda has been looking to increase her ownership in the club, so she decides to "buy out" Samantha's share. She comes up with $1,600 for the club, and she now owns two shares out of the total 15. The money Linda pays is put into the club's account, and then the club gives it to Samantha.

➤ **The club can sell some of its stock to finance the payoff.** This might be necessary in the event that the exiting member owns a large share of the club's portfolio and the payoff is high. This involves tax considerations, though, and there are expenses associated with selling securities, so consult your broker before deciding to go this route.

Joe is leaving the investment club because he no longer has the time necessary to devote to it. This club has been around for a while and has done well with its investments. Joe's share is worth $15,000.

None of the other members can find the money to buy out Joe, so the club decides to sell some stock to do so. According to the club's operating agreement, expenses incurred in selling the stock are taken out of Joe's $15,000. The operating agreement should also stipulate whether Joe will be responsible for paying capital gains taxes if the stock is sold at a profit, or if the club will cover that cost.

➤ **The club can transfer securities to the departing member's ownership.** This allows the club to avoid paying taxes, as it would have to if it sold stocks at a profit. The departing member can decide whether to hold the securities or sell them.

Another option the club has when Joe leaves is to transfer securities from the club's name to Joe's name. If the club has 10 members, and it owns 20 different stocks, then one tenth of the total number of each stock owned would be transferred to Joe's name. If the club owns 100 shares of AT&T stock, for instance, 10 of those shares would be put in Joe's name.

This is attractive to many clubs, because it avoids them having to pay taxes by selling stock at a profit.

➤ **A new member can contribute the amount of the exiting member's share.** If you have a new member who's willing to invest the amount that the exiting member is taking out, you've got a win-win situation. The new member is on par with other members regarding his share of the portfolio, and the member who's leaving is satisfied with the payment.

Vicky is leaving the club because she's about to have a baby and won't be able to attend the meetings for a while. Vicky has a good friend, Marie, who's been dying to join the club, but wasn't able to because the club had 15 members and wanted to remain at that number.

Marie joins and invests $2,200 up front—just the amount of Vicky's share of the club. Marie's contribution is put into the club's account, and the club writes Vicky a check for her share. The status of ownership among other members doesn't change, and everybody's happy.

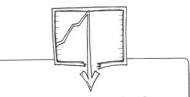

Heading for a Crash

If a member of your club dies, or becomes incapacitated, don't assume anything when it comes time to pay his share of the club's portfolio. It's important to determine who is entitled to his share of the money before it's dispersed. You may need to hold the money in a bank account designated for that purpose if there is question about ownership.

Regardless of what method you use to generate the money needed to pay off the departing member, be sure that you keep accurate records, and consult your broker or an accountant, if necessary, to make sure you're doing what's best for the club, as well as the departing member.

Dealing with Shifting Group Dynamics

Just when you think everyone has settled into the club and everything's going smoothly, you can just about bet that something will happen to shake things up.

Group dynamics change constantly, regardless of what the group may be. Think about groups to which you belong. Church groups, your family, professional organizations, social clubs, even circles of friends—the dynamics of these groups change all the time, as they will within your investment club.

Understand that it's natural for this to happen. In fact, if your group never changed, it would become stagnant. Many things will contribute to, or cause your group's dynamics to shift and change. Every time you elect new officers, accept new members, say goodbye to old members, or move your meeting place, you'll change the dynamics of the club.

Changing of the Guard

It's easy to get stuck in a rut. Let's say that your investment club is moving along just fine. Everybody's been doing his homework, researching companies and analyzing stock. As a result, you've been making some really good choices and your portfolio has done extremely well.

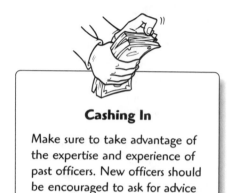

Cashing In

Make sure to take advantage of the expertise and experience of past officers. New officers should be encouraged to ask for advice from those who have held the same posts in the past.

The meetings are lots of fun, well run, and organized. Your president keeps things moving, and you're able to get home in time to see the kids before they go to bed, or to watch your favorite 10 o'clock television show.

Everybody seems to be getting along, and they're fairly agreeable about most issues. Yep. Things are going just great.

If that's the case, there may be a very strong temptation to keep everything just the way it is. After all, if it's not broken, don't fix it, right? You're thinking that you'd like to just keep rolling along—just the way you are. You may even be thinking that maybe your club should pass on election of new officers this year. Or that maybe you should just re-elect the same team, so you can maintain the momentum of the current club.

Take This to the Bank

Your investment club can take a lesson from the top as far as changing officers is concerned. Even the top elected office in the United States—the presidency—has a two-term limit.

Well, sorry to have to tell you, but it's probably not a good idea to succumb to that temptation. Changing the guard is healthy—even if the club is running smoothly.

Bringing new officers on board keeps things interesting, and gives the club a chance to do things differently. It keeps you out of the rut.

How Often Should You Elect New Officers?

It's common for organizations, including most investment clubs, to elect officers annually. Electing new officers gives different members the opportunity to share their ideas and skills. Sure, it could be that some of those ideas don't work. It might even be that some of those ideas really stink.

It also could be, however, that there's somebody sitting quietly at club meetings, who has terrific ideas for making your group more dynamic and successful.

Your club's operating agreement should state when and how new officers are selected. It might say, for example, "Officers will be elected annually, during the January meeting. A majority vote is required."

It's a good idea to remind members of when elections will take place and urge them to take the matter seriously and make it known if they want to be considered for an elected position.

Don't discourage anyone who might be interested from running for office, and don't let one person or group control the elections.

Heading for a Crash

Warning bells should sound if you notice factions appearing within your investment club. It's not unheard of for several people with an agenda to join forces. If they're organized and get enough support, these groups can get the people they want elected and effectively end up running the club. It would be unusual for this to happen in an investment club, but, if you notice cliques forming, keep a close watch on what happens.

Identifying the Best Candidates

We talked some about electing officers in Chapter 7, "Getting Your Investment Club off to a Good Start," so we won't spend much time reviewing the discussion here. We will say, however, that it's very important to find the right people to serve as officers of your investment club.

In addition to paying attention to the nuts-and-bolts type of issues, such as preparing for meetings and keeping track of financial matters, your officers may pretty much set the tone for the rest of the club.

In many instances, officers establish the mood, or type of atmosphere, in which the club will operate. If your president is the serious, let's-get-down-to-business type, then your club meetings most likely will be efficient, to the point, and businesslike.

On the other hand, if your president is the relaxed, let's-see-what-happens type, then your meetings are likely to be more laid-back and informal.

As long as members are comfortable and your club is running effectively, it doesn't really matter what type of atmosphere you have. If a laid-back attitude works best for your club, then laid back is fine. If your club operates more effectively within a businesslike atmosphere, then businesslike is what you should be.

Your club officers should be conscious of the type of atmosphere they're creating, and aware of whether or not the rest of the members are comfortable with it.

Most clubs have a president, vice president, secretary, and treasurer, although they may call the positions by different names.

The treasurer very well may be the most important person in an investment club. Unless you hire an outside person to do some of the financial work, and, in many cases, even if you hire someone to help, your treasurer will have many responsibilities.

Cashing In

Club members will be far more willing to serve as officers if other members are supportive and helpful. Clubs in which officers are overloaded with work and receive little help from other members, often have trouble getting people to serve.

Needless to say, your club should choose its treasurer carefully, making sure that whoever takes the job has the time, knowledge, and expertise to devote to it.

All potential officers should be made aware of the responsibilities associated with each position before elections are held, and nobody should be pressured to be an officer if they don't want to be.

If you have trouble getting club members to agree to serve as officers, take a look at the position and what it entails. Members might be reluctant to be elected to a post that requires a great deal of time, for instance. If that's the case, you may have to divide the responsibilities of that position and create another office.

Some clubs have a treasurer and an assistant treasurer, splitting the responsibilities of the job in order to make it less time-consuming and overwhelming.

It would be ideal for a club to have a treasurer and an assistant treasurer who is in training to replace the treasurer at the end of his or her term. The assistant treasurer would serve as something like an apprentice to the treasurer, helping out while he developed skills and acquired knowledge.

If the president is overwhelmed with too many responsibilities, think about shifting some of them to the vice president. It's easier for everyone to do a little than for a few people to have to do everything.

If you're finding that club members are reluctant to serve as officers, try making the positions as a little more palatable and attractive.

You could have an occasional night out for officers, with the cost of dinner taken from the club's miscellaneous account. The purpose of the evening would be for officers to get to know one another better, and also may serve to make the offices more enticing to other members.

Make sure that officers are treated with respect, and that other members recognize the amount of work they do for the benefit of the club.

You might think about designating one of your meetings as "officer recognition night," during which officers would be duly recognized and their efforts acknowledged.

How's Your Hired Help Working Out?

Most clubs need some outside help from time to time—lawyers, accountants, and so forth. We discussed in Chapter 8, "Establishing Operating Rules," how important it is to find the right help, and how to go about doing so.

Once you have people helping you, it's important to evaluate your relationship with them every now and then. You need to make sure everything is working, and that you're getting the help you need. If your lawyer or accountant is too busy, or not dependable, or not cooperative when asked to do something, then you'd better think about finding somebody else.

It can be a hassle to find a new lawyer or accountant, and sometimes it's tempting to stick with whom you know instead of making the change. If those you've hired aren't doing what you're paying them to do, however, or not doing it satisfactorily, then you need to find new help.

Some clubs even appoint a committee to monitor and evaluate relationships with outside help. Legal and financial matters are extremely important to investment clubs, and you need to be able to depend on the people you hire to help you. If you can't, then it's time to start looking for replacements.

The Least You Need to Know

➤ Your investment club will undergo many changes as it grows and evolves.

➤ One of the most significant changes your club will experience will be in membership.

➤ Members who leave the group can receive their share of the club's assets in several different ways.

➤ It is good and healthy to elect new officers regularly.

➤ All club members should support and be willing to help the officers they elect.

➤ If your hired help isn't performing satisfactorily, it's time to start looking for someone else.

Chapter 25

What Happens If Your Club's Not Working?

In This Chapter

➤ Understanding that failure's not all bad

➤ Solving the problems that can be solved

➤ Facing up to the problems that can't be solved

➤ Knowing when it's time to call it quits

➤ Legal and emotional aspects of disbanding

➤ Using your experience to start another club

We live in a society that loves to win—at everything.

As a nation, we've traditionally envisioned ourselves as winners. Ever since we clobbered the Brits during the American Revolution, we've thought that there's no stopping us.

In many ways, that attitude has served this country well. It has led us westward-ho and into space. It has fueled our belief that, as a country, there's no problem that we can't overcome—nothing that we can't beat.

While this must-win, can't-lose attitude has moved us ahead as a country, it's not without a nasty downside.

Take a look sometime at a little kids' soccer game, or a junior high football game, or a sixth-grade swim meet. Look closely at the parents on the sideline. No doubt you'll see some act as though their kids are competing for a world championship, rather than a third-grade soccer win.

Their message to their kids is hit harder, run faster, maybe even cheat a little bit. Just do whatever you have to do to win the game.

Kids quickly get the picture. They learn that in our society, winning is good and losing is bad, and you do what you have to do to come out on top. This attitude doesn't stop with kids' sports, either.

We hate to fail at relationships, in business, and in school. We even hate to fail in our extra-curricular activities—such as investment clubs.

If your club isn't working—and there have been many cases in which investment clubs have failed—don't think that it's the end of the world. As we'll see in this chapter, you will have gained much by being in a club, even if the club eventually fails.

Failure Isn't a Dirty Word

We have, and you probably have, too, known people who are so worried about failing that they refuse to try at whatever it is they want to do.

There are some folks who are so afraid of being rejected that they refuse to ask someone they care about to go to a movie, or meet for a cup of coffee.

They won't apply for a new job because they're sure that they won't get it. Some people even put aside life goals because they're afraid of failing.

We know of a man—Scott—who wanted to be a doctor. All through junior high and high school, he talked about being a doctor. He worked hard and got pretty good grades—not great, but pretty good. He participated in extra-curricular activities and hoped he'd have enough going for him to get into a really good medical school.

As it got close to the end of high school, Scott became more and more worried that he'd be rejected by the colleges with good pre-med programs. It became almost an obsession—he worried about it all the time.

One day, Scott informed his friends that he decided he wasn't going to be a doctor. He was going to get a business degree at a nearby state university, then go to work for his dad's business, instead.

His friends knew this really wasn't what Scott wanted to do, and tried hard to get him to change his mind. Scott, however, was stubbornly determined to go to work for his father.

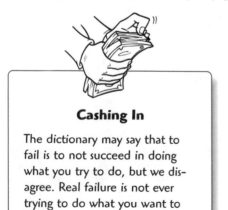

Cashing In

The dictionary may say that to fail is to not succeed in doing what you try to do, but we disagree. Real failure is not ever trying to do what you want to do.

Years later, he admitted that he had been terribly afraid that he wouldn't get into medical school, so he opted for the easy way out. After more than 20 years, he still thinks about what it would have been like to be a doctor.

Scott failed big. He didn't fail because he didn't get accepted into medical school, he failed because he didn't try. Not trying to do something doesn't save you from failing—it guarantees that you will fail.

Webster's dictionary says that failure is "to be unsuccessful in obtaining a desired end." We think, however, that real failure is not having the heart and soul to give something a try.

Just because you fail at something doesn't mean you're a failure. That's really important to remember—especially if your investment club isn't working out and it looks like it's going to fall apart.

If your club fails, it'll be a shame. You'll feel bad, and other members probably will, too, but it's not by a long shot something that you should dwell on, or get depressed about.

Take This to the Bank

Failure is held in such low esteem in our society that for 24 years no failing grades were allowed to be issued at Stanford University. The policy was revoked in 1994 when university President Gerhard Casper said, "Unless you dare something and admit that you may fail, you are living in an illusionary world." Good for you, Gerhard!

Everybody fails sometimes. Even basketball great Michael Jordan was cut from his high school basketball team the first year he tried out. The important thing is how you deal with failure, and what you take away from it. You can be like Jordan and decide that you'll work harder so that the next time tryouts come around the coach will be begging you to be on his team. Or, you can roll over, feel sorry for yourself, and take up needlepoint instead of basketball.

Dealing with Solvable Problems

If your investment club is in trouble, you'll need to pinpoint what's going wrong. Then, you'll need to decide if the problems can be fixed.

Let's have a look at some of the problems that occur from time to time in club settings and how it might be possible to solve them.

Clashing Investment Philosophies

Clashing philosophies is one of the most common problems that occur within investment clubs and can be one of the most difficult to fix.

We've warned several times previously in this book about mixing conservative and high-risk investors. It really isn't a good idea, because there's just too much chance for conflict between these types of people.

If you have both kinds of investors in your club, however, and it's causing problems, there are some steps you can take to try to improve the situation.

➤ **Work out a compromise.** Sit down with the investors who are clashing and address the problem. Don't forget to involve other officers or representatives of the club. You could suggest that the club only consider buying stocks that are neither too high-risk, nor too conservative. Suggest that a stock selection committee be put in place, and give the committee the final say in which stocks get considered, and which ones don't.

➤ **Make sure both types of investors get equal opportunity to present stock choices.** If you're not going to limit the type of stock that the club will consider buying, then make sure that conservative and high-risk investors have equal opportunity to present stocks to other club members. The last thing you want is for one "side" to be able to claim that you're giving unfair advantage to the other.

Heading for a Crash

If your investment club is in trouble, don't try to fix it by yourself. Involve other members and ask for ideas. Trying to solve all the problems yourself can make you look like you're assuming control of the club and other members will resent you and your efforts.

➤ **Suggest that some members leave the club.** This is tricky, but it could work, especially if you know of another club where some of your members would be happier. If your entire club is made up of conservative investors, for instance, with the exception of two who fall into the high-risk category, it's quite possible that the risk-takers would be happier in another club of like-minded investors. You'd need to be very careful about how you present the idea, because you don't want to give the impression that you're kicking members out of your club. Simply say that you know of a club that might be a better fit and then let the risk-takers decide. Hopefully, they'll take the bait and your problem will be solved.

If your club members are committed to the group and are willing to work to see the club continue, they should be agreeable to try these or other ideas that you come up with on your own.

Personality Conflicts

Sometimes people within a club clash, and it has nothing to do with investment philosophies. Sometimes people clash because they just don't like each other.

In this politically correct, kinder-and-gentler society that we live in, it may be considered poor form to not get along with fellow club members. The expectation seems to be that when you're in the same group with someone, you really ought to see eye to eye on club issues.

We all know, however, that expectation isn't always met in real life. Did you ever meet someone to whom you took an immediate and intense dislike? It's not a pleasant feeling, but sometimes, for whatever reasons, it happens. Maybe there's something to that reincarnation thing, and the person to whom you so strongly object bears a strong resemblance to the guy who stole your oxen when you were trying to eke out a living by growing coffee in the Republic of Yemen back in the 1800s.

Anyway, if there are members of your club who don't get along, and the relationship is causing problems within the club, address the issue. Don't make a bigger deal about it than is necessary, but don't let it go. There are a couple of tactics you might try:

➤ Point out that the poor relationship between the people who can't get along is causing problems for the rest of the club. Perhaps the troublemakers simply don't realize that they're making other club members uncomfortable, or taking up club time to argue, or whatever it is that they're doing. They could be so wrapped up in their dislike for one another that it hasn't occurred to them that it's affecting other people. Pointing this out could serve as a wake-up call, or might embarrass them to the point that they'll just get over it, and get on with business.

➤ If the situation is intolerable, you may have to ask the members to leave the club. You could, if you're able, steer them to other groups (but not the same one!). You would need to explain that you're very sorry to have to ask them to leave, but that their relationship is making it impossible for other members to conduct business in a pleasant setting and is causing conditions within the club to

Cashing In

If you're serious about getting members of your investment club to work and cooperate together, read *Building Team Spirit: Activities for Inspiring and Energizing Teams*, by Barry Heermann, Ph.D. The book offers practical ideas for getting people to work together.

deteriorate. If the members who are causing the problems decline to leave, you should have a clause in your operating agreement that allows you to remove them from the club. Again, make sure you have the backing of the rest of the club before you do this, and don't think about trying to do it on your own. You need a majority vote—or maybe even a unanimous one, depending on your operating agreement—to remove a member.

Loss of Interest

Loss of interest starts out as a seemingly benign club condition, but if it continues, it can turn into a real killer.

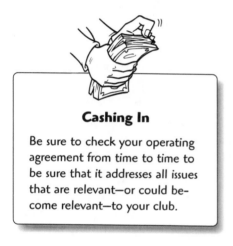

Cashing In

Be sure to check your operating agreement from time to time to be sure that it addresses all issues that are relevant—or could become relevant—to your club.

It's pretty normal for a couple of club members to lose interest. Hopefully, when that occurs, they'll simply leave the group. Your operating agreement should include direction about what to do when someone quits the club, and no problems should arise from their withdrawal.

If more than a few members lose interest and want to leave the club, however, several things might happen. A mass exodus could wipe out your club. Unless you quickly recruit new members, your club membership could drop so low that you can't effectively conduct business or raise enough capital to make investments. If you have a large club, however, and, say, half of the members quit, you could actually end up with a stronger club.

If 12 out of 25 members quit because they lose interest in the club, you'd still have 13 committed members, who presumably are interested in making the club work. If that occurs, consider your club to be better off, reorganize, and get busy investing.

All of these problems—clashing philosophies, personality conflicts, and loss of interest—can be tough to deal with. Sometimes they're solvable, and other times they're irreconcilable.

Often, the trick is recognizing which is which.

Recognizing Problems That Can't Be Solved

If you've tried every way you can think of to solve a problem, including seeking—and listening to—advice from other members of your club and members of other clubs, and you still can't figure out how to make the situation right, you may have an unsolvable problem.

Some people say that there's no such thing as a problem that can't be solved, and maybe they're right. Sometimes, though, it just takes too much time, or too much energy, or it's too much trouble to keep trying. At that point, you may have to be willing to admit that it's time to quit.

It's an awful feeling to have started something—whether it's a big project, or a club, or a business—and to have put your heart and soul into it, only to watch it fall apart.

Sometimes, though, the best and kindest thing you can do is call it quits and move on.

If everyone in your club agrees that your problems are unsolvable, and it's time to disband, you really have no choice but to agree.

Having the Courage to Disband the Club

If you and the rest of your club members decide that it's time to call it quits, don't try to hang on, or drag it out. If it's time to break up the club, go ahead and get it over with.

Delaying the inevitable will only make the situation worse by allowing problems to intensify and members to become demoralized. Refusing to admit that it's time to disband is sort of like staying too long at a party. Eventually, things wind down to that embarrassing moment in which you realize you should have called it quits long ago.

Legal Aspects of Disbanding

Your operating agreement should clearly state how your club may disband, and what happens if it does.

Remember that if your club is a partnership, as most are, you're legally terminating a partnership, not just saying goodbye to fellow club members.

Depending on the terms of your operating agreement, you'll need a majority vote, or a unanimous one, to terminate the partnership. While some investment clubs give

Heading for a Crash

Many people are unwilling to admit that a problem can't be solved, especially when they're personally invested in the organization that's affected by the problem. The danger in that is the problem tends to drag on and intensify, eventually bringing everybody down with it. If you sense a problem can't be solved, be willing to let go of it.

Cashing In

If a very important matter, such as vote to disband, is going to come up at your next meeting, it's a good idea to notify each member in writing. Follow up the written notice with a phone call to make sure everyone received the note. You don't want someone coming to you after the fact and saying he didn't know the vote was going to occur.

each member one vote, regardless of the value of his or her capital account, others give votes according to the amount of capital each member holds.

If your club awards votes depending on the amount of capital, you'll need to consider that when looking for a majority vote. If the vote is based on the partners' capital accounts, you don't just count hands or "ayes." You need to consider the worth of each partner's vote, depending on the value of his or her capital account.

If Sharon's capital account is worth four votes, and Sharon votes for the club to disband, for instance, Sharon's vote negates those of Bill and Andrea, whose capital accounts are worth only two votes each. Some clubs are set up in that manner to give more voting power to members who have been in the club for a long time, or who have contributed larger sums of money.

Your broker should have been notified about the pending breakup of the club. He'll have to close your brokerage account, if you have one. You'll also need to close out any bank accounts that you might have opened.

If your club was required to register as a partnership with your county or state, you'll want to contact—in writing—the agency with which you did so.

Let the agency know that the partnership has been dissolved, provide the date on which the vote was taken, and a list of the names of club members.

You also should notify the Internal Revenue Service that your club has disbanded so that there won't be any confusion concerning taxes. Make sure to notify all members before the meeting that a vote to disband will be occurring. If you vote to dissolve the partnership, all members should be notified in writing, and the vote should be recorded in the minutes of the meeting.

After the vote, your club should first pay off any debts that the it may have, then distribute the remaining assets among members or their personal representatives in proportion to each partner's capital account.

Emotional Aspects of Disbanding

While legally terminating a partnership is not all that difficult, the emotional aspects of doing so can be a little more complicated.

It might be no big deal. Many people belong to groups and organizations to which they have little loyalty. Some of your members might belong to your investment club because it meets on Tuesdays, and that's a good day for them. Or they became members because it was the only club they could find that was accepting new members, or because they liked the companies you invested in, or they like the name of the club, or whatever.

Some members, however—especially those who are founding members or have been in the club for a long time—are likely to be upset when the group disbands. At least some of the members of your club probably have made emotional investments, as well as monetary ones in the group.

Be sympathetic and feel free to commiserate with other people who feel bad. While it's a good idea to talk about why you're disbanding and how you feel about it, however, don't become overly dramatic or make more of an issue about it than is necessary.

There Are Worse Things in Life

Failing at a club, or a business, or a job, isn't one of the worst things that can happen in life. Failing at these things can make us feel bad, but certainly is no tragedy.

Tragedy is when a loved one is killed in a car crash, a child becomes terminally ill, or your home and everything in it is destroyed by fire—not the failure of an organization.

Sure, you might be upset—especially if you started the club and put in more hours than you care to remember organizing it and getting it up and running. Your ego might even be a little bruised if you take the breakup of the club personally.

Take This to the Bank

Don't be too worried about failing—there have been some pretty impressive failures before you. Remember that when Bill Gates introduced Windows 1.0 and 2.0, they both flopped. His product didn't take off until Windows 3.0 came out in 1990. Gates made mistakes and failed, but he didn't give up.

You might even be tempted to try to blame it on somebody else. If Jenny hadn't always wanted her own way when it came to stock selection, or if Bob and Rob hadn't argued all the time, or if Robert would have showed up to meetings now and then .... Blaming others and making excuses, however, are unproductive.

What you must do is put the matter in perspective and move on. Remember that failure is really more of an inconvenience than a tragedy. "Oh, heck," you might say. "Now I've got to pick up the pieces and start over."

And that's exactly what you can do.

Using the Experience to Start Another Club

We should make it clear right now—and perhaps should have done so earlier—that we're not expecting your investment club to fail. On the contrary, we expect that your club will be sound, successful, and long lasting. You have the edge by reading this book.

Having said all that, however, if your club *should* fail, there's something very important that you should do.

Cashing In

Sports broadcaster Wayne Root had more than his share of failure and rejection. He started several businesses that failed and was rejected by hundreds of television stations before finally getting a break and starting on his way to great success. Root learned so much from his failures that he wrote a book about it. It's called *The Joy of Failure!*

If your investment club fails, be sure to pay close attention to the experience and learn everything you can from it. While it might not seem to be so at the time, failure is a very valuable learning tool, and can be of great benefit in the future.

Talk to other members of your club and to members of other clubs. Find out what they think went wrong and why. Read over your club minutes to see if you find any clues as to when problems started, or how they might have been avoided.

Don't dwell only on the negatives, however. Think about some good things that happened while the club was together. Then, ask yourself some questions and answer them as honestly as you can.

➤ **Was the club experience educational?** Jot down some of the things that you learned while your club was together. You might be very surprised at the amount of knowledge you've accumulated.

➤ **Was the club experience profitable?** Hopefully, you came out of the club with at least as much, or more, than you put into it. If so, great! If not, find out where the losses occurred.

➤ **Was the club experience fun?** We feel that time spent having fun is rarely time wasted, although some people may disagree. Think about the people you got to know through your investment club. Maybe some of them have become friends and you enjoy each other's company in settings other than club meetings.

Compare your list of the negatives with the positives of your club's experience. If you feel that there were more good things than bad about the time you spent in the club, then the experience wasn't a failure. If you come up with more negatives than positives, you'll have to look more closely to figure out why.

Having gained much useful knowledge from your first investment club experience, you very well may decide to try another one. We're hoping that you will.

If you do decide to form another club, you'll definitely be better equipped than you were with your first effort. The experience you will have gained from starting a club from the ground up will be invaluable, and the second time around will seem easy.

Sure, you'll encounter obstacles and problems, probably some of the same ones as the first time around. What you'll have, however, are the knowledge and tools you'll need to deal with, and overcome the hurdles more easily than you were able to do before.

So, chalk up your experience to experience, and use the knowledge you've gained to your advantage when starting another club.

While we felt it was important to cover this information, we certainly don't want you to feel discouraged, or think that your club doesn't have a chance of succeeding.

Chances are that your investment club will prosper and grow for years to come, and that you'll come out both wiser and financially better off as a result.

Keep your sights set high, and enjoy the experience.

The Least You Need to Know

➤ We're programmed in our society to win, but failing at something isn't anything to be terribly ashamed of.

➤ Some problems within the club can be solved, and there often are several ways to do so.

➤ It may not be possible to solve other problems, and you'll need to recognize what they are.

➤ If your club decides to disband, you'll need to deal with both legal and emotional issues.

➤ Having your club break up may be disappointing, but it's hardly a tragedy.

➤ Using the experience and knowledge you've gained from starting one club will make starting another one much easier.

Glossary

401(k) A retirement plan into which employees can contribute a portion of their salaries (usually before taxes). Contributions can grow tax deferred until they are withdrawn upon retirement.

activity ratios These capture the way the company is utilizing its assets by comparing company sales to various asset categories.

adjusted gross income (AGI) The gross income less certain allowed business-related deductions. These deductions include alimony payments, contributions to a Keogh retirement plan, and, in some cases, contributions to an IRA.

adjuster An individual who inspects damage as reported on an insurance claim and determines a settlement amount for the claim.

ADRs (American Depository Receipts) Trust receipts for shares of a foreign company purchased and held by a foreign branch of the bank. The ADRS are legal claims against the equity interest that the bank holds. ADRs are an excellent alternative to direct investing in foreign companies.

aggressive growth fund A type of mutual fund that has a primary investment objective of seeking capital gains. It is understood that the potential for above-average returns in such an investment is countered by above-average risks.

amendment Change, alteration, correction, or addition to an agreement or document setting up an investment club.

American Stock Exchange (AMEX) At one time, AMEX was the second largest stock exchange in the U.S. AMEX has recently been merged with NASDAQ. Currently, the two exchanges still remain independent.

amortization Reducing the principal of a loan by making regular payments.

amortization schedule   A schedule of regular payments to repay a loan. The schedule indicates to the borrower the amounts of each payment that are principal, interest, and the remaining balance of the loan.

analysis   *See* fundamental analysis.

annual dividend   A share of a company's net profits that are distributed by the company to a class of its stockholders each year. The dividend is paid in a fixed amount for each share of stock held. Although most companies make quarterly payments in cash, dividends also may be made in other forms of property, such as stock. Dividends must be approved by the company's directors before each payment is made.

annual fee   The amount a cardholder pays to a credit card company for the right to hold a particular credit card.

annual report   A source of operating data on a company published annually by most publicly held firms (also known as a shareholders' report).

annuity   A stream of equal payments, as to a retiree, that occur at predetermined intervals (for example, monthly or annually). The payments may continue for a fixed period or for a contingent period, such as the recipient's lifetime. Annuities are most often associated with insurance companies and retirement programs.

adjustable-rate mortgage   A mortgage set up with an interest rate that can change at specific intervals, as determined under the initial contract.

arbitration   The hearing and determination of a dispute between parties by a third party.

ask price   The lowest price at which a given security is offered for sale.

asset allocation   The process of determining the assignment of investment funds to broad categories of assets. It's when you (or your broker) decide what percentage of your stock should be in technology investments.

at the market   Refers to a security transaction that occurs at whatever price the broker can get for you at the time of the trade. You either buy or sell a stock at a set price, or you give an order to buy the security at whatever price the security happens to be at when the order is placed.

Baby Boomer   A common term used to define individuals born between 1946 and 1964.

balanced mutual fund   A mutual fund whose primary objective is to buy a combination of stocks and bonds. These middle-of-the-road funds balance their portfolios to achieve both moderate income and moderate capital growth. These funds tend to be less volatile than stock-only funds. Balanced funds tend, on average, to be invested as 45 percent bonds and 55 percent stocks.

bear market   An extended period of general price decline in the stock market as a whole.

beneficiary   The person who is named to receive the proceeds from an investment vehicle, trust, or contract. A beneficiary can be an individual, a company, or an organization.

beta (B)   A mathematical measure of the risk on a portfolio or a given stock compared with rates of return on the market as a whole. A beta of less than 1 is less volatile than the general market. A beta above 1 is more volatile than the market.

bid price   The highest price offered to purchase a given security.

blue chip investment   A high-quality investment involving a lower-than-average risk. Blue chip investment is generally used to refer to securities of companies having a long history of sustained earnings and dividend payments.

blue chip stock   This is the common phrase for stock of well-established companies that historically pay dividends in both good and bad years. Some examples of blue chip stock are General Motors, ExxonMobil, and IBM.

bond   A debt instrument. The issuer promises to pay the investor a specified amount of interest for a certain period of time and to repay the principal at maturity.

bond fund   A mutual fund that invests in bonds and passes current income to its shareholders, with capital gains as a secondary objective. Some bond funds purchase long-term securities providing a relatively high current yield, but varying substantially in price with changes in interest rates. Other funds choose short-term securities having lower yields, but fluctuating little in value.

broker   A person who earns a commission or fee for acting as an agent in making contracts or sales.

budget   A schedule of income and expenses commonly broken into monthly intervals and typically covering a one-year period.

bull market   An extended period of generally rising prices in the market as a whole.

business risk   The degree of uncertainty associated with a company's earnings and its ability to pay interest, dividends, and other returns that are owed investors.

C corporations   C corporations get a double whammy when it comes to paying federal income tax. The corporation has to pay a tax on its earned profit, and the people who get corporate salaries or dividends have to pay taxes again.

capital expenses   Expenses spent to improve property.

capital gain   Profits from the sale of an investment or asset. Tax on this gain is usually due when the asset is sold.

capital gains exclusion   An exclusion to the practice of taxing capital gains that applies to the sale of real estate.

capitalization   The sum of a corporation's long-term debt, stock, and retained earnings. Also called invested capital.

cash flow   Shows the ability of a company to meet its day-to-day operating expense and satisfy its short-term obligations as they come due. It's a measure of how well they can pay their bills, and it's important for your club to know this information.

cash-value life insurance   In this insurance, part of the premium is used to provide death benefits, and the remainder is available to earn interest. Cash-value life insurance is both a protection plan and a savings plan that charges significantly higher premiums than term insurance.

certificate of deposit (CD)   A receipt for a deposit of funds in a financial institution that permits the holder to receive interest plus the deposit at maturity.

certified financial planner (CFP)   A professional financial planner who has completed a series of correspondence courses and passed a 10-hour examination in subject areas such as insurance, securities, and taxes. The designation is awarded by the College for Financial Planning in Denver, Colorado.

certified public accountant (CPA)   An accountant who has met certain state requirements as to age, education, experience, residence, and accounting knowledge. Accountants must pass an extensive series of examinations before becoming CPAs.

chartered financial consultant (ChFC)   A professional financial planner who has completed a series of 10 courses and examinations in subject areas such as economics, insurance, investments, and tax shelters. The designation is awarded by the American College of Bryn Mawr, Pennsylvania.

charting   Technical analysis activity of plotting the behavior of everything from the DJIA (Dow Jones Industrial Average) to share-price movements of individual stock in contrast with others.

churning and burning   Trading securities very actively in a brokerage account in order to increase brokerage commissions rather than customer profits. Brokers may be tempted to churn accounts because their income is directly related to the volume of trading undertaken by the customers. Churning is illegal and unethical.

close-ended fund   A type of mutual fund in which only a limited number of shares can be sold.

collateral   Assets pledged as security for a loan. If a borrower defaults on the terms of a loan, the collateral may be sold, with the proceeds used to satisfy any remaining obligations. High-quality collateral reduces risk to the lender and results in a lower rate of interest on the loan.

commercial banks   Financial institutions, either chartered by the federal or state government that take deposits, loan money, and provide other services to individuals or corporations.

commission   The sum or percentage allowed to a broker (agent) for his services.

common stock   Shares of ownership of a company; a class of capital stock that has no preference to dividends or any other distributions.

common stock fund A mutual fund that limits its investments to shares of common stock. Common stock funds vary in risk, from relatively low to quite high, depending on the types of stocks in which the funds invest.

compound interest Interest paid on interest from previous periods in addition to principal. Essentially, compounding involves adding interest to principal and any previous interest in order to calculate interest in the next period. Compound interest may be figured daily, monthly, quarterly, or annually.

consumer price index (CPI) A measure of the relative cost of living compared with a base year (currently 1967). The CPI can be a misleading indicator or inflationary impact on a given person because it is constructed according to the spending of an urban family of four. Used as a measure of inflation.

consumer price indicators Consumer price indicators are changes in prices for a fixed market basket of about 360 goods and services. The changes are used as a measure of inflation.

co-payment The amount the insured is responsible to pay at each time of service under a health insurance contract.

corporate bond A bond issued by a corporation as opposed to a bond issued by the U.S. Treasury or a municipality.

corporation An association endowed by law with the rights and liabilities of an individual.

credit history The record of an individual's past events that pertain to credit previously given or applied for.

credit unions Alternatives to commercial banks, credit unions are nonprofit organizations that provide many of the same services as banks. Generally, credit unions can offer better rates on loans and savings because they don't pay federal taxes.

customer service representative (CSR) A front-line bank employee who opens checking and savings accounts, certificates of deposit, and so forth. They know the products their financial institutions provide.

cyclical stock Common stock of a firm whose earnings are heavily influenced by cyclical changes in general economic activity. As investors anticipate changes in profits, cyclical stocks often reach their high and low levels before the respective highs and lows in the economy.

debit card A plastic card used for purchasing goods and services or obtaining cash advanced in which payment is made from existing funds in a bank account.

deductible The amount the insured must pay before an insurance company pays a claim.

deduction An expenditure permitted to be used in order to reduce an individual's income tax liability.

default   Failure to live up to the terms of a contract or to meet financial obligations. Generally, the term is used to indicate the inability of a homeowner to pay interest or principal on a debt when it is due.

defensive stock   A stock that tends to resist general stock market declines and whose price will remain stable or even prosper when economic activity is tapering.

defined benefit plan   A qualified retirement plan that specifies the benefits received, rather than contributions into the plan, usually expressed as a percentage of preretirement compensation and number of years of service. The responsibility for the benefit is on the company, not the employee.

defined contribution plan   A qualified retirement plan that specifies the annual contributions to the plan, usually expressed as a percentage of the employee's salary. Contributions can be made by the employer, the employee, or both.

disability   The lack of competent power, strength, or physical or mental ability.

disability insurance   Insurance intended to cover loss of income due to a disability.

discount broker   A broker that charges a lower commission than a full-service broker. In exchange, the service is less than with a full-service broker.

discretionary expenses   Expenses that are incurred for nonessentials; money spent as a person chooses.

disposition charges   Expenses charged to a leasee for selling the vehicle or property leased at the end of the lease.

diversification   The acquisition of a group of assets in which returns on the assets are not directly related over time. Proper investment diversification, requiring a sufficient number of different assets, is intended to minimize risk associated with investing.

dividend   A share of a company's net profits distributed by the company to a class of its stockholders. The dividend is paid in a fixed amount for each share of stock held. Dividends are usually fixed in preferred stock; dividends from common stock vary as the company's performance shifts.

dividend reinvestment plan (DRP)   Stockholders may automatically reinvest dividend payments in additional shares of the company's stock. Instead of receiving the normal dividend checks, participating stockholders will receive quarterly notification of shares purchased and shares held in their accounts. Dividend reinvestment is normally an inexpensive way of purchasing additional shares of stock because the fees are low or are completely absorbed by the company. In addition, some companies offer stock at a discount from the existing market price. Normally, these dividends are fully taxable as income even though no cash is received by the stockholder.

dollar cost averaging   Investment of an equal amount of money at regular intervals, usually each month. This process results in the purchase of extra shares during market downturns and fewer shares during market upturns. Dollar cost averaging is based on the belief that the market of a particular stock will rise in price over the long term and that it is not worthwhile (or even possible) to identify immediate highs and lows.

Dow Jones Industrial Average (DJIA)   One of the measures of the stock market that includes averages for utilities, industrial, and transportation stocks, as well as the composite averages. *See* index.

down payment   Funds the purchaser puts down when property is sold. Remaining funds for purchase are borrowed.

dwelling coverage   The part of your homeowner's insurance that covers the structure in which you live.

dwelling insurance   *See* renter's insurance.

earned income   Salary, wages, and self-employment income derived as compensation for services rendered. Unearned income includes the return you receive from investments.

emerging growth fund   The common stock of a relatively young firm operating in an industry with very good growth prospects. Although this kind of stock offers unusually large returns, it is very risky because the expected growth may not occur, or the firm may be swallowed by the competition.

emerging market stock   The term which broadly categorizes countries in the midst of developing their financial market and financial economic infrastructures.

employer identification number (EIN)   A nine-digit number assigned to corporations, partnerships, estates, trusts, and other entities for tax filing and reporting purposes.

enrolled agent   A designation given by the IRS. Enrolled agents are licensed and can represent clients in front of the IRS in the event of an audit. Enrolled agents generally have more training than tax preparers, and they're required to participate in continuing education. As a group, they charge more than tax preparers.

equity   The value of ownership in property or securities. The equity in your home is the difference between the current market value of the home and the loan still owed on the mortgage.

escrow   The holding of assets (for example: securities, cash, a collection) by a third party, which delivers the assets to the grantee or promissee on the fulfillment of some condition. Some parts of mortgage payments are held in escrow to cover expenses owned, like property taxes and insurance.

fair market value   The price at which a buyer and a seller willingly consummate a trade; the prevailing price of a security or property.

Fannie Mae   A security issued by the Federal National Mortgage Association (FNMA) that is backed by insured and conventional mortgages. Monthly returns to holders of Fannie Maes consist of interest and principal payments made by the homeowners on their mortgages.

Federal National Mortgage Association (FNMA)   A privately owned profit-seeking corporation that adds liquidity to the mortgage market by purchasing loans from lenders. It finances the purchases by issuing its own bonds or by selling mortgages it already owns to financial institutions.

finance charges   Interest expense incurred from lending or leasing.

financial adviser   A professional who guides individuals to arrange and coordinate their financial affairs.

financial consultant   Someone who provides an overview of financial information and options, in order for you to choose products and services from which you will benefit.

financial planner   A person who counsels individuals and corporations with respect to evaluating financial status, identifying goals, and determining ways in which the goals can be met.

financial planning   The process of defining and setting goals to achieve financial security.

fixed-interest rate loan   A loan that has a set rate throughout the period of the loan. Payments are usually set at a specified, equal payment throughout the loan.

fixed-rate mortgage   A mortgage in which the annual interest charged does not vary throughout the period of the loan.

foreclosure   When a lender claims a property on which the loan has been defaulted.

Freddie Mac   A security issued by the Federal Hoe Loan Mortgage Corporation that is secured by pools of conventional home mortgages. Holders of Freddie Macs receive a share of interest and principal payments by the homeowners.

full-service broker   Normally works for a major brokerage firm. She receives commissions on the trades an individual makes, or she gets a fee based on the value of funds within an account.

fundamental analysis   The process of comparing the fundamental properties of an investment.

gap insurance   Insurance purchased to pay the difference between the value your auto insurance will pay if a leased vehicles is stolen or totaled and the amount required to terminate the lease.

Generation X-ers (Gen X-ers)   The name given to the 46 million Americans between the ages of 19 and 30.

global fund   A mutual fund that includes at least 25 percent of foreign securities in its portfolio. The value of the fund depends on the health of foreign economies and exchange-rate trends. A global fund permits an investor to diversify internationally.

GNP (gross national product)   The market value of all goods and services produced by a country over the period of a year.

334

good-til-cancelled order   A limit order that remains outstanding until it is executed or cancelled. Also called an open order.

Government National Mortgage Association (GNMA)   A government-owned corporation that acquires, packages, and resells mortgages and mortgage purchased commitments in the form of mortgage-backed securities.

government obligations   A debt that is backed by the full taxing power of the U.S. government. Direct obligations include Treasury bills, Treasury bonds, and U.S. savings bonds. These investments are generally considered to be of the very highest quality.

government securities   Bonds, bills, or notes sold by the federal government to raise money.

gross income   All income except that specifically exempted by the Internal Revenue Code.

group insurance   Insurance offered only to members as a group, such as employees, often for only as long as they remain members of the group.

growth fund   An investment company whose major objective is long-term capital growth. Growth funds offer substantial potential gains over time but vary significantly in price, depending on general economic conditions.

growth stock   The stock of a firm that is expected to have above-average increases in revenues and earnings. These firms normally retain most earnings for reinvestment and therefore pay small dividends. The stocks, often selling at relatively high price-to-earnings ratios, are subject to wide swings in price. Object of investment is capital appreciation and long-term capital growth.

guaranteed replacement cost provision   An insurance provision that promises to pay the total cost to replace property upon loss or damage.

high-yield/junk bond   A high-risk, high-yield debt security issued by corporations or municipalities that are of lower quality. Junk bonds have a greater risk of default than higher-rated bonds. These securities are most appropriate for risk-oriented investors. They usually pay a higher interest rate than higher-rated bonds.

home equity loan   A loan in which property is used as collateral. Usually a second mortgage on a property.

homeowner's insurance   Insurance obtained by a property owner to protect the property and contents. It also provides liability coverage for accidents that occur on the property.

housing starts   A pickup in the pace of housing starts follows an easing of credit conditions—the availability and the cost of money—and is an indicator of improvement in economic health. Housing starts include the number of new building permits issued across the country, which is an even earlier indicator of the pace of future construction.

335

hybrid funds   Mutual funds that have characteristics of several types of securities. An example would be a convertible bond, which is a bond that has a conversion feature that permits the investor to convert the security into a specified number of shares of the company's common stock.

income fund   An investment company the main objective of which is to achieve current income for its owners. Thus, it tends to select securities such as bonds, preferred stocks, and common stocks that pay relatively high current returns.

income stocks   A stock with a relatively high dividend yield. The stock's issuer is typically a firm having stable earnings and dividends and operating in a mature industry. The price of an income stock is heavily influenced by changes in interest rates.

index   The measurement of the current price behavior of a representative group of stocks in relation to a base value set at an earlier point in time. The best-known indexes are the Dow Jones Industrial Average and Standard & Poor's 500 Index.

index fund   A mutual fund that keeps a portfolio of securities designed to match the performance of the market as a whole. The market is represented by an index, such as the Standard & Poor's 500 index. An index fund has low administrative expenses; it appeals to investors who believe it is difficult or impossible for investment managers to beat the market.

individual retirement account (IRA)   A retirement savings plan in which you can contribute up to $2,000 per year. Funds can grow tax-deferred until they are withdrawn at retirement. Contributions may or may not be tax-deductible depending on income level and participation in other retirement plans.

inflation   A general increase in the price level of goods and services.

inflation rider   Additional insurance coverage that is purchased to provide that the underlying policy coverage increases with inflation.

initial public offering (IPO)   A company's first sale of stock to the public. Securities offered in an IPO are often, but not always, those of young, small companies seeking outside equity capital and a public market for their stock. Investors purchasing stock in IPOs generally assume very large risks for the possibility of large gains.

insurance   A mechanism that permits individuals to reduce risk by sharing in the losses associated with the occurrence of certain events.

intangible personal property   Property that attains its value from what it represents, not from what it's worth. An example is a stock certificate.

insurance bond   An insurance policy guaranteeing that funds will be retained as pledged.

interest   The cost for the used of borrowed money. Also known as interest rate.

interest-sensitive stock   A stock that tends to move in the opposite direction of interest rates. Interest-sensitive stocks include nearly all preferred stocks and the common stocks of industries, such as electric utilities, banks, and insurance companies. A common stock may be interest-sensitive because its dividend is relatively fixed (as with an electric utility) or because the firm raises a large portion of its funds through borrowing (as with a savings and loan).

international fund   A mutual fund that invests only outside the country in which it is located.

international stock   This is stock of companies located outside the United States.

investing   Buying something with the expectation of making a profit.

investment   The process of purchasing securities or property for which stability of value and level of expected returns are somewhat predictable.

investment club   A financial entity formed to pool resources to buy investments.

investment return   The return achieved on an investment, including current income and any change in value during an investor's holding period; also known as total return.

IPOs (initial public offerings)   The stock offering of a company when it goes public.

itemized deduction   An expenditure permitted to be used to reduce an individual's income tax liability.

Keogh   A federally approved retirement program that permits self-employed people to set money aside for savings up to $30,000 (or up to 25 percent of their income). All contributions and income earned by the account are tax-deferred until withdrawals are made during retirement.

large-cap stocks   Stocks in companies with over $10 billion in capitalization—the largest companies.

leading indicator   A statistic, data indicating that the economy is pointing in a direction opposite of where the economy currently is.

lease   A contract under which someone obtains the use of an object, such as a vehicle or property for a specified time and for a specified amount of money.

lending instrument   A debt instrument; companies borrow money from investors and agree to pay a stated rate of interest over a specified period of time, at the end of which the original sum will be repaid.

leverage   Measures different types of financing for firms and indicates the amount of debt being used to support the resources and operations of the company.

leverage ratios   These are the amount of debt being used to support the company, and the ability of the firm to service its debt. Debt-to-equity ratio measures the amount of financial leverage being utilized by a company.

limit order   An order to buy at a specified price (or lower) or sell at (or above) a specified price.

liquidity   The ability to quickly convert assets into cash without significant loss.

liquidity ratios   These are current ratios and net working capital. You measure the ability of the company to meet its day-to-day operating expenses and satisfy short-term obligations as they come due.

long-term capital gains   Profits from the sale of investments that you've held for more than a year. Long-term capital gains are taxed at either 7 or 10 percent, depending on your income tax bracket. Investors in the 15 percent bracket pay only a 10 percent tax on their capital gains, while all others pay a 20 percent tax of their long-term capital gains.

long-term stock   A stock that you keep for more than a year before selling.

majority consent   Means that more than half of all members must be in favor. Some clubs require a 75 percent majority vote.

marginal tax bracket   The percentage of extra income received that must be paid in taxes or the proportional amount of taxes paid on a given income or the given dollar value of an asset. If the tax is calculated on the basis of total income, it is the average tax rate. If the tax is calculated only on the extra units of income, the rate is the marginal tax rate.

market measures   *See* common stock.

marketing timing   Buying or selling stock, in part or in whole, depending on when an investor feels it's advantageous to get in or out of the stock market.

market order   An order to buy or sell stock at the best price available at the time the order is placed with the broker.

market value   The prevailing market price of a security or property; an indication of how the market as a whole has assessed the security's or property's worth.

maturity   The termination of the period that an obligation has to run (bonds); mortgages have a date of maturity when they are due to be repaid in full.

mid-cap stocks   Stocks in companies with $1 billion to $10 billion capitalization.

misrepresent   To represent a financial product incorrectly, improperly, or falsely.

money manager   A person who is paid a fee to supervise the investment decisions of others. The term is usually used for management of individual portfolios as compared to institutional funds (*see* portfolio manager).

money market accounts   Accounts held in banks on which you receive interest.

money market fund   A mutual fund that sells shares of ownership and uses the proceeds to purchase short-term, high-quality securities, such as Treasury bills, negotiable certificates of deposit, and commercial paper. Income earned by shareholders is received in the form of additional shares of stock in the fund (normally priced at $1 each). Although no fees are generally charged to purchase or redeem shares in a money market fund, an annual management charge is levied by the fund's advisers. This investment pays a return that varies with short-term interest rates. Money market fund is relatively liquid and safe, but its yields and features vary.

mortgage   A conditional conveyance of property to a creditor as security for the repayment of money.

mortgage life insurance   Term insurance that will pay the outstanding balance on the insured person's home loan should he or she die.

municipal bond   The debt issue of a city, county, state, or other political entity. Interest paid by most municipal bonds is exempt from federal income taxes and often from state and local taxes. Municipal bonds with tax-exempt interest appeal mainly to investors with significant amounts of other taxable income.

municipal bond fund   A mutual fund that invests in tax-exempt securities and passes through tax-free current income to its shareholders. Some municipal bond funds purchase long-term securities providing a relatively high current yield, but varying substantially in price as interest rates change. Other funds choose short-term securities having lower yields but fluctuating little in value.

mutual fund   An open-ended investment company that invests its shareholders' money in a diversified group of securities of other corporations. Mutual funds are usually diversified and professionally managed.

NAIC (National Association of Investment Clubs)   A nonprofit organization that helps investors organize and run investment clubs.

NASDAQ (National Association of Security Dealers Automated Quotation System) A system (exchange) providing up-to-date bid and ask prices on thousands of over-the-counter securities.

net income   The income you have after you've paid taxes and any and all other liabilities, expenses, or charges against that income.

net working capital   An absolute measure of a company's liquidity.

net worth   The amount of wealth calculated by taking the total value of assets owned and subtracting all liabilities.

New York Stock Exchange (NYSE)   The largest, oldest, key organized trading exchange in the United States for stock and bond transactions, accounting for over 50 percent of the total volume of shares traded on organized exchanges.

no-load fund   A mutual fund sold without a sale charge. No-load funds sell directly to customers at net asset value with no intermediate salesperson charging a fee.

nondiversifiable risk   *See* systematic risk.

nontaxable income   Income specifically exempt from taxation on federal income tax returns. Examples of nontaxable income include interest from most municipal bonds, life insurance proceeds, gifts, and inheritances.

odd lot   Less than 100 shares of a stock.

open-ended fund   A mutual fund with no limit on the number of shares it can offer for sale.

open order   *See* good-til-cancelled order.

operating agreement   The formal agreement designed and agreed to by members of an investment club.

partnership   A legal relationship between two or more persons contractually associated as joint principals in a business.

pension plan   An employer-sponsored retirement plan in which a retiree receives a fixed periodic payment made in consideration of past services, injury or loss sustained, merit or poverty, and so on.

performance   The level of profit you make from a particular investment. Performance is measured for a period of time—either a quarter-year, half-year, or annual rate of return.

personal finance   Every aspect of one's life that deals with money.

personal income   This is the before-tax income, received in the form of wages and salaries, interest and dividends, rents, and other payments such as Social Security, unemployment, and pensions. This report helps explain trends in consumer buying habits. When personal income rises, it often means that people will increase their buying.

points   Prepaid interest paid as a fee to a mortgage lender to cover the cost of applying for the loan. One point is 1 percent of the loan's value.

portfolio   A group of investments assembled to meet an investment goal.

portfolio manager   A person who is paid a fee to supervise the investment decisions of others. The term is normally used in reference to the managers of large institutions, such as bank trust departments, pension funds, insurance companies, and mutual funds.

preferred stock   A security that shows ownership in a corporation and gives the holder a claim prior to the claim of common shareholders on earnings and also generally on assets in the event of liquidation. Most preferred stock issues pay a fixed dividend set at the time of issuance, stated in a dollar amount or as a percentage of par value. Because no maturity date is stipulated, these securities are priced on dividend yield and trade much like long-term corporate bonds. As a general rule, preferred stock has limited appeal for individual investors.

premium   The amount paid, in one sum or periodically, for a contract of insurance.

price-to-earnings ratio (P/E ratio)   A common stock analysis statistic in which the current price of a stock is divided by the current (or sometimes the projected) earnings per share of the issuing firm.

principal   The capital sum, as distinguished from interest or profit.

producer price index   If this index goes up, it means that producers are raising prices on the products they sell. Sometimes these increases are passed along to consumers, but depending on things such as competition and the state of the general economy, they cannot be.

producer prices   These indicate price changes of goods at various stages of production—from crude materials such as raw cotton to finished goods such as clothing and furniture. An upward surge may mean higher consumer prices later. Watch for changes in the prices of finished goods. These don't fluctuate as widely as crude materials, which makes them a better measure of inflationary pressure.

profitability ratios   These measure the company's success as based on its profit.

prospectus   A formal written document relating to a new securities offering that delineates the proposed business plan or the data relevant to an existing business plan. Investors need this information to make educated decisions about whether to purchase the security. The prospectus includes financial data, a summary of the firm's business history, a list of its officers, a description of its operations, and a mention of any pending litigation. A prospectus is an abridged version of the firm's registration statement, filed with the Securities and Exchange Commission.

redemption fee   A fee charged to an investor if mutual fund shares are sold before the end of a previously agreed upon time period.

refinancing   Reapplying for a new mortgage, usually to receive a lower interest rate. Refinancing is done for consolidation, lower interest rate, or additional funding.

renter's insurance   Similar to homeowner's insurance, it provides insurance protection for a resident's personal property, along with liability coverage.

residual value   The value of a vehicle when it comes off a lease; the value you need to pay to acquire the vehicle.

retail sales   These are total sales at the retail level, including everything from cars to groceries. This figure gives a rough clue to consumer attitudes, and can indicate future conditions. A long slowdown in sales can lead to cuts in production. If retail sales are dropping, your club shouldn't rush out and buy stocks of Gap, Limited, Sears, and so on.

return on equity (ROE)   *See* return on investment (ROI).

return on investment (ROI)   Measures the return to stockholders by relating profit to shareholders' equity.

return on total assets (ROTA) ROTA looks at the amount of resources used by the firm to support operations. It reveals management effectiveness in generating profits from the assets it has available, and is perhaps the single most important measure of return.

rider An addition or amendment to a document.

risk The chance that the value or return on an investment will differ from its expected value. Business risk, financial risk, purchasing power risk, interest rate risk, market risk, default risk, and foreign currency risk are all types of risks associated with investments.

Roth IRA New in 1998, an individual retirement account in which the funds placed into the account are nondeductible; if held for more than five years, all funds withdrawn are received tax-free.

round lot The standard unit of trading in a particular type of security. For stocks, a round lot is 100 shares or a multiple thereof, although few inactive issues trade in units of 10 shares.

S corporations S corporations get special tax status from the Internal Revenue Service (IRS), and they don't pay tax on the corporate level. All profits and losses are passed along to members or shareholders, who have to include the income on their personal tax returns. If there's a loss, shareholders write it off on their personal taxes.

S&Ls *See* thrifts.

S&P 500 A composite of the 500 largest companies in the United States.

SEC (Securities and Exchange Commission) A federal agency that registers securities and investment advisers. The agency is in charge of the administration of federal securities law. They regulate the organized securities exchanges and over-the-counter markets by extending disclosure requirements to outstanding securities.

sector fund Securities or other assets that share a common interest. Sector funds permit an investor to concentrate on a specific investment segment and yet diversify investments among various issuers. Sector funds entail more risk, but offer greater potential returns than funds that diversify their portfolios.

security An investment that represents evidence of debt, ownership of a business, or the legal right to determine the intrinsic interest in a business.

SEP-IRA A retirement plan for the self-employed that permits contributions up to $30,000 per year, or 15 percent of your income, whichever is lower. Similar to an IRA, except that the contribution limits are higher.

settlement The settling of property and title on an individual or individuals; the transaction when you purchase a security or property.

shareholder One who holds or owns a share or shares of a corporation.

short-term capital gains   Profits that come from the sale of investments that you've held for less than a year. Any gain made as a result of the investment is taxed at the income tax rate of all other income of the taxpayer.

short-term stock   A stock that you buy, then sell within a year.

simple interest   Interest paid on an initial investment only. Simple interest is calculated by multiplying the principal by the annual rate of interest by the number of years involved.

simplified employee pension plan (SEP)   A special type of joint Keogh-individual retirement account, permitting contributions from employees and employers. The SEP was developed to give small businesses a retirement plan that is easier to establish and administer than an ordinary pension plan.

small-cap stock   Companies that have less than $1 billion capitalization.

speculation   Taking above-average risks to achieve above-average returns, generally during a relatively short period of time. Speculation involves buying something on the basis of its potential selling price rather than on the basis of its actual value.

standard deduction   The minimum deduction from income allowed a taxpayer for calculating taxable income.

stock   Shares of ownership in a company. These shares include common stock of various classes and any preferred stock outstanding.

stock certificate   Physical proof issued by the corporation that an investor owns shares in the company. These documents can be certificated (in paper form that you would hold in your lockbox) or uncertificated (held in dividend reinvestment plans and with your broker).

stock market   The organized securities exchange for stock and bond transactions.

stockbroker   A broker who, for a commission, buys and sells stocks (and commonly other securities) for customers.

stop-loss order   An order to sell a stock when its market price reaches or drops below a specified level, a suspended order used primarily to protect the investor against rapid declines in prices and to limit loss.

systematic risk   Also known as the nondiversifiable risk. The risk of a stock following the market. Systematic risk is attributable to forces that affect all investments, and are therefore not unique to a given investment.

target price   What you anticipate your investment will be worth at a future time. If you expect your $1,000 investment to double in five years, for example, your target price is $2,000.

tax attorneys   Used to complete your tax return if your club's financial situation gets incredibly complicated, with all kinds of legal ramifications. Be prepared to pay—big time! Many tax attorneys charge a minimum of $300 an hour.

tax number   *See* employer identification number (EIN).

tax preparer   An individual who prepares a tax return according to law.

tax-deductible   An expense that can be used to offset gross income when calculating your taxable gross income.

tax-deferred   Income that is earned but neither received nor taxed until a later date, when the funds are withdrawn or mature. Tax-deferred assets include those within an IRA, 401(k) plan, 403(b) plan, tax-deferred annuity, tax-deferred life insurance, EE savings bonds, and others.

tax-managed   A recent concept for specified mutual funds where the tax consequences are taken into consideration when securities within the mutual fund are sold.

taxable income   Income that is subject to taxation; adjusted income minus standard or itemized deductions and exemptions.

term insurance   Life insurance in which the insurance company pays a specified sum if the insured dies during the coverage period. Term insurance includes no savings, cash value, borrowing power, or benefits at retirement On the basis of cost, it is the least expensive insurance available, although policy prices can vary significantly among firms.

thrifts   These are financial institutions commonly known as savings and loans (S&Ls).

total return   Dividend or interest income plus any capital gains, generally considered a better measure of an investment's return than dividends or interest alone.

trading stock   This is different from investing in stock. Trading stock is buying and selling stock actively, with the intention of turning a profit. Investing is buying stock with the intention of keeping it for a significant period of time.

transaction costs   The expense of buying or selling securities.

Treasury bond   Long-term (over 10 years), interest-bearing debt of the U.S. Treasury, available through a bank or brokerage firm or directly from the Federal Reserve. Treasury bonds are quoted and traded in 32nds of a point.

Treasury note   Intermediate-term (1 to 10 years), interest-bearing debt of the U.S. Treasury. Treasury notes are quoted and traded in 32nds of a point.

Treasury stock   Shares of a firm's stock that have been issued and then repurchased. Treasury stock is not considered in paying dividends, voting, or calculating earnings per share. It may be eventually retired or reissued.

unanimous consent   Means that all members must vote in favor.

unemployment   Measuring the percentage of the work force that's currently involuntarily without jobs, this is a broad indicator of economic health. Another monthly figure available is the number of payroll jobs. This may be a better indicator for spotting changes in business. A decreasing number of jobs is a sign that firms are cutting production.

unrealized losses   *See* unrealized profits.

unrealized profits   The difference between what the club paid for a stock, and the amount it's worth on any given day. Profit doesn't become realized until the stock is sold and the money earned taken by club members. Positive means profit and negative means losses.

unsystematic risk   The portion of an investor's portfolio's risk that can be eliminated by diversification.

value stock   A stock in which the price is considered below normal using valuation measures common to the market.

variable interest rate   Interest, either paid or received (depending on whether you are borrowing or investing funds), that changes periodically, depending on the initial contract.

warranty   A statement of promise or assurance in connection with a contract or purchase.

yield   The percentage return on an investment; also known as return. The dividends or interest paid by a company as a percentage of the current price.

Resources

Personal finance and investing are hot topics these days, and there are many resources available for everyone from the novice to the expert.

This list of additional resources includes books, Web sites, journals, and other publications that may be of value to you as your get started with your investment club. Remember, though, that this is just a beginning. There are thousands of Web sites, with more coming online every day, and your local library has dozens of books dealing with financial-related topics.

Books

Apostolou, Barbara, and Nicholas G. Apostolou. *Keys to Investing in Common Stocks (Barron's Business Keys)*. Barrons Educational Series, 2000.

The Beardstown Ladies' Investment Club with Leslie Whitaker. *The Beardstown Ladies' Common-Sense Investment Guide: How We Beat the Stock Market and You Can, Too.* Hyperion, 1995.

Brown, David L., and Kassandra Bentley. *Getting Started in Online Investing.* John Wiley & Sons, 1999.

Cappiello, Frank. *New Guide to Finding the Next Superstock.* Liberty Hall Press, 1990.

Carlson, Charles B. *Buying Stocks Without a Broker.* McGraw Hill, 1995.

Case, Samuel. *Big Profits from Small Stocks: How to Grow Your Investment Portfolio by Investing in Small Cap Companies.* Prima Publishing, 1994.

———. *The First Book of Investing: The Absolute Beginner's Guide to Building Wealth Safely.* Prima Publishing, 1999.

Engel, Louis. *How to Buy Stocks.* Little, Brown & Co., 1994.

Fisher, Sarah Young, and Susan Shelly. *The Complete Idiot's Guide to Personal Finances in Your 20s and 30s.* Alpha Books, 1999.

Gardner, David, and Tom Gardner. *The Motley Fool Investment Guide: How the Fool Beats Wall Street's Wise Men and How You Can Too.* Fireside Books, 1997.

———. *The Motley Fool Workbook.* Fireside Books, 1998.

Gerlach, Douglas. *The Complete Idiot's Guide to Online Investing.* Alpha Books, 1999.

Heady, Christy. *The Complete Idiot's Guide to Making Money on Wall Street.* Alpha Books, 1997.

Kelly, Jason. *The Neatest Little Guide to Personal Finance.* Plume Publishing, 1999.

———. *The Neatest Little Guide to Stock Market Investing.* Plume Publishing, 1998.

Koch, Edward T., and Debra DeSalvo. *The Complete Idiot's Guide to Investing Like a Pro.* Alpha Books, 1999.

Lowell, James. *Investing from Scratch: A Handbook for the Young Investor.* Penguin USA, 1997.

Lynch, Peter, with John Rothchild. *One Up on Wall Street.* Penguin USA, 1990.

Mintzer, Richard, and Kathi Mintzer. *The Everything Money Book: Learn How to Manage, Budget, Save, and Invest Your Money So There's Plenty Left Over.* Adams Media Corp., 1999.

Morris, Kenneth M., Virginia B. Morris, and Alan M. Siegel. The Wall Street Journal *Guide to Understanding Money and Investing.* Fireside Books, 1998.

Naylor, W. Patrick. *10 Steps to Financial Success: A Beginner's Guide to Saving and Investing.* John Wiley & Sons, 1997.

Neff, John B., and Steven L. Mintz. *John Neff on Investing*. John Wiley & Sons, 1999.

O'Hara, Thomas E., and Kenneth S. Janke Sr. *Starting and Running a Profitable Investment Club: The Official Guide from the National Association of Investment Clubs*. Times Books, 1996.

Orman, Suze. *The 9 Steps to Financial Freedom*. Crown Publishing, 1997.

Pond, Jonathan P. *1001 Ways to Cut Your Expenses*. Dell Books, 1992.

Quinn, Jane Bryant. *Making the Most of Your Money*. Simon & Schuster, 1997.

Savage, Terry. *The Savage Truth on Money*. John Wiley & Sons, 1999.

Sethna, Dhun H., and William J. O'Neil. *Investing Smart: How to Pick Winning Stocks with* Investors Business Daily. McGraw Hill, 1997.

Shaw, Kathryn. *Investment Clubs: A Team Approach to the Stock Market*. Dearborn Trade, 1995.

Turkington, Carol, and Sarah Young Fisher. *Everything You Need to Know About Money and Investing: A Financial Expert Answers the 1,001 Most Frequently Asked Questions*. Prentice Hall Press, 1998.

Vujovich, Diane. *Macmillan Teach Yourself the Stock Market in 10 Minutes*. Alpha Books, 2000.

Wasik, John F. *The Investment Club Book*. Warner Books, 1995.

Periodicals

➤ *The Wall Street Journal*. Published Monday through Friday in regional editions by Dow Jones & Company. For more information or to order, call customer service at 1-800-369-2834. An online edition of *The WSJ* also is available. Access it on the Web at www.wsj.com.

➤ *Money*. Well-known and respected, this monthly magazine offers coverage of all aspects of personal finance. In addition to strategies for smart investing and saving, it provides advice about retirement planning, spending for maximum value, travel planning, consumer awareness, tax preparation, and education. Contact *Money* at 1-800-633-9970, or on the Web at www.pathfinder.com/money.

➤ *The Financial Report Card.* This is a monthly publication dedicated to investors who are not in search of "get rich quick" schemes, but would rather make money by following proven, conservative investment strategies. This newsletter adheres to this philosophy, and presents practical, understandable financial information. Contact *The Report Card* at 732-382-9531, or on the Web at www.mdrinf.com.

➤ *Barron's.* This publication covers a wide range of topics related to investing, and digs into what may be coming up in the financial markets. This is a good source of information that can help you anticipate what may happen with your investments. Contact *Barron's* at 1-800-975-8620, or on the Internet at www.barrons.com.

➤ *Forbes.* Offers in-depth coverage about people and issues that affect business today and the trends that could affect business in the future. You can reach *Forbes* at 1-800-888-9896, or on the Web at www.forbes.com.

➤ *Your Money.* Provides down-to-earth information about savings, investing, and other financial matters. Each issue of *Your Money,* which is the sister publication of *Consumers Digest,* also includes *Your Investment Advisor,* the magazine's newsletter. Contact *Your Money* at 312-275-3590, or at www.consumersdigest.com.

➤ *Smart Money.* Calls itself "*The Wall Street Journal* Magazine of Personal Business." Published monthly, it offers investors and consumers expert market analysis, investing strategies, personal finance options, and other tips for financial issues such as retirement planning and car leasing. Get more information or subscribe by calling 1-800-444-4204, or find it on the Internet at www.smartmoney.com.

➤ *Individual Investor.* Devoted to investors, brokers, dealers, and analysts who are interested in over-the-counter and NASDAQ-listed stocks. The monthly magazine covers trends, government regulations, earnings reports, and recent corporate developments impacting the industry. Contact the magazine at 1-800-273-6960, or on the Web at www.individualinvestor.com.

➤ *Kiplinger's Personal Finance.* Geared toward consumers, this magazine provides practical information about how to maximize current assets and anticipate opportunities in the changing economy. The phone number is 1-800-544-0155, and the Web site is located at www.kiplinger.com.

➤ *Business Week.* Presents complicated issues in a clear, easy-to-understand manner. The magazine identifies and analyzes events, trends, and personalities that influence companies and business in general. Contact *Business Week* at 888-878-5151, or at www.businessweek.com.

➤ *Worth*. Provides personal investors with all sorts of expert advice on stocks, mutual funds, the economy, taxes, real estate and retirement. Includes a regular column by Peter Lynch. To order or get more information, call 1-800-777-1851, or go to www.worth.com.

➤ *Dick Davis Digest*. This publication summarizes ideas and opinions from more than 450 newsletters and reports. It's filled with practical investment ideas. For more information or to order, call 1-800-654-1514, or find it on the Web at www.dickdavis.com.

➤ *Market Logic*. This publication is known for its predictions of market trends. It's published by the Institute of Econometric Research. You can contact *Market Logic* at 1-800-442-9000, or find it on the Web at www.marketlogic.com.

➤ *Morningstar Investor*. This is a great source of information about mutual funds. *Morningstar* is widely used and well respected. Call 1-800-876-5005, or find it on the Web at www.morningstar.com.

Web Sites

➤ **The National Association of Investors Corporation (NAIC).** Includes all kinds of information about starting and running an investment club. Includes information on stocks and companies, NAIC products, club contacts, and more. You can even download demonstration software or join NAIC and its computer group. Find it at www.better-investing.org.

➤ **Thomson Investors Network.** Lists top stock performers, shows stock screening, gives multiple quotes. Find it at www.thomsoninvest.net/att/stocks.

➤ **World Federation of Investors Corporation.** The NAIC is a member of this group, which has chapters around the world to support individual investors in many countries. It includes a wide variety of topics that you might find useful. Its Web address is at www.wfic.org.

➤ **Investorama.com Guide to Investment Clubs.** This comprehensive site presents articles, commentary, message boards, a free newsletter, tutorials, and other features. Find it at www.investorama.com/guide/clubs. For a listing of investment clubs by state, go to www.investorama.com/directory/Investment_Clubs/club_web_sites.

➤ **The Canadian Shareowners Association.** This is the Canadian counterpart to the NAIC. It provides data, software and educational tools for investors. It's located on the Internet at www.shareowner.ca.

➤ **The Mining Company: Investment Clubs.** Gives links to investment club resources. Go to it at www.investmentclub.miningco.com.

351

➤ **Gateway Eagles Guide to Personal and Club Investing.** Provides an overview of how to start a club, information about dividend reinvestment plans, investment strategies, and links to some major companies, stock quote services, stock news services, and other investing sites. Find it at www.hometown.aol.com.

➤ **Doug Gerlach on Starting an Investment Club.** All sorts of useful and practical information about clubs and finances can be found here. It can be found on the Web at www.pathfinder.com/money/chat.

➤ **Bombardier/Stock Quote and Performance.** As the name of the site implies, this one gives you quotes and rates performance of various stocks. Go to it at www.bombardier.com/cgi-bin/quotes.

➤ **Investment Club Webring.** Provides a linked list of investment club Web sites. Find it at www.geocities.com/WallStreet/floor/6000/webring/ring_homepage.html.

➤ **Microsoft Investor.** Features a mutual fund screen, based on NAIC's comparison guide. You've got to subscribe in order to get it. Go to www.moneycentral.msn.com.

➤ **The Motley Fool Investment Clubs.** All sorts of entertaining articles. Also has message boards for investment clubs. It's on the Web at www.fool.com.

➤ **Reality Moneynet.** Gives you information on online club portfolio tracking. You can find it at www.moneynet.com/home.

➤ **Jim Dickerson's Stock Screen.** This is a review of stocks that meet NAIC's criteria for buying. It's on the Web at www.ourworld.compuserve.com/homepages/Jim_Dickerson/screen.htm.

➤ **Socially Responsible Investing.** Provides information about socially responsible companies and suggestions for investing in a socially responsible manner. Find it at www.socialfunds.com.

➤ **Corporate Watch.** This site gives you the scoop on which companies operate in a socially responsible manner—and which don't. It's located on the Internet at www.corporatewatch.org.

➤ **BWZine.** An online magazine with articles about socially responsible individuals and companies, environmental issues, and so forth. The site can be found at www.betterworld.com.

➤ **Investors' Compass.** Helps locate information about stocks and mutual funds through company-specific links. Go to it at www.icompass.com.

➤ **Investment Club Central.** This is a comprehensive directory of investment clubs and NAIC-related resources. Find it at www.iclubcentral.com.

➤ **Investor Guide Classic.** Gives lists of investment clubs with Web sites—state by state. Go to it at www.investorguide.com.

➤ **About.com.** Provides lots of links to topics such as how to get an investment club started, listings of clubs, investment software, and stock news. Look for it at www.investmentclub.about.com.

➤ **Internal Revenue Service.** Get information and download forms from this site. It's at www.irs.ustreas.gov.

➤ **Securities Exchange Commission.** Gives information about investing, as well as SEC regulations and resources. Find it at www.sec.gov.

Index

N–P